AF719191

PROBLEMS IN PROGRAMMING

PROBLEMS IN PROGRAMMING

EXPERIENCE THROUGH PRACTICE

Andrej Vitek, Iztok Tvrdy, Robert Reinhardt, Bojan Mohar, Marc Martinec, Tomi Dolenc and Vladimir Batagelj

University of Ljubljana
Yugoslavia

JOHN WILEY & SONS
Chichester · New York · Brisbane · Toronto · Singapore

Copyright © 1991 by John Wiley & Sons Ltd,
Baffins Lane, Chichester,
West Sussex PO19 1UD, England

All rights reserved.

No part of this book may be reproduced by any means,
or transmitted, or translated into a machine language
without the written permission of the publishers.

Other Wiley Editorial Offices

John Wiley & Sons, Inc., 605 Third Avenue,
New York, NY 10158-0012, USA

Jacaranda Wiley Ltd, G.P.O. Box 859, Brisbane,
Queensland 4001, Australia

John Wiley & Sons (Canada) Ltd, 5353 Dundas Road West, Fourth Floor,
Etobicoke, Ontario M9B 6H8, Canada

John Wiley & Sons (SEA) Pte Ltd, 37 Jalan Pemimpin 05-04
Block B, Union Industrial Building, Singapore 2057

Library of Congress Cataloging-in-Publication Data:

Problems in programming : experience through practice / by A. Vitek
... (et al.).
p. cm.
Includes bibliographical references and index.
ISBN 0 471 93017 2
1. Electronic digital computers—Programming. I. Vitek, A.
QA76.6.P7475 1991
005.1—dc20 91-25548
CIP

A catalogue record for this book is available from the British Library.

Printed in Great Britain by Courier International, East Kilbride, Lanarkshire

Contents

II. Problems 35

III. Solutions 85

Literature 321

Index 323

Problems & solutions index 329

Preface

The book present comprises a rich set of problems and solutions in programming. The main emphasis of the book, however, is not on the problems or solutions: the aim is to demonstrate by example some of the difficulties which can be encountered in designing and writing programs and to suggest ways of coping with them.

While the problems presented here were not devised solely by the book authors most were at least "polished" by them. The authors of the book, ranging from university professors to software researchers and systems engineers, all have a rich experience in programming, both theoretical and practical. Many of the problems here originated from some past experience: for example, a resistant bug in a program which turned out to be caused by a couple of more or less trivial mistakes, or in an unusually disguised use of a well-known algorithm or data structure.

We hope and believe that such experience gained in the "school of life" will help students to become "grown-up" computer scientists with much less effort than we had to invest.

The problems presented in this book were devised for a series competitions held over an eleven year period (from 1977 to 1987) in a country called Slovenia, positioned in Europe between Italy, Austria, Hungary and Croatia. The competitions have been the source of much enthusiasm and enjoyment for the authors, for all the various collaborators, and for the participants. Over the years the competitions attracted more and more competitors until in 1987 about 2000 high school students out of the total population of 2,000,000 inhabitants of Slovenia participated in pre-competitions and the finals. The competitions culminated in the International Computer Science Olympiad, held for the first time in Nova Gorica, Slovenia in 1988, (and since in Münster, Germany, and Varna, Bulgaria).

It is impossible to thank all those who have contributed in various ways, nor even to identify the exact source and author of each problem.

We enjoyed our part in preparing the problems for each competition, we enjoyed seeing them solved at the competitions in a variety of ingenious ways, and most of all, we enjoyed solving them again when writing this present book. (The only thing we did not enjoy was hunting for the resistant bug in the original program...)

We hope the readers will experience equal enjoyment in using this book.

The authors

Ljubljana, April 1991

Introduction

The book is divided into three parts. The first is a text to be read as such. It explains the basic general ideas about programming with all the little details which we learned, some during a sleepless night spent at the computer, others from exercises in a number of excellent textbooks on computer science (some of which are mentioned at the end of this book) and which we thought worth explaining. The second part contains the problems from the competitions, presented in chronological order. The main part of the book is the last one, which contains the solutions. Here we tried to explain the background of the problems, the general ideas behind them and the approach used to overcome the potential difficulties when encountering such a problem in practice. This makes the book not only a problem-solution text but also both a story about our (but not only our) programming experience and a text explaining some of the fundamental problems in computer science and the way they are solved.

The solutions are arranged according to their topics in eight chapters, and follow a different order from the problems. Most chapters start with a short introduction presenting the most interesting common details of the problems that follow. The first chapter, **A – Straightforward Problems**, presents a miscellany of short and easy problems of all kinds, which may be found appropriate for a gentle warming up in introductory courses of programming. The second chapter, **B – Computational Problems**, comprises a set of problems requiring some computational tests to be performed. They require some basic knowledge of integer arithmetic (prime numbers, divisibility, etc.) The problems range from easy numeric problems to the presentation of some frequently used aids of a numeric nature. The next chapter, **C – Recursive functions**, leads us to a slightly more theoretical view of computer science, demonstrating its mathematical background; nevertheless it remains at an elementary level. In most cases no programming skills are required. Instead, a basic knowledge of the mathematical induction principle is recommended. Two short chapters follow. The fourth, **D – Reordering**, solves some problems related to sorting and searching and presents a set of most frequently used algorithms related to ordering, while the fifth chapter, **E – Graphs**, describes some basic algorithms for graphs. They are followed by the most voluminous chapter, **F – Controlling Real-Time Processes**, which presents a variety of examples of everyday uses of computers (especially since robots, the Space Shuttle and bar code readers have become almost everyday features of our lives). The next chapter, **G – Computer Graphics** answers some problems in raster graphics; for instance, it explains how to flood a computer screen. The last chapter, **H – Remaining Problems** again presents a group of unrelated problems but more difficult than those in Chapter A. The problems range from macro substitution to the problem of optimum selection of a winner, and to the problem of bootstrapping a compiler.

The special Problems & Solutions Index, printed at the very end of the book, lists all the problem numbers along with the page numbers of the problem text and its solution; a short description of the problem topic is included to ease the search for a particular problem.

All programs in the solutions are coded in standard Pascal. Occasionally, the solutions are illustrated by programs in other languages, mostly when the language is more appropriate for coding (for instance, standard Pascal provides no legitimate way to code interrupt service routines, while Ada or Modula-2 do). We decided to use Pascal for several reasons. The first and most important is that Pascal is the most common programming language in our high schools. Besides, Pascal code is fluent, concise and legible, which makes Pascal surpass most other languages. In addition to programs, Pascal was used to devise the solutions to those problems that required only the formulation of the algorithm. We strongly feel that the algorithm coded this way is at least equivalent to, if not more precise than, the specification in natural language. The third reason was that Pascal compiler is provided by most computer systems from the most basic home computers to the largest mainframes. And last but not least, most programmers agree that Pascal is their *second* favourite language, while their opinions about the *first* are rather different, if not contrary. To read the book, therefore, fair knowledge of Pascal is required.

To code the solutions, we adhered to the style described in more depth later on. Since the book was prepared using a computer, the majority of the programs were inserted into the text directly, the same texts as were passed to the compiler to compile them. We have thoroughly tested all programs. To do that, most solutions had to be embedded in an appropriate program environment, which defined all those procedures and functions that are declared as outside – **external** in the solutions. To save space, the environments were mostly omitted from the book; you may find some in solutions to problems 424A, 823E and 1111B. We encourage the reader to test our solutions on his or her own. We advise you, however, to copy the programs with caution and common sense: some compilers understand slightly nonstandard Pascal, others exercise peculiarities when writing to screen or reading from keyboard (more about that may be found in the solution to problem 813A), and the utmost caution is required to devise an appropriate environment for the solution. Having had some experience in programming, we expect that mistakes may occur in the book, despite the care we have taken to avoid them. We hope the readers can see them as an ever-recurring proof of the human unreliability so well known to all with at least a bit of computer experience.

Part I

Properties of a Good Program

There are many who think it is enough that a program "works", some perhaps add that the program must be as effective as possible. But these two necessary characteristics still lack a lot. Below we will describe some of the properties which a good program should possess.

1. Program correctness

Program correctness means more than just that a "program works". The program must do what it is supposed to do, that is, what it is intended for. If the program computes incorrect results for some valid data, if the operation of the program contradicts the user manual, if the user instructions are inadequate, the program is either unusable or the user must struggle with the mysteries he encounters when using the program.

1.1 Proving program correctness

We might say that the correctness of a program is its most important property. In the last fifteen years, extensive efforts have been invested in methods for formally proving program correctness as well as in the choice of expressive means which assist in writing correct programs (among others, the Pascal programming language is a result of these efforts). It is only rarely possible to state the program requirements in such a way as to enable proof of program correctness. Even where a specification can be expressed formally, unfortunately no practical algorithms exist for proving the program correctness automatically. Although there are appropriate methods for proving correctness, even they cannot be used without human intuition. An example proof of program correctness may be found in solution 922F.

1.2 The program specification

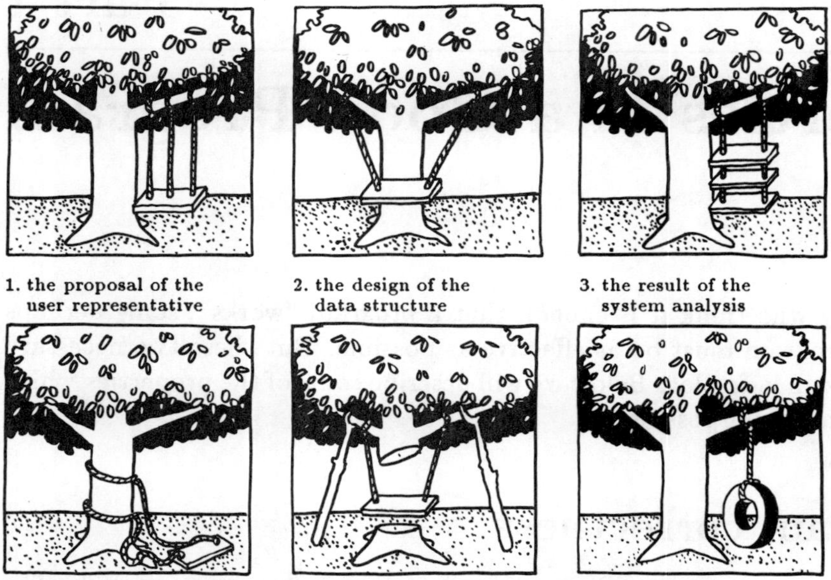

1. the proposal of the user representative
2. the design of the data structure
3. the result of the system analysis
4. the product of the programmers
5. the final implementation after the removal of some minor problems
6. the actual requirements of the users

Figure U1: A communication problem
The picture was adapted from an idea originally printed in University of London Computer Centre Newsletter, No.53, March 1973.

We have already pointed out that it is rather difficult to describe formally what a program must accomplish. But not only that. In many cases, when starting to design a large program, neither the customer nor the program designer have a clear idea what they expect from the program. Moreover, the designer has a different perception of the problem from that of the customer. The computer experts often face the serious problem of learning from the customer what he really wants. If the description of the requirements is left to the customer, they are usually non-systematic, inconsistent and incomplete, and fail to describe a number of important facts which seem like common sense to the customer — but not to the program designer. This specification may only be considered as a starting point for further understanding of the problem. It often happens that only when the customer obtains the first working version of the program, does he discover that although it does conform to the specifications, he had something entirely different in mind originally.

The process of the determination of the problem to be solved by the program is called *system analysis*. Special ad hoc methodologies (the science of methods or ways of doing) are often used in this task, which may significantly assist in understanding the customer problem, but they are not universal. All the time, the program designer (the programmer) must be aware that the customer requirements will change during the program development, as they will change when the program is being used. This cannot be avoided, and the program designer must adapt to it. Programs must therefore be designed to be as flexible as possible, so that they are easy to change and adapt. It is helpful if the program solves a more general problem than the customer presents. The program designer must always anticipate what the customer may need later on but is not yet aware of. If the program does not provide for such additions from the beginning, the designer must at least strive not to make later improvements to the program impossible.

When solving unusually obscure problems which are especially difficult to explain, the designer may often decide to develop a simpler program, which will later be discarded. The purpose of this prototype program is to help the customer understand what is really needed, and to assist in a more detailed specification of the actual program later on.

Particularly in recent times, and exclusively to design large systems, the system analysts use the so-called *formal description methods.* Using these, the specification of the system is clear and concise, since a good formal description method is independent of programming languages and adheres only to the strict rules determining the form (syntax) and the meaning (semantics) of the specification. The system may be described on several levels of abstraction, from a rough general sketch of the system (what the future program should do) down to a very precise description, which may be "transcribed" to a programming language (a recipe of how the program should work). Using such a specification, some tests of correctness and conformance are possible even before it is coded as a program. Since the errors may be detected early, and since the specification is transcribed to a program only once, the implementation of large projects is accelerated and made cheaper. Nevertheless, specification using such formal methods is not universal: the methods may help in analysis and design, but they cannot correct bad decisions by project managers.

1.3 Writing a correct program

Since it is practically impossible at present to prove the correctness of a large program, and since the tools for automatic programming are still in their infancy, other methods must be used to write and test programs. A frequently used method is to write the program and then wonder why it does not work. In spite of more and more powerful tools for automatic testing and for finding and removing programming errors, this is a very unsatisfactory method. The execution of a large program is very difficult to trace, and correcting one error after another is tedious work both for the programmer and for the computer.

A large program may be broken up into smaller parts, and each part tested and corrected separately. Sometimes this method is acceptable, but it has a serious deficiency. For each separate part of the program, an appropriate testing environment must be built, which simulates other parts of the program that have not yet been built and tested. In this way the effort in program development is at least doubled. Besides, not even with the parts tested in this way is there any assurance that the complete program will work correctly.

The entire program itself is the best simulation environment for each part of the program. This fact should be well exploited. But how, if no part of the program has been tested and it probably does not work correctly? The only way out of this is self-discipline and compliance with the rules of good programming. The program must be designed carefully and thoughtfully. All the time, care must be taken to make the program as robust as possible, so that it can survive even some clumsiness and incorrectness caused by other parts of the program (robustness will be discussed in more detail later on). The program must be written to be as correct and as robust as possible at the first attempt. In this way the program provides the testing environment for itself. The result of such a design is that when an error occurs, it does not cause the entire program to crash, instead other parts of the program diminish the error and report it to the programmer in a comprehensible way.

1.4 The use of the goto statement

After the "crisis of programming" (at the end of the sixties), the necessity for program readability and maintainability (modification, improvement, adaptation) became one of the central interests in computer science. In readability, the demand for a simple nested structure of programs originated (O. J. Dahl, E. W. Dijkstra, C. A. R. Hoare: *Structured Programming*, Academic Press, New York 1972), as such a program structure provided better readability, easier optimization, simpler proving of correctness, more effective analysis and compilation of programs. The **goto** statement particularly was considered dangerous (E. W. Dijkstra: *Go to Statement Considered Harmful*, CACM **11**(1968)3, pp. 147–148). This statement is in fact the only control structure which allows free jumps around the program. But if it is to be abandoned, it has to be replaced by some other structure.

Theoretical research has shown that using solely the control structures: the *sequence of statements*, *branching*, *loop*, and with the use of only the program variables, the schemas containing a cycle with two exits cannot be expressed. An example of such a scheme may be seen in Figure U2. It may be proved that these structures suffice to express any schema, if auxiliary logical variables are added to the variables of the scheme (E. Ashcroft, Z. Manna: *The Translation of Goto Programs to While Programs*, IFIP71, Ljubljana 1971).

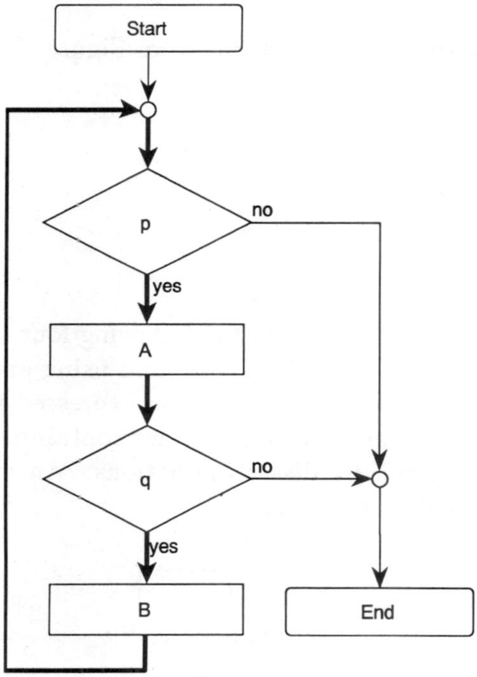

Figure U2: A loop with two exits

The scheme from Figure U2 may thus be written:

```
again:=true;
while p and again do begin
  A;
  if not q then again:=false
  else B;
end;
```

See also solution 514D. There is another answer, which is supported by some modern programming languages as well as by some dialects of Pascal. The following two control structures represent the only correct use of the **goto** statement:

— the infinite loop (**goto** back):

```
loop
  A
end
```

— the exit from a control block *a* (**goto** forward):

```
exit a
```

A control block *a* is designated by preceding the corresponding control statement by the label *a*: .

Using these two structures the scheme from Figure U2 may be written more naturally:

```
a: loop
     if not p then exit a;
     A;
     if not q then exit a;
     B;
   end;
```

It can be proved that using exclusively the following four control structures: the *sequence of statements*, *branching*, *loop*, *exit*, and using exclusively the variables of the scheme, **well-formed schemes** may be expressed without copying parts of the scheme code. These well-formed schemes contain no cycles with multiple entrances; they are obtained by dissecting actions. An example of a *not* well-formed scheme is illustrated in Figure U3.

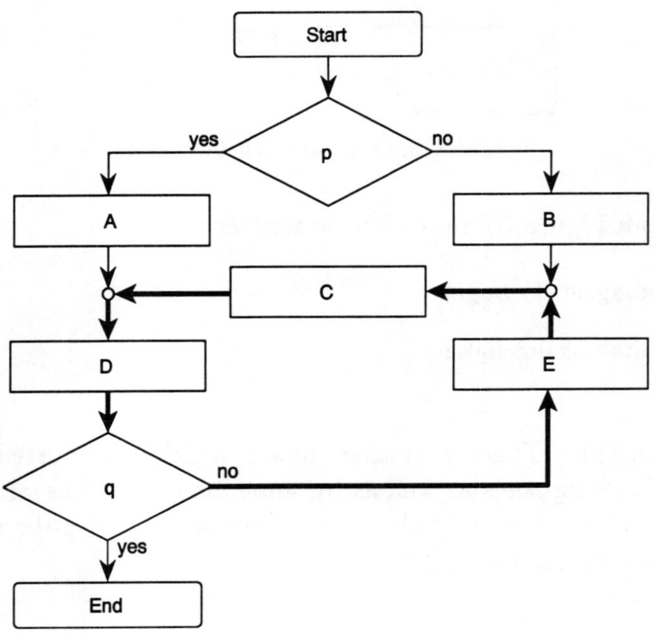

Figure U3: A loop with two entrances

Any scheme may be transformed to an equivalent *well-formed* scheme by copying parts of the scheme . The copied parts of the scheme may be written as subprograms. The scheme from Figure U3 may be rewritten as:

```
    if p then A else begin B; C end;
 a: loop
      D;
      if q then exit a;
      E; C;
    end;
```

In some cases the **goto** or the **exit** statement may be replaced by using special logical operators (see solution 624D) or by using subprograms, which report success or failure as the returned function value (see the paragraph on data correctness in Section 3. and solution 821A).

Although Pascal supports the **goto** statement, many programmers previously accustomed to using the **goto** statement carelessly in programming languages where it was essential, now try to avoid the **goto** statement even when the result is not the most elegant. Their practical experience shows that it is possible to write serious programs without using the **goto** statement, and without copying too much code or introducing artificial new variables. Most programs in this book are written according to this experience. Even experts agree that the **goto** statement is actually unnecessary in Pascal.

2. The documentation

The following documentation is usually provided for serious programs:

— the user manual;
— the installation manual;
— the maintenance manual;
— the documentation on the algorithms and data structures used, on the internal standards adhered to in the program, on file structure, on unusual tricks the program uses, etc.
— the list of possible error messages (diagnoses) the program may report together with the explanation of their probable reasons and with advice to users on how the problems may be eliminated;

and so on.

Some of the documentation is often integrated in the program itself or is in some other way accessible on a computer. This enables the user to access the documentation interactively through a terminal (on-line help).

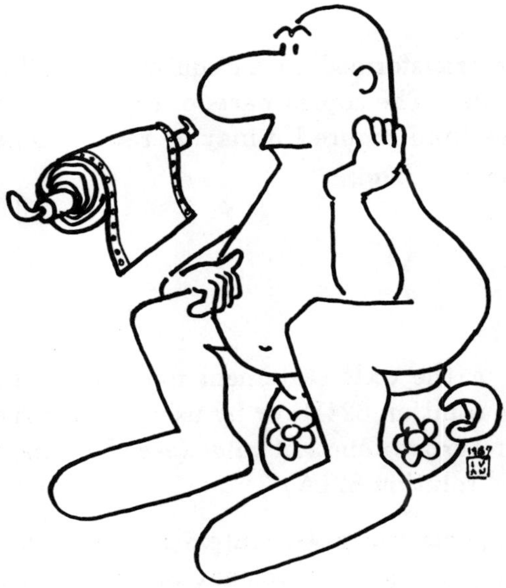

Figure U4: No job is finished until the paperwork is done

A very important part of the documentation is included in the program code. It includes the comments, logically selected names of identifiers (variables, subprograms, etc.) and understandable notation of algorithms. If this task is well done, the program is said to be *self-documented.*

2.1 Self-documented programs

Frequently we hear that the program is its own best documentation. For a nicely written and properly commented program this is doubtless true. We must be aware that the program does not remain the same forever. A useful program experiences many improvements, corrections and changes. Each change in the program must be reflected in its documentation, and if there are lots of it, its maintenance is a tedious job. It is much easier to update the documentation if it is a component of the program—in the form of neatly written comments and understandably coded algorithms. When changing the program, one should be consistent and change the corresponding comments as well. An incorrect (or perhaps out of date) comment may cause more confusion and harm than no comment at all. It is an additional virtue if the program is self-documented, but it may not be used as an excuse for the rest of the documentation to be shallow or even absent altogether.

2.2 The choice of names

Careful choice of names greatly contributes to program clarity. As names we consider (in the Pascal case) the names of programs, subprograms, arguments, constants, types, variables, the record fields, and the elements of the enumeration types — the same syntactic rules hold for all Pascal names. It is all the same to a compiler if a variable is called *i*, or *poO01lIq*, or even *firstElement*. Since the program must be readable for the human in the first place, careful choice of most informative names is very important; often it is more important than the accompanying comments. Carefully chosen names must thus be considered an integral part of the program documentation.

When choosing names, we strive for a reasonable length of name. Very short names are not particularly informative, and so we use them only within particular program portions (for example, for counters of short loops). Very long descriptive names are customary in some programming languages (e.g., COBOL). In this way, the purpose of a name may be precisely described; however, for entirely practical (typing) reasons this should not be exaggerated. Generally, the use of well established abbreviations, prefixes, endings and names works best.

Among established (and sometimes misused) names there are for example: *min*, *max*, *len*, *x*, *y*, *ok*, *str*, *ch*, *inp*, *out*, *from*. Much more misused and less informative are for instance the following names: *i*, *j*, *m*, *n*, *ind*.

Endings of more or less established meaning are often appended to basic names. For instance, to name the variable denoting the number of some elements or the length of the occupied portion of some table, the ending (or prefix) *len*, or *L*, or *num*, or *N* may be used. For the largest allowable length (the declared length) of some data structure, a suitable ending is *max*, or *M*. Anybody can invent his own rules, it is important only that such rules exist and that they are consistently used throughout the program, or even better, that they become the personal or team style of writing programs.

From the variable name *table* we may thus derive the name *tableT* for the table type, *tableL* for the current length of the table (an integer variable), *tableM* for the constant determining the declared length of the table, *pTable* for a pointer to a table, and *pTableT* for the type of a pointer to a table. Although the standard Pascal does not allow the use of the underscore (_) in names, it is permitted by many compilers, which increases readability. If we decide to use the underscore, the above names may be written as *table*, *table_t*, *table_l*, *table_m*, *p_table* and *p_table_t*.

Another practical suggestion: avoid variables similar to numbers. It is sometimes hard to distinguish the letter *l* from the digit 1, the letter Z from the digit 2, the letter S from the digit 5 and the letters *o* or *O* or *Q* from the digit 0.

Often it is worthwhile to adapt the choice of names to the editor used as the primary tool in the program development. Let us observe this in more detail.

During development the program evolves gradually; often it performs some of the functions of the future complete system early in the development stage. The program thus continually changes its form: when the size of a subprogram increases over the controllable limit, it is divided into several subprograms; when some operation (a part of the program) is observed to repeat several times, a new subprogram is devised; the precise meaning of variables, subprograms, and their arguments, which could not be defined in detail in the beginning, gradually settles — more appropriate names may then be chosen — and so on. In such progress, a text editor is of great assistance; this way of working is not possible using only paper, pencils, and an eraser.

A good text editor surpasses the paper and pencil method in many ways. Using paper and pencil, we would think several times before changing a frequently used name, even if the new name was far more appropriate. Also, it is very difficult to find all parts of the program, where a subprogram is called or a particular variable is used. True, the pencil may be better suited to some tasks in programming than a text editor, but the advantage is ever more on the side of a good text editor. The latter usually allows the user to adapt its environment to his taste (commands, keys, search mode, etc.).

When the editor is incapable of performing some operation, this operation is preferably avoided: if the editor is only capable of searching substrings in the text regardless of whether they form a word or are only a part of a longer one, then one-letter names are best avoided, since it will be hard to find them later. (In a large group of Pascal programs we have measured that every tenth letter is an *e* and that it appears twice in each line of a program on average. The situation with the letter *i* is no better.) This problem is avoided, for instance, by using the variable *ii* for loop counters instead of the popular *i*. Also, *j* is much more easily searched for than *i*!

2.3 Documentation standards

Many software producers mandate their own internal standards (specific rules) for coding and documentation of programs. This is the only way of ensuring uniformity of writing and documenting programs in large software projects, where programs are written by a team of programmers. One such internal standard for instance requires for *each program*:

— its title with a one-line functional description;
— the version number;
— the name of the software product;

— the abstract — a short functional description of the program and the description of the conditions which must be met before and during program execution;
— the date of the program creation as well as the name of its author;
— the list of program modifications, each including the sequence number of the change, the author, the date and the description of the modification.

According to one such standard, *each subprogram* must contain:

— the functional description — the purpose of the subprogram (the description of the service it offers) and a description of its communication with the environment in which it executes. Here also the algorithms used must be described along with an explanation of why they were chosen;
— the description of the call of the subprogram — consisting of its name and the list of its arguments;
— the description of its formal arguments: the kind of argument (input, output, input/output), its type, special restrictions and a short description of each argument;
— the description of input and output data, which are not formal arguments (for instance, the use of global variables in Pascal);
— the description of the value returned by a function subprogram;
— the list of called subprograms;
— the list of possible side effects.

The longer the program and the less readable the programming language used, the more necessary is the above described (or similar) outline of the documentation. Unless writing large program systems in a major software house, it suffices that a short description (in a few lines) of the function of each subprogram is provided. The formal arguments should be briefly described, unless their role is evident from the description of the subprogram or from their names. Holding blindly to the standard may sometimes do more harm than good to a program. It must be taken into account that on a normal terminal screen only twenty four lines are simultaneously visible and that there are forty to sixty lines on a single page of computer listing. If a program is continually interrupted by superfluous never-ending comments and decoration, it may become completely illegible.

2.4 The program comments

When writing comments one must be flexible. Just as driving around the city requires constant adaptation to the traffic situation — adjusting speed, changing gear, accelerating and braking, so does writing comments require versatility. The recipes of the "one comment every five lines" kind are quite unsuitable. Simple and evident parts of the program need a single comment, or not even that, if its purpose is evident from the name of the subprogram. Other parts, where unusual algorithms or programming tricks are used, require detailed explanation. Often it is more important that the function of each variable is briefly and precisely described in its declaration, than to describe the algorithm in detail. Extensive comments and "decoration" are best avoided, as they diminish clarity and compactness of the program. If such descriptions are necessary, they are best stored separately in the program documentation.

The programs in this book are sparing with comments. We kept to the convention that the algorithm is best explained in the text of the solution, so the reader should consider programs only in combination with the explanation in the text.

As an example of commenting we borrow the slightly refined *Fill* procedure from solution 622D. It was extended with appropriate comments (here, we have perhaps written more comments than necessary). The program is short enough to fit on a single screen in a text editor.

```
procedure Fill
  (var table: tableT;  { the table of generated random numbers }
   max: integer;       { the table length }
   num: integer);      { the upper bound of the random number range }
{ Fills the table table with distinct random numbers in the range 1..num. }

 var
   len: integer; { the length of the filled portion of the table (at the end=max) }
   k: integer;   { a random number between 1 and num }
   j: integer;

begin
  len:=0;
  while len<max do begin
    k:=1 + trunc(num*Random);                  { generate a new random number }
    table[len+1]:=k;               { put it at the end of the table as a sentinel }
    j:=1;
    while table[j]<>k do                   { check if such element already exists }
      j:=j+1;
    if j=len+1 then                   { if not found, leave it at the end of the table, }
      len:=j;                          {... and increase the length of the filled part }
  end; {while}
end; {Fill}
```

An example of the same procedure but commented *inappropriately* follows:

```
procedure Fill(var table: tableT; max,num: integer);
{ *** Procedure FILL ***

  input data:
max       SCALAR ARGUMENT INTEGERthe upper bound of the loop
num       SCALAR ARGUMENT INTEGERthe range of the random numbers
  output data:
table     ARRAY  ARGUMENT INTEGERthe output table
  input—output data:
    —
  the global variables used:
    —
  the called subprograms:
Random FUNCTION  REAL
  purpose:
    The Fill procedure stores distinct random numbers from
    the range between 1 and num in the table.
}
  var
    i: integer;  { the counter of the first loop }
    j: integer;  { the counter of the second loop }
    k: integer;  { an auxiliary variable }
begin
  i:=0;  { initialize i to 0 }
  while i<max do begin
    k:=1 + trunc(num*Random);  { compute the number  k }
    table[i+1]:=k;  { insert  k  in the table }
{
    the next loop checks whether the table already
    contains an element equal to  k
}
    j:=1;
    while table[j] <> k do j:=j+1;  { increment  j }
{
    if the loop above has found no element equal to
    k in the table, it is inserted
}
    if j=i+1 then i:=j;  { set i to j }
  end; {while}
end;
{ *** end of the Fill procedure *** }
```

The second example of the varFill procedure is more than twice the length of the first example. But is it twice as instructive and readable?

3. Program robustness, safe programming

A program is said to be robust (enduring, stable) if it survives various unexpected events—for instance, incorrect data even if one "knows for sure" that they are "always" correct; or a somewhat incorrect operation of a part of the program. An important guideline in writing a program is that the program attempts to relieve the state into which it unexpectedly arrives. The effort invested in program robustness is well repaid by the time saved in program development and testing, as well as in its use and improvement.

Program robustness does not originate only in program operation. It is also influenced by the way the program is written (for instance, the choice of variable names, indenting, avoiding unusual tricks). This point of program robustness is called *safe* or *defensive programming.* A safely written program is much easier to modify and improve, and it is much less likely to introduce errors during the modification.

What are the typical principles used in writing robust programs?

■ **Separate parts of the program should be as independent of each other as possible**. Distinct parts of the program should communicate with each other in a precisely defined, restricted way. If any part of the program used and modified global variables throughout or carelessly used **goto** statements to various other parts of the program, the program would be on its way to a very vulnerable product, very unlikely to survive later changes and improvements. The concept of carefully partitioning the program into separate parts (modules) with well defined interfaces (principles of communication) is called **modularity**.

Most programming languages provide the concept of a **subprogram**, which is a particularly successful mechanism for writing modular programs. Some programming languages (for instance, Modula-2, Ada, Simula 67) go even further, as they allow combination of data structures and operations on them (subprograms) into units (modules), accessible to other units only through explicitly permitted means, while the interior of a module is hidden from other modules. This hiding of the inner details of a module (its own variables, auxiliary subprograms, etc.) is important for two reasons:

a) the modules are forced to use the prescribed mechanisms for communication with other modules. Neither on purpose nor inadvertently therefore can the internals of another module be accessed in an improper way;

b) a programmer is free to choose and change the names and algorithms within a module. Hiding names suppresses conflicts between identical names of auxiliary subprograms or variables from different modules. Hiding algorithms eases development and maintenance of programs, since in this way one algorithm may be easily replaced by another (for instance faster), without influencing other parts of the program.

We must take care of independence even within a single portion of the program. Observe the following simple (perhaps somewhat exaggerated) example, illustrating what *should not* be done:

```
i:=n;
while i>0 do begin read(a[i]); i:=i-1 end;
for j:=1 to n do i:=i+a[j];
writeln('the sum equals ',i);
```

The first loop reads n numbers into table a. After the loop terminates, the i variable equals 0 (unless n is negative). The second loop adds all the elements of the table read to the i variable. The correct sum is obtained in i only if the value of the i variable is zero prior to the **for** loop. Unnecessarily, the result depends on the correct operation of the first loop. The program would be safer, if the assignment i:=0 was added before the **for** loop; the increase in program length is negligible. What would happen in the above part of the program (with and without setting i to 0), if n was negative? What if somebody later replaced the first **while** loop with

```
for i:=n downto 1 do read(a[i]);
```

■ **Never rely on correctness of the data**, especially not those input or modified by a human. The data read should always be tested to ensure they suit the restrictions imposed by the program. Serious programs should take extreme care in reading data (this is done partly in solution 823E). Often not even reading of numbers may be left to Pascal, since the program is violently terminated if the user types a letter instead of a numeral. A computer proverb says that it is impossible to write a foolproof program, since the fools are so inventive!

The guideline not to rely on correctness of data should be adhered to even when no reading of data is involved. Even the closest part of the program should not be trusted. It is better to write one condition or one statement too many than one too little. The subprograms should first test if all conditions for undisturbed execution are met. Naturally, such testing should not be exaggerated. Only those data should be tested that are easy to check or that are more likely to be incorrect. Such tests should remain in the program even after the development phase is over. A useful program will be typically modified and maintained throughout its lifetime. A slightly larger program and longer execution time will be repaid at the moment the program discovers an error in its operation.

What should be done if a part of the program discovers an error in its operation or in the data it has obtained from another part of the program? Two solutions exist.

The first solution claims that each part of the program should proceed regardless of errors. It should perform at least a part of its duty or ease the problems or, if that is impossible, at least not do more harm. The user will probably notice the errors from the results obtained. This solution is the most appropriate for subprograms at the lowest level of the program structure, for instance for libraries of commonly used subprograms.

The other solution advises that the program should stop immediately after it detects an error and output the reason for stopping. This solution ensures that no error goes unnoticed, but it has the deficiency that an error even in a less important operation prevents the rest of the program from functioning.

It is hard to say which solution is better. Combining the two does not always work, as the good properties of both solutions may be lost. When writing, we should be guided by an awareness of the severity of the error. For serious errors, a detailed description of the problem (together with the output of data) is most valuable. In the case of small defects which may be easily recovered, the program should make no fanfare (for instance: the output of a string of length zero should do nothing; if a part of a picture is outside the screen, the visible portion should be plotted instead of complaining; if during measurement of the duration of an event a negative time is obtained — since somebody set the computer clock back meanwhile — the program may consider the event as momentary).

There are several ways to report an error. In the subprograms at the low level of the program structure an argument is usually added, reporting its success or failure to the calling program. The success may be described by a logical value (usually *true* reports success and *false* reports failure). To report more information, an integer may be used (the value zero denoting no error, and any other value uniquely describing an error). Instead of adding an argument, a procedure may be converted to a function, so that the function value returned describes the success of the subprogram. This technique is often used in our solutions (723F, 821A, 823E, 1111B). Often, a loop with an exit somewhere in the middle (**exit** or **goto**) may thus be transformed into a **while** loop — see Paragraph 1.4. The rules of good programming discourage the use of functions which in addition to their result (the returned value) have side effects on their arguments or even global variables. Nevertheless, our conscience remains clear if the function value is used to report success, and the arguments to return results. Such functions may be considered procedures reporting success and not genuine functions.

An error detected higher in the program structure is usually reported directly to the user. It is often appropriate to write a part of the program responsible for reporting errors. In this way, a uniform way of reporting errors is ensured, which may be improved and modified in one place. Such a part of the program (maybe a single subprogram) may also write all the errors reported to a special file (the error log), which may be used later by program developers in analysis of the reasons for errors encountered by program users.

After a serious error has been detected, the program should terminate, if possible, in the least painful way. This means, for example, that the open files should be closed, and the terminal left in a normal state (and not with the blinking Japanese characters set and with the keyboard locked).

A program which is ready for any trouble, and which continues to work even in the case of small errors or which terminates without much commotion in case of serious ones, is said to **fail softly** (soft failure).

■ **Never forget to initialize variables.** It is safer to initialize a variable too much, say to 0 (or whatever is allowable) at start-up than too little, relying on the fact that it will be initialized later. Some compilers in some cases ensure that the variables are initialized. Standard Pascal does not provide such an initialization, so we may not rely on it. The errors which are due to undefined values of variables are very difficult to discover, since they depend on an unknown value of the variable, which is totally unpredictable. This value may depend on whether a text editor was used half an hour ago, or on how occupied the disk is, or sometimes even on whether it is a full moon or the first quarter today. Also, the debugger, the program which assists in finding errors, usually fails in this case, since programs start to behave quite differently when we start to observe their internals.

■ **Observe the boundary cases.** One such problem is called the "fence-post problem" due to the following popular question: a ten metre fence is to be built from poles a metre apart, how many poles are needed? The answer is "but of course" ten — oh, perhaps it is eleven, if it is not nine accidentally. How many characters are there in a string from the seventh to the twentieth, both inclusive? A useful piece of advice is: check the operation of the program for the boundary cases and for some intermediate value. Building the fence, we would thus consider a fence one metre long (as we can hardly imagine a fence zero metres long). One must be especially careful with boundary cases of a large program, since it is difficult to test all boundary cases occurring in particular parts of the program by testing the entire program.

■ **Express conditions safely**. Observe the following example:

```
const n = 44;
var
  i,s: integer;
  a: array [1..n] of integer;
...
i:=0; s:=0;
repeat
  i:=i+2; s:=s+a[i];
until i=n;
writeln('the sum equals ',s);
```

The program is supposed to compute and output the sum of elements at the even numbered places of table a. And what happens if n is odd (even if we are sure it equals 44 when we are writing the program). The loop counter jumps over the odd n and rushes towards infinity until something goes wrong. It would be easy to terminate the loop with the condition $i \geq n$ or even better $i + 2 > n$. The meaning would be preserved, but the program would be safer. And what happens if n is less than two ("oh, but it is not, it must be 44 ")? Regardless of the corrected condition, the sum is incorrect, if it is computed at all, since the program addresses the nonexistent element a[2]! It is much safer to use a **while** loop, which tests the condition before entering the body of the loop:

```
i:=2; s:=0;
while i<=n do
  begin s:=s+a[i]; i:=i+2 end;
writeln('the sum equals ',s);
```

Is the program any longer, any uglier or less clear? Not a bit! For the price of a bit of thought (which slowly but steadily becomes a habit) we obtained a much safer program. The **while** loop is almost always more appropriate than the **repeat** particularly since it also solves the boundary problem! Remember your program which reads successive data and computes something from them (for instance, the average). Does it work correctly for a single datum? What about no data at all?

■ **Avoid syntactic forms** (expressions, statements) which might be unclear or might even be **misleading**. It is better to put a pair of "superfluous" parentheses around a part of an expression or to put a sequence of logically connected statements between "unnecessary" **begin** and **end**. You have certainly faced the following confusion: to which **if** does the **else** belong in the example below:

```
if expression1 then
  if expression2 then statement1
else statement2
```

The following part of a program is written safely:

```
if expressionA then
  begin if expressionB then statementX else statementY end
else statementZ
```

The **begin** and **end** are unnecessary in this case, but if the "**else** statementY" branch is removed from the example some time later, **begin** and **end** become very important, only that it will be long forgotten by then!

■ **Never declare frequently used auxiliary variables** (for instance i,j,k) **in the main program.** If you are not careful, an unusual error may occur, which is hard to discover. Observe an example:

```
program Factorial(input,output);
  var i,n: integer;

  function F(n: integer): integer;
    var r: integer;
  begin
    r:=1; i:=1;
    while i<=n do begin r:=r*i; i:=i+1 end;
    F:=r;
  end; {F}

begin {Factorial}
  readln(n); i:=1;
  while i<=n do begin writeln(i:3,'! = ',F(i)); i:=i+1 end;
end. {Factorial}
```

The program reads a positive integer n, and it should output the factorials of the numbers from 1 to n. Try to execute the program on a computer. It compiles without errors. Now run it and enter for instance 7. Is the output correct? It is as follows:

```
1! =    1
3! =    6
5! =  120
7! = 5040
```

What about the even numbers? Is it evident where the error lies? Well of course: in the F function we forgot to declare the counter of the loop — the auxiliary variable i. To the compiler, the program seems correct since a global variable i exists, so that both loops use the same variable for the loop counter — with fatal consequences. The lesson of the example is that the main program should be as short as possible, it should preferably contain just calls to two or three subprograms; and most of all it should not use any auxiliary variables. All tasks should be concealed into appropriate subprograms with local variables of their own. Do not worry about a few words more of memory. They will easily be balanced by saving your time and patience in the discovery of errors and testing of the program.

You may find many examples of safe programming in our solutions, for instance in 213F, 623F (the *Deallocate* procedure), 813A, 823E, 832F (the *Typed* procedure) and 1033F. Some solutions in this book, however, disregard the recommendations above, usually since the text of the problem assures the correctness of the data (which should never be trusted in practice).

We have not exhausted the list of desirable properties for a program, and one of them — the program style — will be discussed in more depth in the next section.

4. Program style

In this section, we try to clarify and establish the characteristics of the style of Pascal programs used in the solutions throughout the book. Since we are aware that examples (especially in literature) influence particularly the young reader, who has not yet formed his own style of writing programs as well as his opinion on what is "beautiful" and what "ugly", we wish to encourage good habits by presenting carefully styled programs.

It is a thankless task to prescribe a programming style, since even the opinions of software experts frequently differ significantly. This same problem was encountered by the authors when we wanted to use as uniform a style in the solutions as possible — but which style? We, however, all agree that in writing programs one should constantly keep to the same rules, regardless of what they are. A program of a changing nonuniform style is not only ugly to see, it is also hard to understand, which increases the difficulty in discovering errors and causes problems in maintaining and improving of the program.

Before continuing, let us explain by an example, what we are talking about in what we call the "style of programs". A program to solve the same problem in four styles of writing follows (its purpose is not important at the moment, we concentrate on the style), which we then proceed to review in summary.

The program from example 1 is similar to solution 1024D. The rules of its style will be described later. Above all, observe its indentation, spaces in the program, and the use of capital letters. Regardless of whether you like the style of the program from this example or not, you must admit that it is uniform. Observe now the program in the example 2. At first sight we notice that it is rather luxurious with regard to space, especially when compared to the previous program, which is very terse in this regard. The indentation rules, use of spaces and capital letters, and minimum use of semicolons distinguish it from example 1. Nevertheless, the program is consistent, it has its own style.

Example 1:

```
program Find(tape,output);
  var
    tape: file of integer;
    k,n: integer;
begin
  reset(tape); k:=0; n:=0;
  while not eof(tape) do begin
    n:=n−tape↑; get(tape);
    while n<=0 do begin
      k:=k+1; n:=n+k;
    end; {while}
  end; {while}
  writeln('The missing number is ',n:6);
end. {Find}
```

Example 2:

```
program Find( tape, output );

    var
        tape: file of integer;
        k: integer;
        n: integer;

begin
    Reset( tape );
    k := 0;
    n := 0;
    while not Eof( tape ) do
    begin
        n := n − tape↑;
        Get( tape );
        while n <= 0 do
        begin
            k := k + 1;
            n := n + k
        end
    end;
    Writeln( 'The missing number is ', n:6 )
end.
```

Example 3:

```
program Find(tape,output );
  var
  Tape: file of integer ;
  k,n :           INTEGER;
begin
  reset (tape);
  k:=0; n := 0 ;
  while  not Eof(tape)  do
   begin n:=n −tape↑; get( Tape );
    while n <= 0 do
    begin
        k:= k + 1 ;n :=n+k;
    end {while}
   end;
  writeln('The missing number is ', n:6)
end.
```

Example 4:

```
program  Find  (tape,  output);
var  tape:  file  of  integer;  k,  n:
integer;  begin  reset(tape);  k:=0;
n:=  0;  while  not  eof  (tape)  do
begin  n:=  n  −  tape↑;  get  (tape);
while  n<=0  do  begin  k:=k+1;
n:=  n  +  k;  end;  end;  writeln
('The missing number is', n: 6); end.
```

This is, however, not true for the program of example 3, which constantly *changes* the r u l e s of WRITING. How many inconsistencies can you find? Such a program may definitely be called ugly. What would you think about this book , if it was printed as carelessly as this paragraph is? Many beginners in programming are capable of writing a program exactly like this one and they even have no bad conscience. Unfortunately, this is true of some professionals as well. And how do you like the program in example 4? From two metres away it is probably the most beautiful, and it requires the least space on the screen. And does anybody think that a program in which all statements start in the same column is any more readable than example 4?

To write programs (and their documentation), contemporary computer technology offers programmers effective screen editors, interactive environments on effective computers and many other new software tools. Gone are the days when the programs were developed by punching them on cards, waiting all day for the job to be executed and printed, and examining heaps of computer printout, pencil between teeth. The programmer had to adapt his style of writing programs to these changes. The usual terminal screen can display about 24 lines of programs at the same time. True, a screen editor enables the "window" to be moved up and down the program (and sometimes left and right), but a human most easily perceives what is presented to him at once. Also, it is well known that the appropriate length of a subprogram (representing functionally complete units of the program) ranges from a few to a few dozen lines. This is approximately as much as may be displayed on a screen (or slightly more). Therefore, the space on the screen (and on a sheet of paper as well) must be used carefully.

Now, as we know what the style is all about, let us examine the guidelines which we tried to adhere to in writing the solutions.

4.1 Do not waste space

This rule originates in the technological limitation of screen size and in the human capability of most easily understanding small units of a program at a time. Thus, empty or almost empty lines are best avoided within the code of a single subprogram. A single line separates subprograms. Several short statements can be combined in a single line, especially if they are logically connected. When doing this, never forget to put a space after the semicolon. Programs should be written compactly but never at the price of clarity. In particular, the structure of the program should not be hidden, as it is in the following example:

```
if a<>0 then x:=x/a; writeln(x);
```

To an inattentive eye it seems that the value of x is printed only if $a \neq 0$, which is of course not true. If such saving of space is necessary, two consecutive spaces should be used, as in the following example:

```
for i:=1 to nn do write(aa[i]);  writeln;
```

Observe the following example:

```
if a>b then begin t:=a;
  a:=b; b:=t;
end; {if}
```

All three assignment statements are an equivalent part of the compound statement. Nevertheless, the first is hidden behind the **begin** and is easily overlooked, especially if the statements are a little longer. If we analyze the meaning of the three assignments, we see that they swap the values of the a and b variables; they represent a whole. So, it is better to write them all in the same line. In our case the entire compound statement may be written more clearly in a single line:

```
if a>b then
  begin t:=a; a:=b; b:=t end;
```

In this way, the purpose of this portion of the program is even more evident. Nothing would be wrong if the entire **if** statement was written in the same line.

4.2 Indentation

If the program is to be clearly readable, it is very important that it is properly indented, that the statements of the same level begin at the same column. Any nesting of statements must be emphasized by indenting the nested statements. The only remaining question is, how precisely the syntactic levels of the language are regarded, and by how many characters the statements are indented. Our experience shows that it is best to indent by two characters. Less indentation is not noticeable enough, while greater may cause the statements of a large program to be indented up to the middle of the screen or even deeper, and thus renders writing longer statements or expressions difficult and unnecessarily lengthens the program. It is more difficult to answer the question of when the statements should be indented. Considering the exact Pascal syntax, the proper indentation is as shown in the following example:

```
program T;
  procedure Example;
    var
      i: integer;
    begin
```

```
    if ··· then
      begin
        i:= 0;
        while ··· do
          begin
            ···
          end;
      end;
  end; {Example}
begin {T}
  Example;
end. {T}
```

We may observe that even a very simple program structure causes the deepest statements to be indented by 14 characters to the right. For that reason, we slightly changed the style of the program. The body of the subprogram (starting with **begin**) is written under the **procedure**, and similarly the body of the main program under **program**. Thus, two characters of indentation are saved in the body of the procedure. It is a matter of personal taste whether this rule is preferred to the exact syntactic indentation. A further and more essential gain in indentation as well as in program length is achieved by understanding the syntactic rules of Pascal in a different way. In other more recent programming languages (Algol 68, Modula-2, Ada, Structran), for example, more statements may be nested within an **if**, **while**, **for**, or similar statements, without having to enclose them between **begin** and **end** (as may be done with the **repeat** statement in Pascal). In such languages, the statements are indented approximately as follows:

```
if condition1 then
  statement1;
  statement2;
  statement3;
  while condition2 do
    statement4;
    statement5;
  endwhile;
  statement6;
endif;
```

In Pascal, we can cheat by putting the **begin** immediately after the **then** and consider the **begin** as a part of the **if** statement. At the end of all statements belonging within the **if** we put an **end**, aligned with the initial **if** and imagine that we have written the **endif** of some more pleasant language. In a short comment following each **end** we record to which statement this **end** belongs, which eases the understanding of the program. We admit that one must adapt to this way of thinking, and that the style is not the most beautiful at first sight, but it proves clear enough in practice and saves a lot of space.

Let us now rewrite the previous example using both rules described:

```
program T;

  procedure Example;
    var i: integer;
  begin
    if ··· then begin
      i:= 0;
      while ··· do begin
        ...
      end; {while}
    end; {if}
  end; {Example}

begin {T}
  Example;
end. {T}
```

The indentation has been reduced almost to half of the above at the deepest statement, and the program is shorter as well without losing any clarity—in fact, program readability has even increased due to a more complete appearance of the shorter program (when the first shock of writing the **begin** at the end of the line has passed).

Let us now present three forms of indentation used in our solutions on an example of a **while** loop.

Example 1. The statement is short, it is written immediately after the **while** in the same line:

```
  while condition do statement;
```

This is also appropriate for a short compound statement.

Example 2. The statement is longer than in example 1, so it cannot follow the **while** in the same line, but is short enough to fit within a single line (properly indented):

```
  while condition do
    begin statement1; statement2; ··· statementN end;
```

In this example, a compound statement was used. Observe the exception in writing semicolons (an explanation follows in the *example 3*)—this time we did not put the (unnecessary, but allowed and recommended) semicolon before the **end**. Also, after the **end**, we omitted the short comment explaining that it belongs to the **while** statement. These two exceptions are necessary since each character position is valuable in the almost full line, and the comment after **end**; is unnecessary as the corresponding **while** is close enough.

Example 3. The statement is longer and extends over several lines. Almost certainly this is a compound statement. The loop is written as:

```
while condition do begin
  statement1;
  statement2;
  ...
  statementN;
end; {while}
```

Note the semicolon after the last statement of the compound statement. It is put there for safety. It happens frequently that further statements are added at the end of the compound statement. In such cases we often forget to add the semicolon at the end of the last existing statement. By writing the "unnecessary" semicolon you may often avoid compiling a program with a missing semicolon.

For other statements the same rules hold as explained for the **while** statement. There remains only one point left to explain regarding the nesting of **if** statements.

If we kept to the strict syntactic indentation corresponding to the level of nesting, we would often encounter the following nesting of conditionals:

```
if condition1 then statement1
else
  if condition2 then statement2
  else
    if condition3 then statement3
    else
      if condition4 then statement4
        else
          if condition5 then statement5
          else statement6;
```

This serpentine nesting of **if** statements is sometimes long and the indentation presented is quite inappropriate. To again take an example from other more recent languages, in which the **if** statement may have the following form (anywhere where "statement n" appears in the example, more statements are allowed as well):

```
if    condition1 then statement1
elsif condition2 then statement2
elsif condition3 then statement3
elsif condition4 then statement4
elsif condition5 then statement5
else statement6
endif
```

Thus we prefer writing

```
if      condition1 then statement1
else if condition2 then statement2
else if condition3 then statement3
else if condition4 then statement4
else if condition5 then statement5
else statement6;
```

in Pascal as well

When deciding the sequence of the pairs (condition, statement) we are usually lead by the logic and the optimality of the algorithm. It often happens that the conditions are independent of each other, and that their truth is approximately equally probable. In this case, the shorter statements are best written first, and the longer ones left to the end, again to enhance readability. This is true for a simple **if** statement as well. The condition should be expressed to enable the shorter branch to be written after the **then** and the longer after the **else**.

The next example illustrates an *inappropriate* way of writing an **if** statement:

```
if length>0 then
  begin
    Print(queue[head]); stopped:=false;
    if head<maxQueue then head:=head+1 else head:=1;
    length:=length-1;
  end
else stopped:=true;
```

While reading (and trying to understand) the compound statement after the **then**, when reaching its **end**, we would have forgotten long ago that it was nested in an **if**, and more, what the condition of the **if** precisely was. So, when encountering the **else** during reading, we have to look back for the start of the **if** statement (probably somewhere on the previous screen or sheet of paper) to see what this **if** is all about and what its condition is there for. Such way of writing therefore proves to be difficult to understand later.

If the condition of the **if** statement is inverted:

```
if length<=0 then stopped:=true
else begin
  Print(queue[head]); stopped:=false;
  if head<maxQueue then head:=head+1 else head:=1;
  length:=length-1;
end; {if}
```

the program is much easier to understand, as the meaning of the condition is still evidently clear when we start to analyze the compound statement after the **else**—the statement after the **then** is short and simple enough not to interrupt the line of thought. If the condition must be inverted (negated), care must be taken especially with longer expressions containing the operators **and**, **or**, and **not** — do not forget the De Morgan law — and the negation of the relational operators (see solutions 211A and 414A).

4.3 The use of upper and lower case letters

Experiments have shown that it is easier to read a text written primarily in lower case than a text entirely in upper case. This is an important guideline in the decision to write Pascal programs mostly in lower case as well. Upper case letters are used for special purposes only. Pascal does not distinguish upper and lower case letters; nevertheless, the same way of writing should be used all the way through for the same name (of a subprogram, a constant, a type, or a variable) — it may easily happen that the same name is not considered the same if it is written with a capital in one part of the program and entirely in upper case in another.

The following use of upper case letters has proved fairly clear and legible, so we use it throughout the book:

— the **reserved words** are written entirely in lower case letters (for instance begin, if, array). In literature, they are written in bold face (for instance **begin**, **if**, **array**). When writing by hand, the reserved words are underlined;

— the **program and subprogram names** (the procedures and functions) are written with a capital letter (for instance *Print*, *Search*). If the name is composed of several words, each begins with a capital (for instance: *NewLine*), *ReadSpecialSettings*. When writing a library of related subprograms, a short prefix of lower case letters may precede their proper names (for instance: *fOpen*, *fClose*, *fRead*, *fWrite*, *fEof*). Exceptions to the rule are the predefined subprograms, which may be written entirely in lower case as they resemble the mathematical functions (for instance: *sin*, *cos*, *trunc*, *new*, *chr*, *odd*, *read*, *write*, *eof* and similar);

— the **variable names** are written in lower case. If the compiler allows the use of the underscore character (_) in the names (although not permitted by the Pascal standard) it may be used to increase readability of long variable names (for instance: *in_new_line*, *last_char*). If the underscore may not be used (or it is preferred not to use it) the readability of the names composed of more words may be increased by beginning each word (excluding the first) with a capital (for instance: *inNewLine*, *lastChar*);

— the same rule is used to write the **type names**;

— the same rule is used to write the **constant names** as well, with the exception that some names may be written entirely in upper case. Upper case letters are used, for instance, in control character names (for instance: *CR*, *LF*, *BELL*, *ESC*), for constants denoting the names of actions, commands, states, or similar (for instance: *OPEN*, *DELETE*, *LEFT*, *EMPTY*), for the constants of the enumeration types (e. g., **type** *colour_t* = (*BLACK*, *WHITE*)). In other cases, lower case characters are used (for instance: *max*, *line_length*, *image_m*, *speed*);

— in **comments**, capitals are used as in the ordinary text — statements begin with capital letters, and so do proper names. If a comment does not form a statement, it starts with a lower case letter and is not terminated by a period. If the names from the program occur in the comments, they are written as in the program.

We could continue with further recipes on styling and documenting the program. However we leave it to the reader to find answers to additional questions about programming style in the solutions.

By including this chapter on the programming style we wished above all to clarify why the programs in this book are styled as they are. The rules described are used by the authors of the book in everyday work and so they are founded on practical experience. Again, we would like to stress that we do not impose any strict rules in styling programs, but that we would like to advise and present some useful habits.

5. Software tools

When describing the contents of the book we remarked that it contains a number of very simple problems, intended to stimulate and warm up the competitors at the competitions. Many problems of this kind are encountered in everyday life in computer business. Computer users who are not strangers to programming often write a short **throw-away** program. Using such programs a small problem is solved (which cannot be done using a text editor); the precise operation of a subprogram is tested; a characteristic of some data in a file is computed; a puzzle is solved; a file deleted by error is saved, or something similar. Many problems of this kind follow in the book and they may be easily identified. Numerous such solutions are specially polished for publication in this book and are not good examples of a throw-away program any more. Who would really care to take such pains with the programs in solutions 311A or 225A? Would you not be satisfied with a twenty times slower brute-force solution of problem 721C (in this case you would be much more sure about the correctness of the solution)? Even problem

1123B would be attacked by the brute-force method, if the friendly numbers had to be found among the first several hundred numbers only.

Writing throw-away programs is a fairly frequent activity of computer professionals. For such programs, the efficacy, elegance and other aesthetic and practical virtues of programs are immaterial. Usually, it is most important that they are written as fast as possible. When writing such programs we therefore keep to different rules than those used throughout this book, and described in the previous section, especially the rules about the documentation, the program comments, the generality, the use of tricks, and similar (however, we never forget indentation).

Masters of throw-away programming seem wizards to the uninitiated. In most cases, computer users are not particularly good programmers; usually they know nothing about programming. To enable these users to use such wizardry, various software tools have emerged, which enable the less skilled users to perform unusual tasks. Examples of such tools are the programs for sorting and merging files, searching for text strings, file comparisons, simple text reformatting, macro processors and many others. Probably the most important tool is a suitable text editor, especially if it is capable of being programmed and performing simple reformatting of text. In part, even the general programs for particular tasks (data-base systems, spreadsheets, drafting programs, etc.) may be considered such tools. An important property of such tools is the possibility of combining them. The data-base program must be capable of preparing a text file from the data in a base, a spreadsheet must be capable of reading the data from an ordinary file, etc. A well known example is the use of simple software tools to check proper spelling of words in a text (a part of a good program to perform such task may be found in problem 821A):

1. using a general tool to reformat text, all spaces and punctuation are substituted by new-line characters;
2. the obtained file is alphabetically sorted (thus moving equal words to the same place in the file);
3. using a program to count equal lines, we obtain a file containing each word exactly once;
4. using a program to compare two files, all words are found, which do not appear in the vocabulary of correct words.

Another example of how to use of general software tools and a throw-away program may be demonstrated in the example of problem 514D: determine all anagrams in an English vocabulary.

1. A simple program is written, which copies all words from the vocabulary twice to the output file: first by alphabetically sorting the characters within the word and then adding the original word.

2. The file obtained is then alphabetically sorted by a sorting program using the first words as the sorting key. In this way all anagrams are moved to the same place in the file.
3. Using a program to count unique lines, all words without anagrams (the number of equal lines is 1) are discarded and the anagrams written in a single line.

Using this algorithm, all anagrams may be found in just a couple of minutes; if we had to write a program for the entire algorithm ourselves, this would take much longer; even the execution time would probably be longer, since we would probably not write a program comparable in efficiency to the general sorting program.

Many functions of other software tools may be performed by programmable text editors. How easily a particular computer system is used is largely influenced by the availability of general software tools. The writing of this book would certainly be much more demanding if the tools were not available to format the text, to search through it, to determine changes, to search for cross-references, to produce the index, to prepare the text for printing, to draw most figures, and to carry out a number of other details.

An interesting and pleasant book describing such tools is B. W. Kernighan, P. J. Plauger: *Software Tools in Pascal*, Addison-Wesley, Reading 1981.

6. The user interface

The part of a program which performs the dialog (the interaction) with the user is called the *user interface*. The ease and effectiveness of use of a program depends primarily on the user interface. It is usually intermingled with other parts of the program, but nevertheless, it may be estimated that it represents the majority of the code of serious interactive programs.

Just as it is said that fine feathers make fine birds, it is also true that the user judges the entire program by the user interface. It is not only a question of the first glance, although this may be vitally important for commercial programs. We are usually ready to accept a disorderly man of noble mind after we come to know him well, but a bad user interface will keep on and on making our work more difficult and irritating.

The user interface must be designed to make the use of the program most natural to the user. The quest for effectiveness in program use may be fulfilled in various ways. To choose one of them, the users that the program is intended for must be taken into account.

Recent programs communicate with the user through a graphical terminal and require no extensive training to be used. They help the user with advice and guide him using *menus* (*choices*), and the user directs the program by choosing one of the possible choices or by pointing (the graphical environment). The use of such a program requires no particular knowledge or training. Normally, the user is capable of solving his problems after a short time. Nevertheless, this way has its deficiencies. After a while, the user learns to use the tools perfectly, and so the constant advice and "guiding by hand" become unnecessary. Then, his work would be done faster with short (although less comprehensible) commands. The user may get the feeling that he must constantly explain his wishes to a deaf person by waving hands.

On the other hand, one frequently encounters programs with which the user may only communicate using cryptic commands, unclear at first glance, while the program responds to the commands in an unintelligible way or does not react at all. There may be two reasons for that. Either the authors did not think it worthwhile to provide a better user interface, or the communication is well thought over and is designed to suit specially trained users, who are thus capable of communicating with the program very effectively. In most cases the truth lies somewhere in between (usually it is closer to the laziness of the programmers than to the effectiveness of the users).

In real life, usually no extreme works well. Good programs allow the user to adapt the method of communication to his needs and knowledge. A novice must be provided with the option that the program guides him through the process of solving the problem. The program must be capable of advising him, and sometimes even capable of guessing what the user has in mind. The more experienced the user becomes, the more freedom and the more effective expressive powers he must have at his disposal.

We must remind you of a joke about the programs the manufacturers praise as "user friendly" (which is a virtue, but not one to be exaggerated; frequently it is misunderstood by the authors of the programs):

> The computer flatters the user, saying: "*I'm so user friendly, that I will pose a dozen questions prior to letting you do your work*!"

In writing our solutions, we have intentionally neglected the user interface, since such extensions to programs would conceal the essence of the solutions. An example of a program with a simple user interface may be seen in solution 424A. Some further guidelines for the design of a user interface communicating with the user through graphical input and output may be found in solution 513G.

To illustrate the discussion about the user interface, let us present an unacceptable way of communication found in a game written by some young hackers. The idea of the author was the following:

— first the program should present itself;

— then it should ask the player what is his name;
— since the game is played by pressing various keys representing a number of commands (move left, right, shoot, and so on), and since keyboards are different and so are the tastes of the users, the program should allow the player to choose the keys to be used for particular commands.

Let us first describe what happened in the first game. At start, the program greeted us by writing a welcome over the entire screen. When nothing happened after that for several seconds, we pressed the ⟨RETURN⟩ key, hoping to tell the program we have read the welcome message. Nothing happened for another second, then the program asked for our name and proceeded, without waiting, to ask for the key we want to use for shooting. After thinking over what has probably happened, we imagined that after writing the greeting the program probably waited some time and then proceeded to ask for the name. Since we had already pressed the ⟨RETURN⟩ key, the computer took this as our first answer, and so we accidentally entered an empty name in answer to the request for the player name. "So that is it" we said, "the program waits for the answer and the ⟨RETURN⟩ key, and then it proceeds." With this new knowledge we tried to provide the answer to the question about the choice of the key for shooting. We pressed a space and ⟨RETURN⟩. But it did not work. The space was correctly considered as the command to shoot, while the ⟨RETURN⟩ became the answer to the next question which asked about the key to move left.

What is the lesson to be learned from the above example? First of all, the user interface must be consistent! In the example above, the first event happened after a certain time expired, the second after entering a word and pressing the ⟨RETURN⟩ to terminate it, and the third by simply pressing a key, without terminating the entry with a ⟨RETURN⟩ key: three different methods without any explanation. What could be done here? The welcome message should include the word "WAIT" somewhere. It would be even better the player himself were to request the continuation by pressing the ⟨RETURN⟩ — and that somewhere at the bottom of the screen the initial message would include the statement "Press the RETURN key". This would probably suffice to avoid problems with later questions, although a short outline of the input required would do no harm.

Do not use computer capabilities all over, just to show they are available. Imagine what would be the reaction of the user to various events, and try to make the communication as uniform as possible. Using the program, the user obtains his conception about the representation of the problem which he solves using the program. This conception is called the **user model** (that is, the model of the problem as the user perceives it — and not the model of the user). The meaning of the keys and the commands, as well as the terms that the program uses for specific notions are a part of the user model as well. If, for instance, the user calls some object a "document", the program should use the same term for it, instead of bothering the user with, for instance, a "record in file A". The key, which in some part of the program means "edit the document," should by no means mean "delete the document" in another.

There is another important point in the communication of the program with the user. The user should never be left in doubt about what is happening with the program. To each action of the user (for instance, the entry of a command) the program must respond **immediately**. If the requested operation is to last for more than a second, the program should output at least "yes", or "wait", or even "the operation will last about 5 minutes". Sometimes it is enough that the cursor moves to a new line or that the command entered changes its colour. If this is not done, the user may be left in doubt as to whether he has successfully entered the command or perhaps forgotten to press the ⟨RETURN⟩ key or the key on the mouse, or may even think that the computer does not work.

There are many books on design and development of software, we only mention some:

I. Sommerville: *Software Engineering*, 2nd ed., Addison-Wesley, Reading 1985;

T. Gilb: *Principles of Software Engineering Management*, Addison-Wesley, Wokingham, 1988;

R. S. Pressman: *Software Engineering — A Practitioner's Approach*, 2nd ed., McGraw-Hill Series in Software Engineering and Technology, 1987.

Part II

Problems

The First Competition, 1977

111B **Mark** on the real line the set of numbers for which the following algorithm terminates:

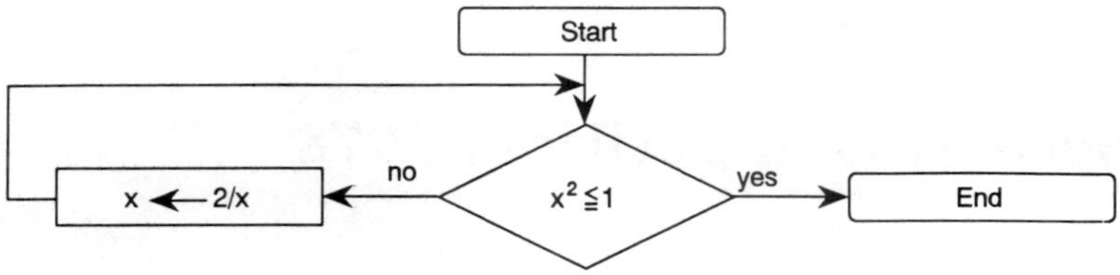

Figure N1: The flowchart of the algorithm

The expression $x \leftarrow 2/x$ in the flowchart indicates that the value of the expression $2/x$ is assigned to the variable x.

112C A function of two variables $f(a,n)$ is defined as follows:

$$f(a,n) = \begin{cases} 1 & \text{if } n{=}0 \\ (f(a,n/2))^2 & \text{if } n \text{ is even} \\ a * f(a,n-1) & \text{if } n \text{ is odd} \end{cases}$$

where a is an arbitrary real number, and n is a nonnegative integer.

a) **Compute** $f(2,5)$!

b) **What does** $f(a,n)$ **compute? Explain!**

113H A card deck is loaded into a computer (comprising a program in a high-level computer language, data for it, and the necessary control cards). **For what reasons** might the expected results not be obtained?

114A Write **a program** to read integers! Each integer occupies one line. Reading should continue until the number 0 or hundred integers have been read. The program should compute and output the average of all positive integers read.

115H An alternative method of writing an arithmetic expression is to precede both operands by the operator (usually it is written between them). Some examples:

the usual way of writing	the alternate way	the result
5 + 2	+ 5 2	7
4 * (9 − 2 * 3)	* 4 − 9 * 2 3	12

a) **Compute** $* \ 2 * + \ 2 \ 2 + 2 * 2 \ 2$!
b) Outline an **algorithm** to compute the value of an expression written in this way!

All operands are nonnegative integers, the operators are $+$, $-$, $*$, and $/$. A blank separates any pair of consecutive integers.

The Second Competition, 1978

Problems for competitors after the first year course

211A Suppose that we use a programming language providing no logical (Boolean) variables and operators. Nevertheless, we would like to use them. To implement that, we use integer variables instead, and assume that the value 0 denotes *false*, (no, non-true), while 1 denotes *true* (yes). **Transcribe** the logical operations **and** (conjunction), **or** (disjunction) and **not** (negation) into arithmetic expressions using only the operators $+$, $-$, $*$ and $/$!

212A A paymaster pays a hundred workers. The salary for each worker is known. Write an **algorithm** to determine how many coins or notes of each value should the paymaster request when collecting the money at the bank, to give each worker the minimum number of coins! The computer must specify the number of coins to be collected for each coin value. The values of all coins are given in a 12-element array *valCoin*.

213F In a warehouse, containers are transported through two lifts. Between both lifts there is a robot transferring the containers from the supply lift at the left to the take-away lift at the right. The robot may also use a temporary store, allowing, at most, ten containers to be stored within.

Draft an **algorithm** to control the operation of the robot, provided it can perform the following actions:

State(x) determines the state of the lift x, which may be *absent*, *empty*, or *full*;
Send(x) sends the lift x;
Transfer(y,z) transfers a container from y to z.

Here, x may be one of the lifts, while y and z may be either one of the lifts or the temporary store. You may assume the temporary store is empty when the robot is started.

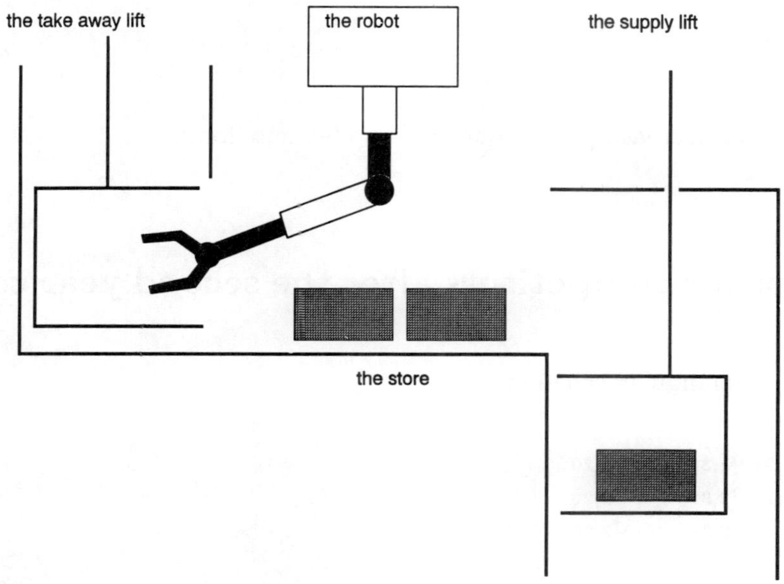

Figure N2: The transport robot

214C The functions f and g are defined for nonnegative integers as follows:

$$f(a,b) = \begin{cases} 0 & \text{if } b = 0 \\ f(a, b-1) + a & \text{if } b > 0 \end{cases}$$

$$g(a,b) = \begin{cases} 0 & \text{if } b = 0 \\ g(2a, b/2) & \text{if } b > 0 \text{ and } b \text{ is even} \\ g(2a, (b-1)/2) + a & \text{if } b \text{ is odd} \end{cases}$$

a) **Compute** $f(5,3)$ and $g(3,5)$!

b) **Which** mathematical operation is defined by f and g? **Explain!**

c) **How many** function calls are necessary to compute $f(m,n)$ and **how many** to compute $g(m,n)$, if computed according to the definition? **Which** of the two functions is more effective?

215D Write a **program** which reads a sequence of real numbers (from cards, each card containing a single number) and determines the length of the longest non-decreasing subsequence! For instance, in the sequence 3, 8, 9, 2, 1, 8, 7, 9, 9, 10, 11, 3, 2 the (maximal) non-decreasing subsequences are:

3, 8, 9,
2,

1, 8,
7, 9, 9, 10, 11,
3, and
2.

The longest non-decreasing subsequence is 5 elements long.

Problems for competitors after the second year course

221H A triangular schema:

$$\begin{array}{cccc} a_{1,1}, a_{1,2}, a_{1,3}, & \ldots, & a_{1,20} \\ a_{2,2}, a_{2,3}, & \ldots, & a_{2,20} \\ a_{3,3}, & \ldots, & a_{3,20} \\ & \ddots & \vdots \\ & & a_{20,20} \end{array}$$

is rewritten in a single line:

$$\begin{array}{l} a_{1,1}, a_{1,2}, a_{1,3}, \ldots, a_{1,20}, a_{2,2}, \ldots, a_{19,20}, a_{20,20} = \\ b_1, \quad b_2, \quad b_3, \quad \ldots, b_{20}, \quad b_{21}, \quad \ldots, b_{209}, \quad b_{210}. \end{array}$$

At which position in the table b_k does the element $a_{i,j}$ appear? At which position in the schema does the element b_k occur (which $a_{i,j}$ translates to b_k)?

222C What does the following program **output**:

```
program Zero(output);
  const m = 21;
  var i: integer;

  function F(n: integer): integer;
  begin
    if n>1 then F:=2*F(n-1)-2**n else F:=2*m;
  end; {F}

begin {Zero}
  i:=1;
  while F(i)<>0 do i:=i+1;
  writeln(i);
end. {Zero}
```

(In this Pascal program ** denotes exponentiation; 2**n thus means 2^n.) The program computes the zero of the function:

$$f(n) = \begin{cases} 2m & \text{if } n = 1 \\ 2f(n-1) - 2^n & \text{if } n > 1 \end{cases}$$

223E On a circular road n cars are positioned arbitrarily. The total amount of fuel in all their fuel tanks allows one car to tour the entire road. It may be proved that a car can be found which can tour the entire road, provided it can transfer all fuel from any car it meets to its own tank. Write an **algorithm** to find such a car! The inputs to the algorithm are: the position of each car on the road (the arc length from a fixed point on the circle measured in the same direction for all cars) as well as the distance the car can travel on its own fuel.

224D Write an **algorithm** to shift all elements in a table of n elements circularly right by k places ($k \leq n$)! The *Swap*(i,j) procedure is provided, which swaps the i-th and the j-th element of the table. No variables may be used except counters.

Example: circularly shifting the table 1, 2, 3, 4, 5, 6, 7, 8 three places right the table 6, 7, 8, 1, 2, 3, 4, 5 is obtained.

Estimate the number of operations (i.e. calls to the *Swap*) procedure depending on n and k! Try finding the algorithm that calls the *Swap* procedure the minimum number of times!

225A Write a **program** to print the following figure on 41 lines:

```
     *
    ***
   *****
  *******
 *********
***********
 *********
  *******
   *****
    ***
     *
```

The Third Competition, 1979

Problems for competitors after the first year course

311A Write a **program** to print the following table of numbers:

```
... 0 0 0 1 0 0 0 ...
... 0 0 1 1 1 0 0 ...
... 0 1 2 3 2 1 0 ...
... 1 3 6 7 6 3 1 ...
```

In the table, the first line contains zeros except for the middle number, which equals 1; each number in any line that follows equals the sum of the three numbers lying adjacent to it in the line above. The table should be printed in 21 columns and should terminate when all numbers in the line become nonzero.

312F Since a bridge is too narrow to allow two cars to meet on it, a traffic signal is installed at each end of the bridge, as well as a sensor which checks whether there is a car waiting to cross the bridge. There is another sensor on the bridge itself, checking if a car is crossing it. Write an **algorithm** to control both traffic signals, taking care that no car waits unnecessarily, and that during rush hours the traffic flows in turn in both directions! The bridge is very short. The devices on either end of the bridge are controlled using the following procedures and function:

Open(*side*) *side* denotes an end of the bridge; *Open* causes the traffic light at the specified end to change to "go";

Close(*side*) *side* again denotes an end of the bridge; *Close* causes the traffic light at the specified end to change to "stop";

Sensor(t) t denotes a sensor to probe whether it senses a car; t may denote a sensor at either end of the bridge or the one on the bridge itself; *Sensor* is a function returning *YES*, when a car is sensed and *NO* otherwise.

The ends of the bridge are denoted by a and b, the sensor on the bridge is denoted by m. a, b, m, *YES* and *NO* are predefined constants.

Examples: *Open*(a) switches the traffic light at the a end of the bridge to "go";
Close(b) switches the traffic light at the b end to "stop";
Sensor(m) equals *YES*, whenever there is a car crossing the bridge;
Sensor(b) equals *NO*, unless there is a car waiting at the b end of the brig

313C Observe the following functions (n is a nonnegative integer):

$$s(n) = \begin{cases} n & \text{if } 0 < n < 10 \\ s(n \textbf{ div } 10) + n \textbf{ mod } 10 & \text{if } n > 9 \end{cases}$$

$$p(n) = \begin{cases} n & \text{if } 0 < n < 9 \\ 0 & \text{if } n = 9 \\ p(s(n)) & \text{if } n > 9. \end{cases}$$

a) **Compute** $s(15324)$ and $p(15324)$!
b) What does the function s compute? **Explain**!
c) **Not obligatory**: **prove** that $p(n)$ equals the remainder of dividing n by 9 for any nonnegative integer n!

314D A programmer of questionable qualities has brought us the following program:

```
program ReverseData(input,output);
  var
    n,i,j,z: integer;
    t: array [1..100] of integer;
begin
  readln(n); for i:=1 to n do read(t[i]);
  j:=n;
  for i:=1 to n do
    begin z:=t[i]; t[i]:=t[j]; t[j]:=z; j:=j−1 end;
  for i:=1 to n do write(t[i]);
end. {ReverseData}
```

What does the program **output** when given the following data:

```
10
9   8   7   6   5   4   3   2   1   0
```

Can you **guess** what the programmer intended to write and **correct** the program?

315C When given a set of data, programs written in a certain programming language may terminate or not. We might consider writing a program T in the same language to compute, when given *any* program and a set of its data, whether the latter program terminates or not. **Prove** that no such program can possibly exist!

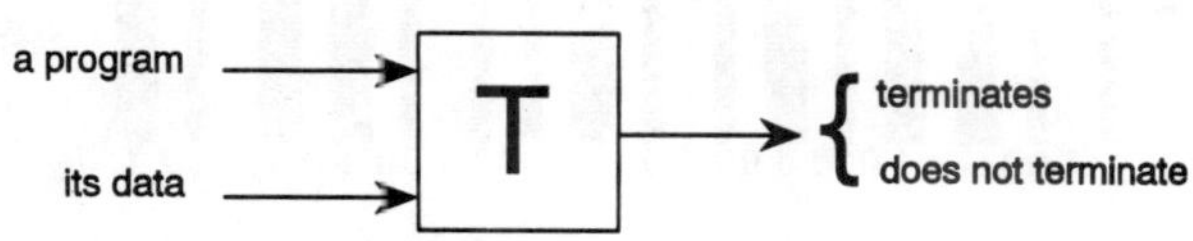

Figure N3: The program T

Hints:

a) Suppose that such a program T exists. Using existing program transforms convert T into another program which cannot exist. If the conversions can certainly be performed, then T cannot exist.

b) A program which terminates according to one reasoning, and never terminates according to another does not exist.

Problems for competitors after the second year course

321A A group of n children wants to play the game of tag. They know a count-out m words long. Write a **program** to compute which child is the catcher! The children are numbered from 1 to n, and the counting starts at the first child. The catcher is the one to remain the last in the circle.

322F Data are printed on paper in a special code, consisting of alternating black and white strips (bars). A thin strip (black as well as white) denotes a zero, and a thick one denotes a one. The thick strips are twice as wide as the thin ones. Draft an **algorithm** to output the sequence of zeros and ones coded on paper! The reading device moves along the paper with constant velocity. To allow measuring of the velocity, a thin black strip is printed prior to the data. The following two functions are provided for reading:

Colour returns the colour currently sensed by the reading device;

Time returns the time elapsed from the start of the program execution in milliseconds.

Example:

Figure N4: An example of the bar code

How would the **algorithm** change, if it should adapt to the changing velocity of the reading device?

323C For nonnegative n the functions f, g and h are defined as:

$$f(n) = \begin{cases} 0 & \text{if } n = 0 \\ 1 & \text{if } n = 1 \\ f(n-1) + f(n-2) & \text{if } n > 1 \end{cases}$$

$$h(a,b,n) = \begin{cases} a & \text{if } n = 0 \\ b & \text{if } n = 1 \\ h(b, a+b, n-1) & \text{if } n > 1 \end{cases}$$

$$g(n) = h(0,1,n)$$

a) **Compute** $f(5)$ and $g(5)$!

b) **Show** that for any a, b, c, d and e the following holds:
$h(a,b,e) + h(c,d,e) = h(a+c, b+d, e)$!

c) **Show** that the equality $f(n) = g(n)$ holds for any nonnegative integer n!

324D A programmer of questionable qualities sent us the following program:

```
program Table(input,output);
  var
    i,j,z: integer;
    a: array [1..10,1..10] of integer;
begin
  for i:=1 to 10 do for j:=1 to 10 do read(a[i,j]);
  for i:=1 to 10 do for j:=1 to 10 do
    begin z:=a[i,j]; a[i,j]:=a[j,i]; a[j,i]:=z end;
  for i:=1 to 10 do begin
    for j:=1 to 10 do write(a[i,j]);
    writeln;
  end;
end. {Table}
```

Create suitable data for this program and **write down** the data and the results! Can you **guess** what the programmer intended to write and **correct the program** to work as you think it should?

325C (see problem 315C).

The Fourth Competition, 1980

Problems for competitors after the first year course

411B n and p are integer data. For the algorithm:

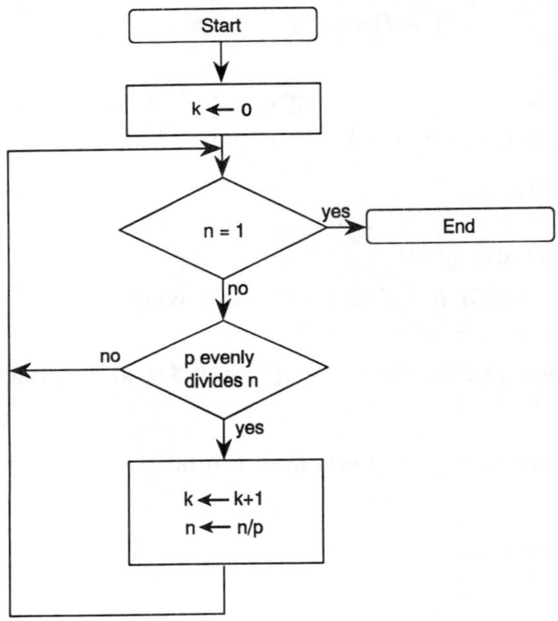

Figure N5: The flowchart of the algorithm

determine:

a) the value of k when the algorithm terminates if at start $n = 81$, $p = 3$;
b) for which values of n and p the algorithm terminates;
c) what is the value of the variable k if the algorithm terminates.

412F Next to a railway, a sensor device is installed, observing whether a carriage is moving by. Carriages are 10 m long, and there is 1 m of space between them. The interval between two consecutive trains never lasts less than one minute. Write an **algorithm** (or a program) to output the velocity of each train moving by! The following functions are provided:

Carriage returns *YES* (1, *true*), if there is a carriage moving by the sensor device, or *NO* (0, *false*) otherwise;

Time returns the time (in seconds) elapsed from a fixed moment.

413B Write a **program** to determine which number from the range between 1 and n has the most divisors. n is an input to the program.

414A In a certain programming language the following logical operators are defined: $\neg$ (**not**, negation), $\wedge$ (**and**, conjunction) and $\vee$ (**or**, disjunction) as well as the relational operator $\geq$ (greater or equal). **Rewrite expressions**: $a < b$, $a > b$, $a = b$, $a \neq b$ and $a \leq b$ using exclusively the operators defined in the language!

415B After the termination of the program segment below, where n and s are integer variables, the value of $s = 10$. **Determine** the smallest possible starting value of n providing this result value!

```
...
s:=0;
while n>0 do begin
  if odd(n) then s:=s+1;
  n:=n div 2;
end;
...
```

Problems for competitors after the second year course

421A Consider the following program:

```
program Chain(input);
  var
    k,i: integer;
    t: array [1..100] of 0..100;
begin
  for i:=1 to 100 do read(t[i]);
  read(k);
  while t[k]<>0 do k:=t[k];
end. {Chain}
```

Write a **program** that reads the data of the *Chain* program above (the values of the elements of the table t in the range from 0 to 100 as well as the starting index)! The program should output whether the *Chain* program terminates for the given data.

422F Next to a railway, a sensor device is installed, observing whether a carriage is moving by. Carriages are 10 m long, and there is 1 m of space between them. The interval between two consecutive trains never lasts less than one minute. Write an **algorithm** (or a program) to output the number of carriages in each train as well as the time when its last carriage moved by! The following functions are provided:

Carriage returns *YES* (1, *true*), if there is a carriage moving by the sensor device, or *NO* (0, *false*) otherwise;

Time returns the time (in seconds) elapsed from a fixed moment.

423E Write a **program** to output the labels of bus stops in the order of their appearance along a bus route if the pairs (bus stop, next stop) are given! There are n stops along the entire route (less than 1980), and the stop labels are numbers in the range from 1 to n. The data describe exactly one circular route and need not be tested.

424A On a table there are n glasses of various volumes. Each of them may be filled with water to a chosen level. The water may be poured from one glass to another in one of the following two ways:

— all the water from one glass is poured to the other, if there is enough space in the latter;

— enough water is poured to the other glass to fill it entirely.

Demonstrate, how you would **present** the problem (the data) **in a programming language**, and write a **procedure** to perform the pouring from one glass to another. The glasses are numbered from 1 to n.

425B (See problem 415B).

The Fifth Competition, 1981

Problems for competitors after the first year course

511H A colour picture sent to the earth by Voyager 1 is composed of three black-and-white pictures. Each of them is in turn composed of 256 × 256 points. In each point, 256 color intensities are distinguished. What is the **transmission speed** of the pictorial data (how many bits are transmitted per second), if 87 minutes (5220 seconds) are necessary to transmit the entire colour picture (i. e. all three black-and-white pictures)?

512B Consider the following program:

```
program Hamming(input,output);
  var x,y,d: integer;
begin
  readln(x,y); d:=0;
  while (x<>0) or (y<>0) do begin
    if (x mod 2)<>(y mod 2) then d:=d+1;
    x:=x div 2; y:=y div 2;
  end; {while}
  writeln(d);
end. {Hamming}
```

a) **Compute**, for some examples, what does the program output!

b) From the values of x and y, the *Hamming* program computes the result d. Write a **program AntiHamming** that inputs the values of x and d, and computes y so that the *Hamming* program would compute precisely d, when given x and y as its inputs (since y is not uniquely determined, AntiHamming may compute any appropriate y.)

513G A raster graphics terminal is connected to a computer, which controls the colour of any point of the terminal screen through a call to the procedure

SetColour(x,y,*colour*), where x and y are the coordinates of a screen point (in the range from 0 to 500), and *colour* is set to 1 to turn the point white, or to 0, if the point should become black.

Furthermore, a small box with a key (called a "mouse") is connected to the computer. It may be moved around on the table by hand. Its movements along the x and y directions are measured by the computer and made available to a program through a call to the procedure

Mouse(dx,dy,*key*), that returns in dx and dy the changes of the coordinates x and y (dx and dy may be negative). The variable *key* is set to 1, if the key on the mouse is depressed, and is 0, if it is not.

Write a **program** to draw white lines on the terminal screen by moving the mouse on the table. The mouse may leave traces only when its key is depressed. The program should react sensibly when the mouse is moved outside the screen area. You may assume that the program executes much faster than the mouse is moved, so that the values of dx and dy are always -1, 0 or 1.

514D Present an **algorithm** to check whether a pair of words are anagrams. Two words are anagrams, if they are composed of the same letters in a different order, e. g. SISTER/RESIST.

515B Write a **program** to print squares of all nonnegative integers up to n (input), which are palindromes. A palindrome is a word (a number) that reads the same backwards and forwards.

Problems for competitors after the second year course

521G Consider a pair of rectangles in the plane with sides parallel to the coordinate axes. Each rectangle is given by the coordinates of its lower left and upper right corner.

a) Write a **procedure** to determine the smallest enclosing rectangle containing both given rectangles!

b) Write a **procedure** to test whether the interiors of the two rectangles have a common point!

522B For **which input** does the program below output a 0? Try several cases first!

```
program Modulo(input,output);
  var a,k: integer;

begin
  readln(a); k:=10;
  while 2*k<=a do k:=2*k;
  while a>=10 do begin
    if a>=k then a:=a-k;
    k:=k div 2;
  end;
  writeln(a);
end. {Modulo}
```

523F The Space Shuttle is a very sophisticated spacecraft and may consequently only be operated with the aid of computers. To increase reliability, 5 equal computers are installed on board, executing the same programs. The computers also supervise each other, and if the majority find out that one of them gives incorrect commands, they may vote to turn it off.

Write the **part of a program** (running concurrently on all computers), that compares the actions of other computers and, if necessary, votes to turn one or more of them off! A computer is turned off by means of special circuitry, if the majority votes to turn it off. The following procedures are available:

WhoAmI(i)	returns in i the number of the computer executing the program;
WhatSays(i,*action*)	i is the number of a computer, and *action* describes a step proposed by the i-th computer in a given moment; if *action* equals 0, the i-th computer has been turned off;
VoteAgainst(i)	i is the number of a computer to be turned off.

Is it possible to write this **part of a program** without the *WhoAmI* procedure? How?

Remark: this problem is a simplification of the actual implementation, which differs somewhat from the one described.

524D A palindrome is a sequence of characters that reads the same backwards and forwards (e. g. MADAMIMADAM).
Write a **program** which finds the longest palindrome in a given string of characters starting from the first given character on. The string is terminated by a space.

525E In the Cartesian coordinate system, n points are given; among them the starting and final points are selected. Describe an **algorithm** to test whether the starting point may be connected to the final one with segments not longer than a! All line segments should end at the points given. It is not necessary to find the sequence of points leading from the starting to the final point, but only to find out whether such a sequence exists.

The Sixth Competition, 1982

Problems for competitors after the first year course

611A Two sequences of numbers in the range from 0 to 9 are given. Describe an **algorithm**, which counts

— the number of equal elements at the same positions in both sequences, assigning it to the variable *black*;

— the number of all other equal elements of both sequences (not lying at the same positions), assigning it to the variable *white*!

Each element may be counted only once!

Examples:

sequence 1	sequence 2	*black*	*white*
1 2 3 4 5 6 7 8 9 0	1 2 3 1 1 1 1 1 1 1	3	0
1 1 1 2 3 3 3 3 3 3	0 1 1 1 1 7 7 3 7 3	4	1
1 2 3 4 5 6 7 8 9 0	0 0 0 0 0 0 0 1 2 3	0	4

Remark: the problem originates in the game MEMO (the numbers from 0 to 9 represent colours).

612A At the end of a production line in a beverages factory there is a robot that places bottles into boxes. The robot has a sensor detecting whether there is a bottle on the line or not. Each box can hold 12 bottles. The coordinates of compartments in the box are given in figure N6. Write a **program** to control the robot! Assume that there is an empty box waiting initially. The following procedures are provided:

Sensor a function that returns 1 if there is a bottle on the line, or 0 if there is none;

Take the robot takes a bottle from the line;

Put(x,y) puts the bottle into the compartment (x,y) in the box;
NewBox removes a box and brings in a new, empty one.

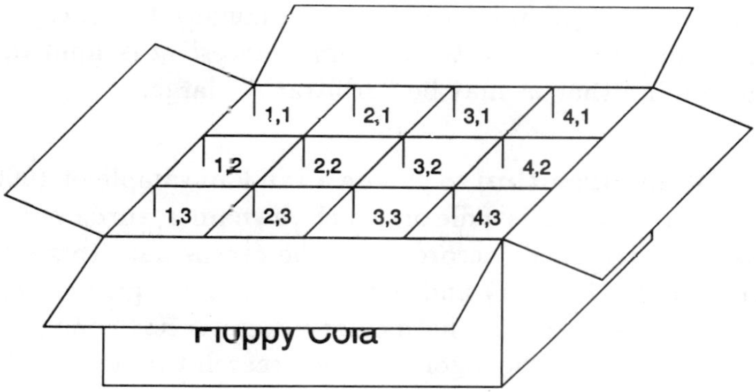

Figure N6: The coordinates of compartments in the box

613B The majority of small computers can only deal with integers in the range from −32768 to 32767. On such a computer we would like to perform computations with twenty-digit numbers. How can we represent such a number in a computer, if only addition and subtraction will be performed? Sketch the **algorithms** to add and to subtract a pair of such numbers. Pay attention to signs!

614B Write a **program** to compute all lucky numbers smaller than 1000! The lucky numbers survive the following procedure:

Place n nonnegative numbers in a sequence. Leave 1 out, and start with 2, removing every second number from the sequence. The first number after 2 in the sequence obtained is 3, so every third number is removed from the sequence. The next remaining number after 3 is 7, etc. The next remaining number after 7 is 9, then 13, etc. This procedure is repeated until no number can be removed. The numbers are always counted from the start of the sequence, that is, from 1 on.

A few starting steps:

1 **2** 3 4 5 6 7 8 9 10 11 12 13 14 15 16 17 18 19 20 21 22 23	
1 **3** 5 7 9 11 13 15 17 19 21 23	(every second element removed)
1 3 **7** 9 13 15 19 21	(every third element removed)
1 3 7 **9** 13 15 21	(every seventh element removed)
1 3 7 9 13 15 21	(As there are less than nine elements the process terminates.)

Problems for competitors after the second year course

621B Write a **program** to read a pair of nonnegative integers and output their quotient precise to m decimal places! m is input to the program as well. Keep in mind that m may be "arbitrarily" large.

622D Draft an **algorithm** to choose a random sample of 1000 Slovenians! At your disposal is a file on which the names, surnames and addresses of all Slovenians are recorded (according to the census data there were 1 891 864 Slovenians on March 31, 1981) and a random number generator — a *Random* function, $0 \leq Random < 1$. In the memory there is not enough space for the data about all Slovenians. The algorithm may search through the file only once!

623F We would like to build a simple electronic organ. There are 60 keys with switches available, 5 oscillators (tone generators) with adjustable frequency (pitch) as well as a computer, which is due to control the oscillators and the keyboard. Since there is a limited number of oscillators available, at most five tones may sound simultaneously. The following two procedures are provided:

Key(number)	a function returning 1 if the key *number* (in the range from 1 to 60) is depressed, and 0, if not;
Freq(oscillator,number)	a procedure to set the oscillator *oscillator* (between 1 and 5) to sound the tone *number* (between 1 and 60) or to cease, if *number* equals 0.

a) it is possible that more than 5 keys are pressed simultaneously. In this case the longest sounding tones must be shut off although corresponding keys are still depressed. In other words: pressing any key must immediately sound its tone for at least some time. Write a **program** to control the circuitry of the organ using the procedure (**a**)!

In case of trouble, you may use the procedure (**b**), bringing less points:

b) simplify the procedure (**a**) by considering at most five keys pressed simultaneously, and ignoring the excess keys.

624D **Find out** what the following program does! **Test** it on an example! **Explain** how it works (the algorithm)!

```
const n = 10;
type table = array [1..n] of integer;

procedure WhatDoIDo(var a: table; n: integer);
  var
    i,j,x: integer;
    again: boolean;

begin
  for i:=2 to n do begin
    x:=a[i]; j:=i-1; again:=true;
    while again do
      if j<1 then again:=false
      else if a[j]<=x then again:=false
      else begin a[j+1]:=a[j]; j:=j-1 end;
    a[j+1]:=x;
  end; {for}
end; {WhatDoIDo}
```

The Seventh Competition, 1983

Problems for competitors after the first year course

711B The sequence *seq* is defined as follows: $a_0 = a$, while a_{k+1} is computed by inverting the order of the decimal digits in $a_k + 4$. Example: for $a = 4$:

4, 8, 21, 52, 65, 96, 1, 5, 9, 31, 53, 75, 97, 101, 501,...

Write a **program** to determine which element of the sequence equals 1 (in our case it outputs $k = 6$)! The program should read the starting value a.

712G A black and white photograph is represented by a two dimensional table of 512 × 512 points, and the intensity in each point by an integer in the range from 0 to 127. We would like to transform the picture to avoid halftones; if possible, half of the points should become 0 and the other half 127. Write a **part of a program** to first determine the limit value below which the points will become 0 and above which 127, and then modify the picture accordingly!

713A What does the following program **output**? **Verify** the answer appropriately!

```
program Ball(output);
  const
    xmax = 31;
    ymax = 23;
  var
    x,y, dx,dy, j: integer;

begin
  x:=1; y:=1; dx:=1; dy:=1; j:=1;
  repeat
    x:=x+dx; y:=y+dy;
    if (x<1) or (x>xmax) then begin dx:=-dx; x:=x+dx end;
    if (y<1) or (y>ymax) then begin dy:=-dy; y:=y+dy end;
    j:=j+1;
  until (x=1) and (y=1) and (dx=1) and (dy=1);
  writeln(j);
end. {Ball}
```

714F In a warehouse, automatic trucks are used. Their routes are drawn on the floor with a black line of uniform width. Each truck carries two optical sensors at the bottom that are less than the line-width apart. A truck is guided by a computer. To observe the guiding line, the *Sensor*(*side*) function is provided, returning the value 1 if the sensor senses it, and the value 0 if not. The argument *side* may only assume two values: L for the left sensor, and R for the right one. To drive the truck, the computer uses the *Turn*(*side*) procedure, directing the truck to turn left, turn right, or to proceed in the same direction. The argument *side* may have the value L, R, or M.

a) Write an **algorithm** to guide a truck along a route!
b) Write an **algorithm** to allow a truck to take the left (or the right) branch of a Y fork!

Problems for competitors after the second year course

721C Write a **program** to compute all five-digit integers n such that all decimal digits appear in the decimal notations of n and $2n$, each digit appearing exactly once.

Example:

n	$2{\cdot}n$
09327	18654
20679	41358
48651	97302

722E In a labyrinth, each crossing is labelled by a distinct positive integer. A path through the labyrinth was found, starting at a certain starting crossing, and terminating at the exit crossing. The labels of all intermediate crossings were recorded. Write a **program** to remove all unnecessary loops from such a description (i. e. all portions of the path that start and end at the same crossing)!

723F In a bottling plant, filling of bottles is handled by a robot. There are n filling posts. The robot must deliver a bottle to the filling post, turn filling on, turn it off, and remove the bottle. The filling speed varies, it is however never excessive. Outline an **algorithm** to control the robot! The following operations may be used (in all cases i is in the range from 1 to n):

Open(i) opens the supply pipe at the i-th filling post; the operation completes immediately.

Close(i) closes the supply pipe at the i-th filling post; it completes immediately;

Remove(i) removes the bottle from the i-th filling post; the operation lasts three units of time, and during that time the robot is incapable of doing anything else;

Deliver(i) delivers an empty bottle to the i-th filling post; the operation lasts two units of time, and during that time the robot is incapable of doing anything else;

WhenFull(i) returns the minimum number of time units left to fill the bottle at the i-th filling post; if it returns 0, the bottle is already full; if it returns -1, the filling post is empty; the answer is delivered immediately.

The robot should never attempt to fill a bottle which is already full, and the filling posts should be as optimally utilized as possible. The number of filling posts and the minimum time to fill an empty bottle are not known in advance.

724B What does the following program do for positive inputs a and b? **Explain** the answer appropriately!

```
program Puzzle(input,output);
  var a,b: integer;

  function Mac(a,b: integer): integer;
    var x,c: integer;
  begin
    x:=1; c:=0;
    while (a<>0) or (b<>0) do begin
      if odd(a+b) then c:=c+x;
      x:=2*x; a:=a div 2; b:=b div 2;
    end;
    Mac:=c;
  end; {Mac}

begin {Puzzle}
  readln(a,b);  a:=Mac(a,b); b:=Mac(a,b); a:=Mac(b,a);  writeln(a,b);
end. {Puzzle}
```

Problems for experienced competitors

731B For a positive integer m, $1/m$ is a periodic fraction. Write a **program** to compute for any m in the range from 1 to 1000 the non-periodic and the periodic part of the fraction!

Example (the number in parentheses repeats periodically):

$$1/7 = 0.(142857)$$
$$1/100 = 0.01(0)$$
$$1/22 = 0.0(45)$$

732G In a table of size $n \times n$, the elements may assume only the values 0 or 1. A picture is "drawn" in this table with elements of value 1, composed of several parts. Write a part of a **program** which inputs the location of a point in the picture and deletes (changes ones to zeros) any point connected to the given point from the picture! A point is connected to its four (and not eight) neighbours. The picture in the table is mainly composed of lines and has little or no coloured areas.

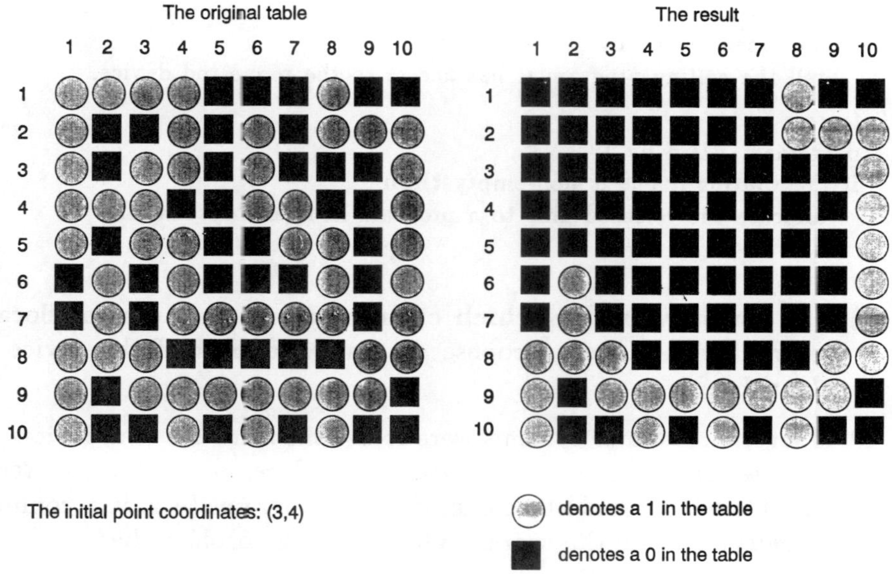

Figure N7: Example — a table 10×10

733C A very long line of text has been printed on paper. Several copies of it were found separately, torn to small pieces. Describe an **algorithm** to reconstruct the original line from the above information,

a) knowing that no piece was lost and that all characters at joints are uniquely readable;

b) in the case that condition (**a**) does not hold!

If there are more solutions, the algorithm should be able to find at least one. The number of the copies found is arbitrary (at least two). The copies were found in such a way that it is evident which pieces belong to a particular copy.

734F To a computer, n tape units (or similar devices) are attached. Several programs execute (essentially) simultaneously in the computer. When a program wishes to use a device, it must request it by a call to the *Request* procedure. When it does not need the device anymore, it releases it by a call to the *Release* procedure. Both procedures are parts of the operating system, which takes care that the entire procedure always executes without interruption. The procedures use a common variable *nDev*. They work as follows:

Request:
  if *nDev* $\geq$ n **then**
    place the calling program into the waiting queue

else
  increment *nDev* by 1;
  tell the calling program it has access to the requested device.

Release:
  decrement *nDev* by 1;
  if the waiting queue is non-empty **then**
    allocate the released unit to a program in it and restart it.

a) Can you show **under which circumstances** such device allocation leads to trouble? Can you propose an **improvement** of the device allocation algorithm?

b) If several computer systems were to use the same set of n devices, one could use the same *Request* and *Release* procedures on each computer, only the variable *nDev* should be common to all programs (e.g. in a common part of memory). Would this work? Where does the problem lie?

The Eighth Competition, 1984

Problems for competitors after the first year course

811G A table of size $m \times n$ contains only the numbers 0 and 1. The ones in this table constitute the edge of a figure, while its interior and exterior are represented by zeros.

The edge of the figure is a simple connected line. Altogether a point has four neighbours (left, right, above, below). Any point on the edge has exactly two neighbours that belong to the edge as well (two of the four neighbours equal 1, the other two are 0).

Write an **algorithm** which, given the coordinates i and j of a point in the table, determines whether the point is inside, outside, or on the edge of the figure!

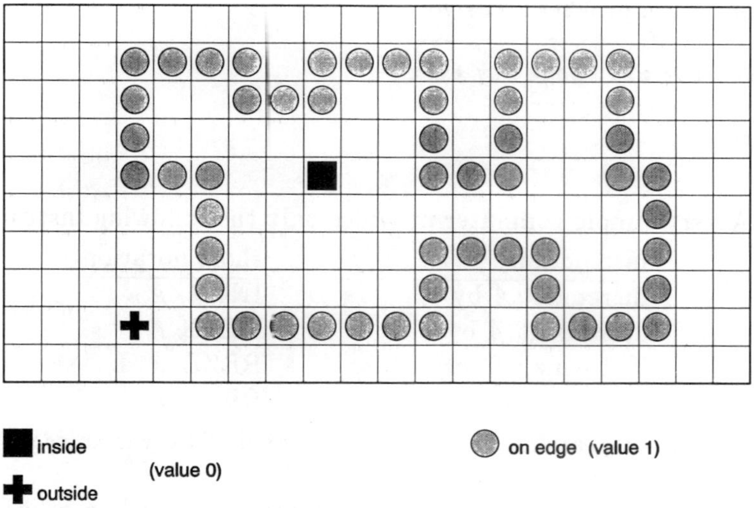

Figure N8: An example

812F A telephone sends the dialled number to the exchange as a sequence of pulses for each digit. The digit n is represented by n pulses, save zero, which is denoted by 10 pulses. A pulse is sent by interrupting the line for 1/20 seconds and then waiting the next 1/20 seconds before sending the next pulse. Before choosing the first digit, as well as between two consecutive digits the line must be closed for at least 1/3 seconds.

A computer is connected to a telephone line, and we need a program to dial numbers keyed in. The following procedures are available:

Lift connect the line;
Drop interrupt the line;
Wait(n) wait for n milliseconds.

Write a detailed **algorithm**!

813A Write a **program** that copies the input text double-spaced to the output, underlines the text between the double quotes (") in the intermediate lines, and removes the quotes! The input lines are at most 60 characters long, and the program must preserve the line structure of its input.

Example: the input text

```
The competition problems are "very
easy". Not for all. "Some" may even
be solved.
```

should be copied to

```
The competition problems are very
                             ----
easy.  Not for all. Some may even
----                ----
be solved.
```

814H A very simple computer provides only the following instructions:

instruction	short notation
increment A by 1	INCR A
decrement A by 1	DECR A
if A equals 0, branch to L	BRZE A, L
branch to L	BR L

where A is any variable, and L any instruction label. The variables of this computer can hold small unsigned integers.

In the variables X and Y specific values are stored, while other variables hold unknown values. Write a **program** for this computer, which exchanges the values of the variables X and Y!

Problems for competitors after the second year course

821A On a file, alphabetically sorted words are stored. To save space in the file, we observe that some starting letters of two consecutive words are usually equal. Instead of these initial letters we precede the rest of the word by a digit between 2 and 9, which specifies how many letters should be kept over from the previous word. No digit in front of the word means the same as 0. Words are delineated by spaces.

Example:

```
abacus 3ndon 7ed 2normal 8ly 9ity
2solute 8ly admiral 7ty beginner
```

Write a **program** to read a file encoded in this way and output the full (decoded) words!

822F A one way character transmission is to be established from a computer, called the TRANSMITTER, to another computer, called the RECEIVER. The TRANSMITTER exposes a character by a call to *Expose*(*ch*) procedure. The RECEIVER may examine the exposed character by call to *Examine*(*ch*) procedure.

Two more control wires allow the computers to agree when a character has been exposed or examined. The first is controlled by the TRANSMITTER using the *Signal*(i) procedure (where i may equal 0 or 1), and inspected by the RECEIVER using the *State*(i) procedure (where i becomes 0 or 1). The other wire is controlled by the RECEIVER using the *Signal*(i) procedure, and inspected by the TRANSMITTER using the *State*(i) procedure.

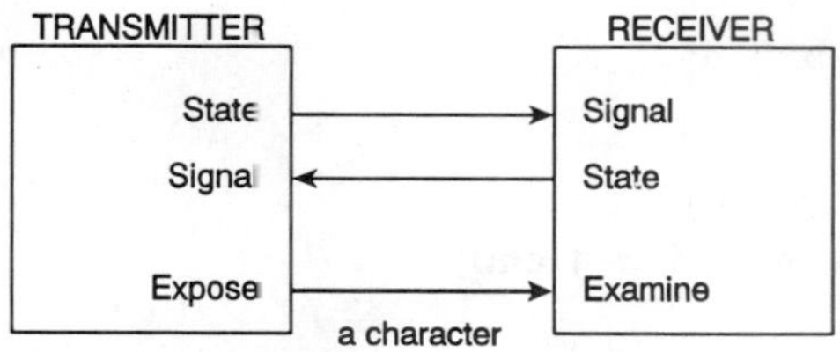

Figure N9: An outline of the computer interconnection

Establish the rules for managing the control wires during the character transmission! Outline an **algorithm** for the TRANSMITTER, which reads characters from a file and transmits them! Also, write an **algorithm** for the RECEIVER, which receives characters and writes them to a file!

Take into account that the computers may execute at different speeds. You may assume that the state of both control wires is 0 initially.

823E There are n towns on an island. From every town a road leads to each other town; however, all roads are one-way. The towns are numbered from 1 to n. For each town k a list is given, specifying the towns to which a road leads from the town k. (Evidently, from all towns not listed in the list of the town k roads lead from them to the town k). Write an **algorithm** to find any route leading through all towns on the island, through each exactly once! **Propose** a suitable data structure! The algorithm should be as efficient as possible.

Example: there are 5 towns on the island,

from town 1 there is a road to towns 2, 3, 4, and 5;
from town 2 there is a road to towns 3 and 4;
from town 3 there is a road to towns 4 and 5;
from town 4 there is no road;
from town 5 there is a road to towns 2 and 4.

A suitable route leads through towns 1, 5, 2, 3, and 4.

824B On a small computer, the following program terminated due to integer overflow. What does the program **output** on computers with larger integers? **Prove** the answer!

```
program Circle(output);
  const orwell = 1984;
  var a,b,f,k: integer;

begin
  f:=0;
  for k:=1 to orwell do begin
    a:=k; b:=k;
    while a>0 do begin
      if odd(a) then f:=f+b;
      a:=a div 2; b:=b*2;
    end;
    for a:=1 to k do f:=f-2*a+1;
    if f>0 then begin writeln(f); f:=-f end;
  end; {for}
end. {Circle}
```

Problems for experienced competitors

831F The telephone company offers a wake-up service to its subscribers. An operator accepts the orders and enters them into a computer by typing-in the telephone number and the time when the number should be called. Wake-up calls may be ordered for at most 24 hours in advance. The computer must register all requests (there may be plenty of them), dial the number at the requested time, and delete the request.

Describe a **data structure** suitable for an effective representation of the requests, and write an **algorithm** for the wake-up service, provided the following procedures are given:

Read(*dataReady*,*number*,*time*)	checks whether a new wake-up request has been typed in; if there is a new request, *dataReady* equals 1, and the requested telephone number and wake-up time are given in *number* and *time*; if there is no new request, *dataReady* equals 0, and the other arguments are not defined.
Dial(*number*)	dials the telephone number given by *number*; the procedure executes immediately;
Clock(*time*)	returns the current day-time in hours (a real number $0 \leq time < 24$).

832F A keyboard and a printer are attached to a computer. The characters typed in on the keyboard must be printed on the printer. The typing speed may sometimes exceed the speed of the printer; however, on average the printer is fast enough.

Each time a key is pressed on the keyboard, the *Typed*(*ch*) procedure is automatically called.

If the printer is idle, a character may be sent to be printed by calling the *Print*(*ch*) procedure.

Each time the printer finishes printing a character, the *Printed* procedure is called. After that the printer is certainly idle.

Write the *Typed* and *Printed* **procedures**! You may assume that the architecture of the computer prevents the execution of one of the procedures during the execution of the other.

833A In a given text, words are strings composed exclusively of letters. All other characters delimit adjacent words. When the last nonblank character of the line is a '–' and it immediately follows the last word of a line that means that a word continues (carries over) to the next line. Write a **program** to inspect the given text and output

— the number of words in the text, and

— the average length of the words (number of letters per word) in the text!

834B What does the following program **output**?
Why; **explain**!

```
program Reverse(output);
  const k = 10; n = 1023;  { n = 2**k-1 }
  var
    t: array [0..n] of integer;
    a,f,i,j,m: integer;

begin
  t[0]:=0; f:=1; m:=(n+1) div 2;
  while f<=n do begin
    for i:=0 to f-1 do t[i+f]:=t[i]+m;
    f:=2*f; m:=m div 2;
  end;
  for i:=0 to n do begin
    a:=t[i]; t[i]:=0;
    for j:=1 to k do begin t[i]:=2*t[i]+a mod 2; a:=a div 2 end;
  end; {for}
  for i:=0 to n do if t[i]<>i then writeln(i,t[i]);
end. {Reverse}
```

The Ninth Competition, 1985

Problems for competitors after the first year course

911D Andy and Charlie are ardent programmers. Each of them has data about all his programs recorded in his computer. For each program, its name, as well as the day, month, and year of the last improvement are stored. The program lists are sorted alphabetically by the program names. Each program appears only once in a particular list (no two programs have the same name).

a) Specify, in more detail, the **data structure** you find most appropriate to record the data about the programs!

b) Write a **program** which compares both lists of programs and tells which programs Andy should lend to Charlie, since he does not have them or has an outdated version of them!

912F A drum printer comprises a line of hammers and a rotating cylinder. On the perimeter of the cylinder all characters are arranged . Equal characters are all aligned in the same line along the cylinder. The cylinder is 132 characters wide. The characters are printed by striking appropriate hammers against the paper at a particular moment. In this way, all F-s get printed first, then all G-s, then all H-s, etc.

Write a **program** that reads a text and prints it on the printer! Assume that the computer is considerably faster than the printer. The following procedures are available:

Advance advances the paper forward one line;

Location(ch) returns the character currently under the hammers; ch changes when the new line of characters is properly positioned for printing; since spaces are not printed, there is no space on the drum;

Strike(i) strikes the i-th hammer; i is an integer between 1 and 132; striking is fast compared to the rotational speed of the drum.

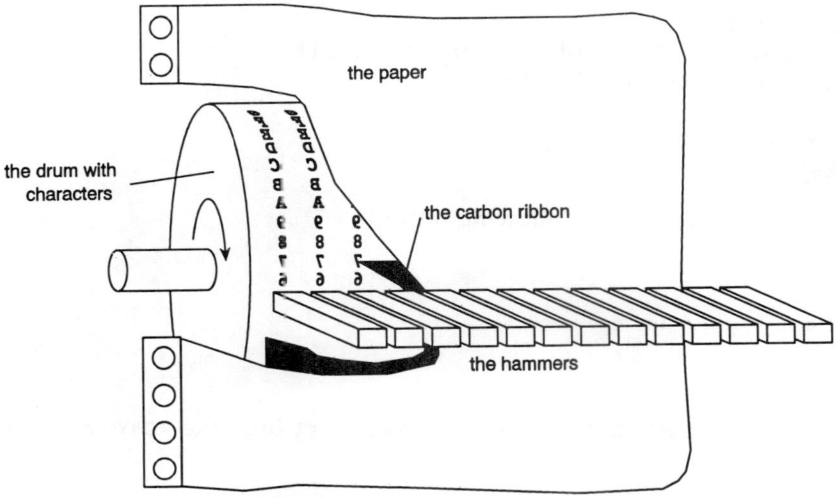

Figure N10: The drum printer

913A We obtained a new printer, which is not clever enough to know that the spaces at the end of a line need not be printed. Since we do not want to modify existing programs, we intend to put a simple microcomputer between the computer and the printer, which will be responsible for removing the unnecessary spaces.

Propose an **algorithm** for the microcomputer! The lines may be of any length, and the end of line is denoted by a special character. The following procedures are available:

Receive(*ch*) receives the next character from the computer;
Transmit(*ch*) sends the character *ch* to the printer.

Take into account that the microcomputer has *very little memory* (a few characters in size).

914A The following program was run

```
program Bla(input,output);
  const n = 10;
  var
    b: array [1..n] of integer;
    i,first,last: integer;
begin
  for i:=1 to n do read(b[i]);
  i:=1;
  while i<>0 do begin
```

```
    first:=i; write(first:2);
    repeat last:=i; i:=b[i] until (i=0) or (i<>last+1);
    if last<>first then write(' –',last:2);
    writeln;
  end; {while}
end. {Bla}
```

The program produced the following output:

```
1 - 4
9
6 - 8
10
5
```

What were the **input data** to the program? **Explain** the answer in detail.

Problems for competitors after the second year course

921G At a computer fair in Nowherton, a new computer is to be introduced. A commercial for it is to be displayed on its screen, which is 80 columns wide and 24 lines high (each line in the file with the commercial corresponds to a line on the screen). The text should be copied to the screen gradually, making the characters appear at their correct places in a random order. In the end, the entire commercial should be displayed. The following procedures are available:

WriteAt(x,y,ch) writes the character at the x-th column of the y-th line, $(x=1, y=1)$ is the upper left corner of the screen;

Random(r) returns in each call a random number r in the range $0 \le r < 1$.

Write this **program**! Remember that the visitors expect the display to be fast enough and unchanging in speed.

922F Three wires connect to a computer: OUTPUT, INPUT1 and INPUT2.

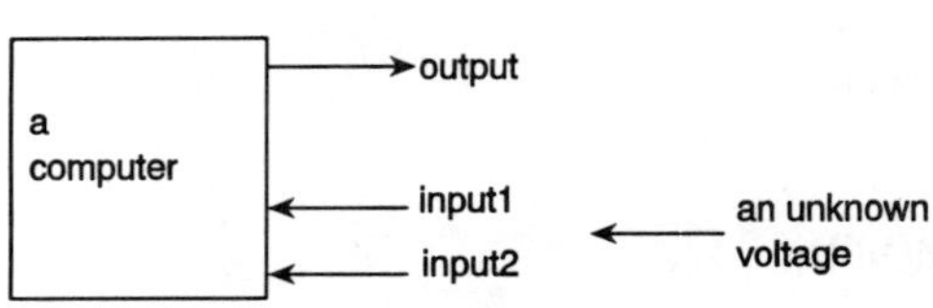

Figure N11: Measuring the unknown voltage

The following procedures are available:

SetOutput(n) sets the voltage on the output wire to n millivolts; n must be an integer between 0 and 1023;

Compare(*which*) compares the voltage on both input wires and returns in the variable *which* the value 1, if the voltage on the wire INPUT1 is higher than the voltage on the wire INPUT2, and returns 2 otherwise.

a) How would you measure an unknown voltage (between 0 V and 1,023 V) using such a computer? Describe the **algorithm**! Explain **where** the unknown voltage should be connected, **how** should the other lines be attached, and **how** the program should function!
b) **Which** is the fastest way to measure the unknown voltage (with the minimum number of calls to both procedures)?
c) **How** would you continuously measure a slowly changing voltage?

923D When entering a highway, each driver receives a card which must be returned at the exit toll-station. Due to various reasons some of the cards are never returned. The cards returned are collected at the exit toll-station in an arbitrary order. All cards in a series are labelled with sequence numbers from 1 to 30 000. The toll collector wants to know which cards are missing.

Write a **program** to output the numbers of all cards missing in a series!

924H A program is wanted to copy input characters to the output. During the copy, it must replace each pair of characters "AA" with the character "B", each pair of characters "BB" with the character "A", and leave all other characters unchanged. When replacing, it must take care that a replacing character may form a pair with the preceding character. **Is it possible** to write a program, which would be able to copy an arbitrary text (of arbitrary length)? The program may read the input text exactly once, and has a limited memory available. **Explain** the answer!

Examples: the first line contains the input text, intermediate phases follow below, and the last line contains the output text (the strings before replacement are printed in bold face, the replacement characters are underlined):

example 1:	example 2:	example 3:
AABCABBD	ABA**BB**	**BB**BCABBA
BBCABBD	AB**AA**	ABCA**BB**A
ACA**BB**D	A**BB**	ABC**AA**A
AC**AA**D	**AA**	ABCBA
ACBD	B	

Problems for experienced competitors

931B 7-bit characters are stored on a file. The device to which the text is directed requires the parity bit as well. The parity bit is the eighth bit in a character, chosen to make the number of ones in the new character (including the parity bit) even.

Example:

character='A', ord('A')=$65_{(10)}$=$1000001_{(2)}$
parity bit=0, new character=$01000001_{(2)}$=0+65=65

character='F', ord('F')=$70_{(10)}$=$1000110_{(2)}$
parity bit=1, new character=$11000110_{(2)}$=128+70=198

a) Write a **program** that copies an existing file to a new one, adding the parity bit to each character copied!

b) Computing the parity bit for each character of a file is time consuming even for a computer; can you **speed up** the program?

932F On two computers (1 and 2), the same program is needed to enable the computers to communicate with each other. The characters typed must be sent to the neighbour, and the characters received from it displayed on the screen. Both computers have access to a *single common memory location* (e.g. an integer variable). The computers may assign a new value to it, as well as inspect its current value. The following procedures are available:

Assign(n)	assigns a new value to the common location;
Inspect(n)	returns the current value of the common location (an integer n);
WriteCh(c)	writes the character c on the screen;
ReadCh(c,p)	checks whether there is a typed character available; if there is, its value is returned in the variable c and p is set to 1; otherwise the value of p is 0, and c is not defined;
Computer(r)	returns in r the number of the computer: 1 or 2.

Describe the **algorithm** for communication! Take care to synchronize the computers, as they may run at different speeds. The characters typed-in should appear on the neighbour's screen as soon as possible. You may assume that the initial value of the common memory location equals 0 and that there are more integers than characters.

933G A square raster picture of $n \times n$ points is given (where n is a power of 2). The colour of each point is represented by an integer. The picture stored in this form (as a matrix) must be converted to a tree, as the following example shows:

```
1 1 · · 1 1 · ·
1 1 · · · · · 2        3 4   the order of
2 2 · · 3 · 2 2        1 2   numbering of the squares
2 2 · · · 2 2 2
· · 1 · 2 2 2 2
· · · 1 2 2 2 2        (in the raster the colour 0 is represented
3 3 · · 2 2 2 2         by a dot for better readability)
3 3 · · 2 2 2 2
```

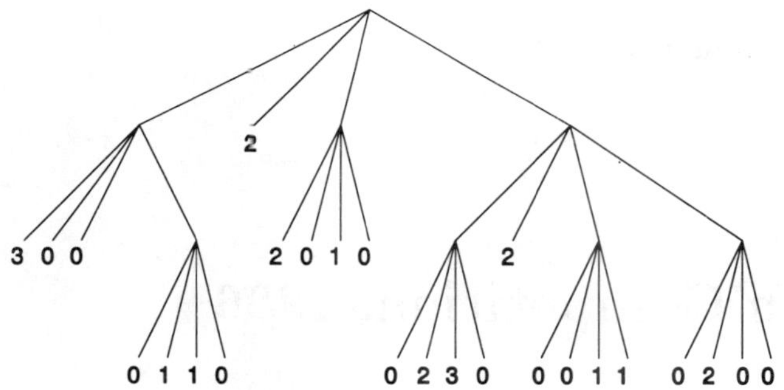

Figure N12: The tree corresponding to the data in the table

A square area entirely of the same colour is represented in the tree by a leaf node containing the colour number; otherwise the area is split into four squares — it is represented by a branching node consisting of four successors; for each square the procedure is repeated.

a) Propose a **data structure** to represent such a tree!
b) Write an **algorithm** that converts the matrix form of the picture to the proposed data structure!
c) Write an **algorithm** to determine the colour of a point (x,y) of the raster picture, given the proposed data structure!

934D The input data for the following program are:

12 18 9 27 48 11 98 54 54 69 12 13 1 15 16 17 80 50 51 50

What does the program output for these data? **Explain** the answer!

```
program FindOut(input,output);
  const n = 20;
  var
    tab: array [1..n] of integer;
    i,j,k,x: integer;

begin
  for i:=1 to n do read(tab[i]);
  i:=n;
  while i>1 do begin
    k:=1;
    for j:=2 to i do
      if tab[j-1]<=tab[j] then
        begin x:=tab[j-1]; tab[j-1]:=tab[j]; tab[j]:=x; k:=j end;
    i:=k;
  end; {while}
  for i:=1 to n do write(tab[i]:1,' ');
  writeln;
end. {FindOut}
```

The Tenth Competition, 1986

Problems for competitors after the first year course

1011F Using a digital voltmeter, a voltage is continuously measured. The voltmeter is attached to a microcomputer which constantly inputs the voltage currently measured (an integer between 0 and 255). Occasionally, the voltage fluctuates; in that case the program is (manually) told to stop reading the measurements and output the last 1000 measurements input (or all of them, if less than 1000 have been input). The measurements must be output in the correct chronological order.

It is important that during measurement the consecutive inputs follow as fast as possible. The duration of measurement prior to the interrupt may be arbitrarily long (there may be less than thousand measurements or many more than the memory is capable of storing). The following two procedures are given:

Measurement(*voltage*) inputs the current value of the voltage measured by the digital voltmeter; *voltage* receives a value between 0 and 255;

State(*s*) — *s* may have the value *MEASURE* (0) or *PRINTOUT* (1); initially the value of *s* is *MEASURE*.

Write a **program** to perform the measurement and output! After the output is finished, the program should forget all data measured and restart. **Estimate** how many **measurements** your program can perform **in a second** if running on an average 8-bit microcomputer and if written as effectively as possible! Assume that the calls of the two procedures do not consume any time.

1012B A sequence of four digit numbers is formed in the following way: from the digits of a given number the largest and the smallest number are produced. Their difference is used to proceed with the sequence. Write a **program** which reads the starting number and prints the sequence until it starts to repeat!

1013F A spring balance is loaded by a changing force (weight) which moves the measuring scale. The scale is a bar of alternating black and white strips of equal width. The width of a strip corresponds to the change of the force for one newton.

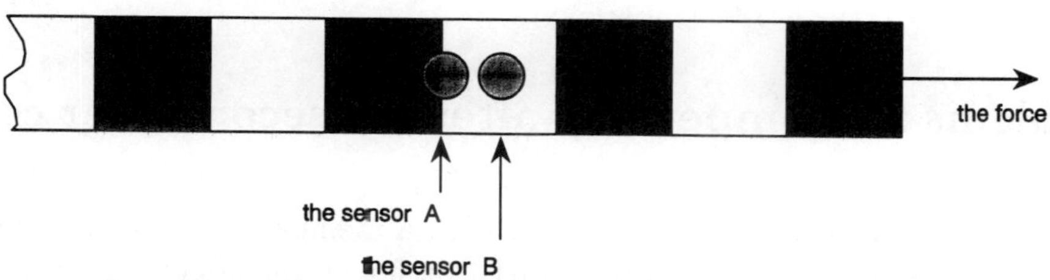

Figure N13: The measuring bar

Next to the bar, two sensors (photocells) are installed half the strip width apart (see figure N13). To read the state of the sensors the *SensorA* and *SensorB* functions are available, returning:

0, when the corresponding sensor senses a black strip; and
1, when there is a white strip next to the sensor.

Describe an **algorithm** to print the weight at any measurable change! Assume that the weight on the balance equals 0 initially. The execution of the program is much faster than the movements of the measuring bar.

1014A With the program below, the first 1000 elements of the sequence c_n were attempted to be printed, where

$$c_1 = 0, \quad c_2 = 0, \qquad c_n = n + \frac{1}{n}\sum_{j=1}^{n-1} c_j, \quad n = 3, 4, \ldots$$

Can you **modify** the program below so that it would require less space and time to execute? **How many** additions and subtractions does the given program perform, how many are needed by your program?

```
program Waster(output);
  const
    m = 1000;
  var
    c: array [1..m] of real;
    sum: real;
    n,j: integer;
begin
  c[1]:=0; c[2]:=0;
  for n:=3 to m do begin
    sum:=0; for j:=1 to n−1 do sum:=sum+c[j];
    c[n]:=n+sum/n;
  end; {for}
  for n:=1 to m do writeln(n,c[n]:10:3);
end. {Waster}
```

Problems for competitors after the second year course

1021H The Passionate Dicers Club, with a membership of several hundred members, organized a competition for all members according to the following rules:

In each round, a player throws a die ten times; the score of the round is the sum of points in all throws. The final score of a player is the sum of points in 30 rounds.

The players are numbered from 1 to n. In the competition, the only objective is to find the winner, the placement of other players is irrelevant. Due to the large number of players, the players who cannot possibly win must be eliminated as soon as possible. Describe the **algorithm** which, based on the results of individual rounds, selects the player for the next round, using the minimum number of trials to determine the winner.

1022G A picture is represented in a computer by a table of integers (a matrix) a of size $n \times n$. A rectangular subpicture (a part of the matrix a) is given by its width w, its height h and the indices x and y of its upper left element.

Write a **part of a program** that copies a given subpicture to some other position in the same picture. The new position is given by the indices nx and ny of the upper left corner of the copy.

The copy may overlap the original; in this case, the copy must overlay the original. You may assume that both the original and the copy are entirely inside the picture. Due to the shortage of space no auxiliary tables may be used during copy.

1023F A Geiger-Müller tube is attached to a computer and measures the radioactivity of the air. The pulses from the measuring tube generally occur every few seconds, but their frequency varies in time.

Describe an **algorithm** to detect pulses and continually output the average number of pulses during the last hour! The following two functions are provided:

Time returns the time elapsed since midnight in minutes;

Pulse returns 0, if the measuring tube did not detect any new pulse since the last call to this function; and 1, if the tube detected one or more pulses; to avoid the possibility of detecting more pulses, the *Pulse* function must be called frequently enough.

1024D On a magnetic tape, the integers between one and one million are written in arbitrary order, with a single integer missing. Describe an **algorithm** to find the missing number on a computer with 64-bit words, considering that only a few words of memory are available!

Problems for experienced competitors

1031D On a magnetic tape a million 20-bit integers are stored. A computer is available with three tape units and little memory. Write an **algorithm** to determine any integer not stored on the tape! The algorithm proposed should finish in a reasonable time. A tape may only be read or written sequentially from the start to the end. A command to rewind a tape to its beginning is available.

1032B A set of n elements has 2^n subsets. Write a **program** to output all the subsets of a n element set for any given n in such order that two adjacent subsets differ in a single element! Example: the elements of the base set are denoted by A, B, C, and D; in the printout the commas and braces are omitted; the following sequence conforms to the above requirements:

$\{\,\}$, A, AB, B, BC, ABC, AC, C, CD,
ACD, $ABCD$, BCD, BD, ABD, AD, D

Hint: try **proving** first that the subsets may always be ordered so that the first and the last subset also differ in a single element.

1033F A computer is capable of executing several processes simultaneously. Several processes execute programs that use (read and modify) files on a disk unit.

To prevent two processes changing each other's data, simultaneous access to the disk unit by any pair of processes must be inhibited. To accomplish this, the process must allocate the disk unit prior to using it. When the unit is needed no longer, the process must release it.

This technique must guarantee that a unit already allocated to a process cannot be allocated to any other process. In such a case the other process must wait until the current user releases the unit. You may assume that all processes use the disk unit in the proposed way.

To implement the technique, a portion of memory is available, common to all processes. In a program, it is represented by a table of integers. The following procedures are provided as well:

Wait(*time*) the program waits *time* milliseconds;

Random is a function returning a random value in the range from (inclusively) 0 to (exclusively) 1;

WhoAmI returns the process number; all processes running (there are never more than 10) are numbered from 1 to 10.

Write the **procedures**:

Allocate which allocates the disk unit; this procedure is called by each process before using the unit; if the unit is already allocated, the procedure should wait until the current user releases the unit and then allocate it;

Release releases the disk unit; this procedure is called by each process when the disk unit is no longer needed; if no disk unit is allocated by the process, this is an illegal operation!

Note: you may assume that the common portion of the memory is initialized to zeros initially.

1034D The program below reads n (1000) integers between 1 and m (100) and attempts to find a number x such that half of the data read are smaller than x and the other half greater than or equal to x. This is not always possible; however, it is always possible to find x such that the above holds approximately, so that the difference of the numbers of the data less than x, and the data greater than or equal to x is minimal. The program below works correctly in most cases; in some singular cases, however, it chooses a very unusual value for x. Determine **which are these cases** and describe how the program should be **improved** to work better.

```
program Boundary(input,output);
  const n = 1000; m = 100;
  var
    f: array [1..m] of integer;
    i,s,t,x: integer;
begin
  for i:=1 to m do f[i]:=0;
  for i:=1 to n do begin readln(t); f[t]:=f[t]+1 end;
  x:=1; s:=0;
  repeat s:=s+f[x]; x:=x+1 until s>=(n div 2);
  writeln('x = ',x);
  writeln('The number of data less than x:          ',s);
  writeln('The number of data greater or equal to x:',n-s);
end. {Boundary}
```

The Eleventh Competition, 1987

Problems for competitors after the first year course

1111B In a computer, the relief map of a mountainous terrain is represented by a table of $m \times m$ points. For each point, its elevation from sea-level is given. A ball is placed at the point (x,y) on the surface and its rolling down the terrain observed. To prevent the ball from escaping outside the table, the edge points are assigned a very high elevation (the terrain is surrounded by a high wall). From each point the ball moves to the neighbour towards which the descent of the terrain is the steepest (if there are more alternatives any of them is taken). The ball stops when it reaches the bottom point (when no neighbour lies lower). The inertia of the ball is ignored during the roll-down. Write a **part of the program** that reads the coordinates of the starting position of the ball, leads it down the valley, and outputs the position of the point where the ball stops. The terrain relief is stored in the table *height*.

1112F A voltmeter is attached to a computer, continuously measuring a changing voltage. At any given moment, a program can input the voltage currently measured (in the range from -1 V and $+1$ V). The voltage measured changes periodically, and is approximately sinusoidal in shape, implying that it changes its sign twice in each period.

Write a **program** that outputs the effective voltage at end of each period. The effective voltage equals the square root of the average of the squared voltages measured in a single period (provided the measurements are done often enough at uniform time intervals).

The following procedures are provided:

Measure(u) returns the current value of the voltage measured (a real number between -1 and $+1$);

Delay waits for a fixed short period (an appropriate pause between two consecutive measurements).

You may assume that the program executes very fast relative to the change of the voltage.

1113B On a magnetic tape 8-bit characters are stored. To enable the discovery of possible errors in the records, each 8-bit character is supplied with the ninth bit, whose value is chosen to make the number of ones in the extended (9-bit) character odd. The additional bit is called the *transverse parity bit.*

Consecutive characters on tape are grouped into blocks of equal even length. To ease error detection, a 9-bit character is appended to each block. This character represents *nine longitudinal parity bits.* Each bit in it is chosen to make the number of ones among the same numbered bits of the characters in the block, together with the parity bit, odd.

Example of a block with parity bits appended:

```
0 0 1 0 1 0 0 1 1 1 1 0 1 1   1
0 0 0 0 0 0 0 0 0 0 0 0 0 0   1
0 0 0 1 0 0 0 0 1 1 0 1 1 1   1
1 0 0 0 0 0 0 0 0 0 0 0 0 0   0
1 1 1 0 1 1 1 0 1 0 0 1 0 1   0
1 1 1 1 1 1 1 1 1 1 1 1 1 1   1
0 1 0 1 1 1 0 0 1 0 1 0 0 1   0
1 1 0 0 1 1 0 1 0 1 1 1 1 1   1

1 1 0 0 0 1 1 0 0 1 1 1 1 1   0  ← Transverse parity bits
                              ↑
          Longitudinal parity bits (the character appended)
```

When the characters are recorded on tape or read from it, an error may occur, changing the value of one or more bits. An error may also occur among parity bits.

- **How many** incorrect bits may occur in a block and still allow the error to be detected?
- **How many** incorrect bits may there be to allow the error to be recovered?
- Explain the **algorithm** to recover the block read (if necessary), or notify that the error is irrecoverable!

1114A

The program below should read a sequence of n integers and output the length of the longest subsequence of equal numbers in it.

Example: in the sequence 3 3 1 1 1 1 1 7 7 1 the longest subsequence of equal numbers is 5 numbers long.

Find a sequence of integers, for which the program computes an incorrect length of the longest subsequence. **Modify** or **improve** the program so that it will work correctly for all cases.

```
program Sequence(input,output);
  const n = 10;
  var
    i,d,dmax: integer;
    t: array [1..n] of integer;

begin
  for i:=1 to n do read(t[i]);
  d:=1; dmax:=1;
  for i:=2 to n do begin
    if t[i]=t[i-1] then d:=d+1
    else begin
      if d>dmax then dmax:=d;
      d:=1;
    end; {if}
  end; {for}
  writeln('The longest subsequence contains ',dmax,' integers');
end. {Sequence}
```

Problems for competitors after the second year course

1121A In a large warehouse, containers are labelled with computer readable numbers. To implement that, the numbers are written in binary notation using bar code, which is a sequence of alternating black and white strips of two different widths. A strip of width equal to the previous strip represents a zero (regardless of its colour), while a change in width represents a one. Furthermore, the sequence always starts with a *wide black* strip, (not representing any bit) and ends with a *black* strip of appropriate width, (representing the last—least significant bit of the number).

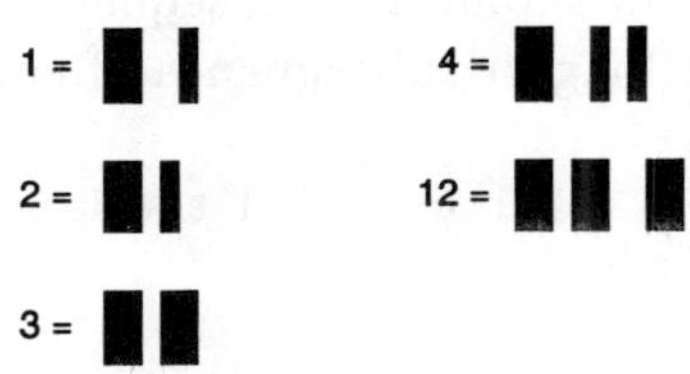

Figure N14: Examples of the bar code

Write a **program** that inputs a positive integer and prints the corresponding bar code! The following procedure is provided:

DrawBar(*colour*,*width*)	which prints a strip of requested colour (0=*white*, 1=*black*) and of requested width (0=*thin*, 1=*wide*).

1122F Eight terminals, situated in Dover, are to be connected to a mainframe in London. Leasing eight telephone lines and buying sixteen modems proves too expensive, while a pair of modems and one line could be afforded.

The problem is solved by connecting the terminals to a simple microcomputer and linking the latter through a modem to the telephone line to London. At the London end, a similar microcomputer is installed, communicating with the Dover one, while behaving as eight terminals attached to eight ports to the mainframe.

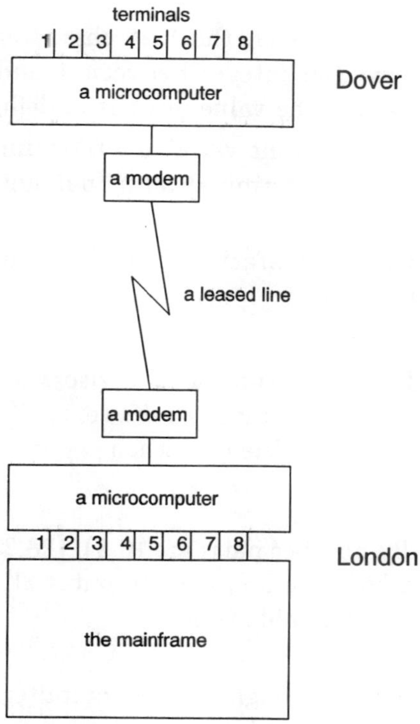

Figure N15: Connection scheme

The duty of both microcomputers is to transfer the characters typed in at the terminals to the London mainframe ports and to return the responses of the London mainframe to appropriate terminals in Dover. The characters must be transmitted as soon as possible. When all terminals are active at the same time, the modem line must be evenly shared: each terminal should be entitled to approximately 1/8 of the modem line transmission capacity. When some terminals are inactive, their rights may be allocated to other active terminals.

Write that **part of a program** for the Dover microcomputer which reads the characters from the terminal keyboards, provides the accumulated characters with appropriate data about their origin (e.g. the terminal number) and sends the characters so supplied to the modem line.

Describe how your program informs the London microcomputer about the origin of characters.

When providing the characters with the data about their origin you should be as terse as possible, as these data additionally load the not-so-fast modem line.

The following procedures are provided:

ReadChar(term,ch) returns in *ch* the first character waiting at the terminal *term* (an integer between 1 and 0); if no characters are waiting the value of *ch* is undefined.

Waiting(term,n) returns in the variable n the number of characters, received from the terminal *term*, but not yet read with the procedure *Read*.

SendChar(ch) sends a character through the modem line from Dover to London.

1123B Let $S(a)$ denote the sum of all divisors of the integer a, including 1 and excluding the number itself. (e. g. $S(28) = 1 + 2 + 4 + 7 + 14$). The numbers a and b are called friendly when

$$S(a) = b \quad \text{and} \quad S(b) = a.$$

Examples of friendly number pairs are (6,6), (28,28), and (220,284). Write a **program**, which (on a home computer) computes all pairs of friendly numbers between 1 and 30 000 in reasonable time.

1124H Professor Hasting bought a new computer. Later he discovered that no Pascal compiler existed for his computer. Therefore he decided to write the compiler himself. Like most of his previous programs he wrote it in Pascal. Once finished he discovered that his computer could not compile Pascal programs.

It was then that he remembered his old friend, Professor Branes, who had a computer with a different processor, but with a working compiler for Pascal. Also he was able to transfer an arbitrary file between the two computers in any direction.

Can Professor Branes help Professor Hasting in supplying a working Pascal compiler for his computer? **Explain** why!

Problems for experienced competitors

1131G A picture is represented by a raster of 1000 × 1000 points. In the memory, it is stored as a matrix of 1000 × 1000 integers. We want to rotate it counterclockwise by the right angle. Write a **program** to rotate the picture in the matrix using minimum additional memory!

1132F The calculator keyboard consists of 20 keys arranged in an array of 4×5 keys. Each key is a switch, which, when pressed, connects a horizontal wire passing under the key to the vertical one. The voltage of each of the five horizontal wires may be set by a program to either 0 V or to 1 V (the intermediate voltages cannot be set). The voltage on each of the four vertical lines can be read by a program (0 V or 1 V). The voltage on a vertical wire not connected to a horizontal wire equals 1 V. When the vertical wire is connected to any number of horizontal ones, its voltage drops to 0 V, if the voltage of at least one of the horizontal wires equals 0 V, and remains 1 V, if all the horizontal wires are at 1 V.

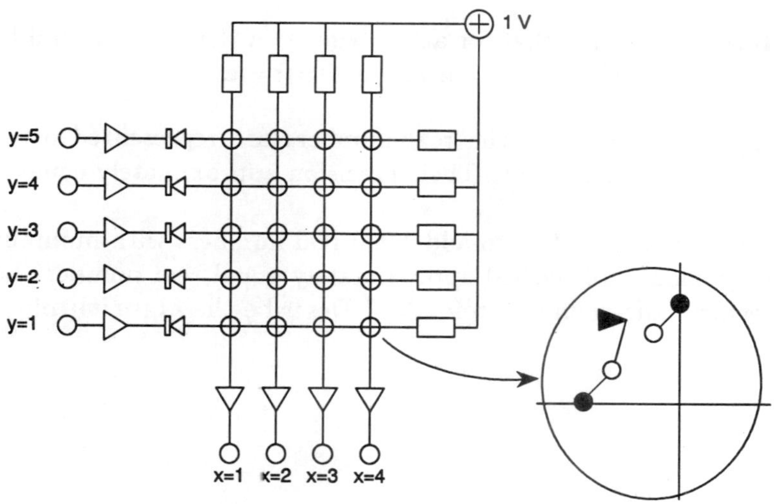

Figure N16: The calculator keyboard

Write a **program** to continuously observe the state of the keys, and output the coordinates of a key whenever one is pressed .

Note: although a key may be pressed for a long time, the output is needed only once. Also consider the possibility that several keys may be pressed simultaneously.

The following procedures are available:

SetState(y,*state*) sets the voltage on the horizontal wire y (an integer between 1 and 5) to *state* (0 or 1);

ReadState(x,*state*) reads the voltage on the vertical wire x (an integer between 1 and 4) and returns the result in the argument *state* (the integer value 0 or 1).

1133B For any integer in the range from 0 to 32 767 the following function computes an integer in the same range.

```
function f(r: integer): integer;
  var i,n,l: integer;
begin
  n:=0;
  for i:=0 to 14 do begin
    l:=r mod 2; r:=r div 2; n:=2*n;
    if odd(r)<>odd(l) then n:=n+1;
  end;
  f:=n;
end; {f}
```

Write a **function** g such that for any integer x in the range from 0 to 32 767 the following will be true: $f(g(x)) = x$ and $g(f(x)) = x$.

1134B In a computer, the real numbers are represented using the floating decimal point. Their precision approximately equals six decimal places.

Describe an **algorithm** to add 1 000 real numbers with minimum error! **In which way** should 10 000 000 approximately equal real numbers be added, so that the error made would be tolerable? Describe the **algorithm**!

Part III

Solutions

Chapter A

Straightforward Problems

The present chapter assembles the problems, which are solved in a "straightforward" manner, without much complication. From the logical point of view, they are usually clear and simple, and generally have no deeper background. At the competitions they typically represented the silly problems one has to give to allow less skilled competitors gain at least some points.

114A The requested program probably presents one of the easiest problems of all. Reading integers requires no particular expertise. Anybody can count to a hundred, and almost everybody knows that positive integers are greater than zero. Also, everybody knows that the arithmetic average of a set of numbers equals their sum divided by their number. If there are no positive numbers in the sequence read, the arithmetic average is not defined (zero divided by zero!), so it cannot be computed. The program follows:

```
program Numbers(input,output);
{ Computation of the arithmetic average of positive integers read. }
  const
    max = 100;                         { at most this much numbers will be read }
  var
    number: integer;                                  { the current number read }
    numAllNum: integer;                          { the number of all numbers read }
    numPosNum: integer;                 { the number of all positive numbers read }
    sumPos: integer;                       { the sum of all positive numbers read }

begin
  NumAllNum:=0; numPosNum:=0; sumPos:=0;
```

```
  repeat
    readln(number); numAllNum:=numAllNum+1;
    if number>0 then
      begin sumPos:=sumPos+number; numPosNum:=numPosNum+1 end;
  until (number=0) or (numAllNum>=max);
  if numPosNum<>0 then writeln(SumPos/numPosNum)
  else writeln('No positive numbers.');
end. {Numbers}
```

211A

Before solving the problem, let us consider some basic tools of propositional calculus. They will aid us also in the solution of problem 414A.

Let P and Q denote arbitrary propositions (e. g. "Cindy cooks celery", or "it is sunny today"; the exact meaning of the statements is irrelevant). Then $P \wedge Q$ denotes a statement which is true only if both P and Q are true. This composite proposition is called the **conjunction** of the simple propositions. The formula $P \vee Q$ denotes a proposition which is true when either P or Q is true, or both; it is called the **disjunction** of the two simple propositions. And finally, to allow us to peek outside the world of eternal truth, there is the **negation**, $\neg P$, a statement, which holds if and only if P is false. Mathematicians sometimes write & instead of $\wedge$, and put a vinculum over the proposition instead of $\neg$.

The truth of a composite proposition is usually illustrated by its *truth table.* For the conjunction it is shown below; the zeros denote that the proposition is false, and the ones that it is true. Instead of 0 and 1 one might write *false* and *true* in the table.

P	Q	$P \wedge Q$
0	0	0
1	0	0
0	1	0
1	1	1

The second line of the table reads: if the proposition P is true, and the proposition Q is false, then the conjunction of both propositions is false. Try writing the truth table for the disjunction and the negation yourself. (If it proves too difficult, you will find the tables later on.)

Any propositions may be combined to form more complicated statements, for instance $\neg(\neg P \vee \neg Q)$. (Writing them, we keep to the custom that the priority of $\neg$ is higher than either $\wedge$ or $\vee$, so that $\neg P \vee \neg Q$ means $(\neg P) \vee (\neg Q)$.)

If you write the truth table for this proposition, you will find it is the same as the one for the conjunction. When two propositions have the same truth table, they are called **equivalent**. The **equivalence** (a composite proposition stating the member propositions are equivalent; it may be true or false;) is a composite proposition as well; usually it is denoted by $\Leftrightarrow$ — try writing its truth table. The above statement may then be written as:

$$P \wedge Q \Leftrightarrow \neg(\neg P \vee \neg Q).$$

This equivalence is called De Morgan law. Try finding another such law: in the equivalence above exchange $\vee$ with $\wedge$ and vice versa.

To get better acquainted with the basic elements of the propositional calculus, you may find useful the following textbook: R. R. Stoll: *Set Theory and Logic*, Freeman, San Francisco 1961.

Let us now solve our problem. First, observe the results of the logical operations for the selected values of the operands. To do that, we first write the truth tables for all three operations, along with the table of the two basic arithmetic operations:

A	B	$\neg A$	$A \wedge B$	$A \vee B$	$A * B$	$A + B$
0	0	1	0	0	0	0
1	0	0	0	1	0	1
0	1	1	0	1	0	1
1	1	0	1	1	1	2

From the table it is immediately obvious how the negation and disjunction are expressed:

$\neg A$ is expressed as $1 - A$

$A \wedge B$ is expressed as $A * B$.

The disjunction requires slightly more reasoning: the addition almost works, the only incorrect result 2 is obtained in the case when both operands equal 1. To correct that, an operation on A and B must be subtracted, which is equal to 1 when both operands are 1 and zero otherwise. But this is exactly the conjunction, the multiplication of both operands:

$A \vee B$ is expressed as $A + B - A * B$.

Try now expressing in a similar way the *exclusive disjunction*, $A \veebar B$, which equals 1 if and only if its operands are different. (Solution: $A+B-2*A*B$). Using the arithmetic representation, can you prove that $A \veebar B \Leftrightarrow (A \wedge \neg B) \vee (\neg A \wedge B)$?

212A The table *valCoin* holds the values of available coins and notes, as the problem statement specifies. We introduce another table, *numCoin*, which holds the required number of the coins.

The sketch of the algorithm follows:

```
Initialize the tables valCoin and numCoin;
for each worker
    read wages,
    compute the numbers of coins,
    add the number of coins to appropriate components of numCoin;
endfor
output the results (the table numCoin)
```

We assume that the values in the table *valCoin* are ordered decreasingly, so that the largest value is at the beginning of the table, and the smallest is at its end. The values of bank-notes and coins are as in 1991. To avoid fractional arithmetic, the coin values are given in (British) pennies. Also, we assume all values in the table *valCoin* are positive. We do not distinguish between bank-notes and coins of the same value. The paymaster does not pay amounts less than *valCoin*[12], and, for simplicity, we assume all wages are already rounded. The detailed algorithm is evident from the program below:

```
program PayWages(input,output);
{ Computes the number of particular coins to pay wages. }
  const
    nWorkers = 100;                         { the number of all workers to pay out }
    nValues = 12;                           { the number of distinct coin values }
  var
    valCoin: array [1..nValues] of integer;                     { the coin values }
    numCoin: array [1..nValues] of integer;                  { the numbers of coins }
    wages: integer;           { the wages of the current worker—last amount read }
    nCoin: integer;                         { the number of coins of current value }
    i,k: integer;
begin
  valCoin[1]:=5000; valCoin[2]:=2000; valCoin[3]:=1000; valCoin[4]:=500;
  valCoin[5]:= 200; valCoin[6]:= 100; valCoin[7]:=  50; valCoin[8]:= 20;
  valCoin[9]:=  10; valCoin[10]:=  5; valCoin[11]:=  2; valCoin[12]:= 1;
  for i:=1 to nValues do numCoin[i]:=0;
  for k:=1 to nWorkers do begin
    read(wages);
    for i:=1 to nValues do begin
      nCoin:=wages div valCoin[i]; numCoin[i]:=numCoin[i]+nCoin;
      wages:=wages-valCoin[i]*nCoin;
    end; {for}
  end; {for}
  writeln( 'The paymaster requires:');
  for i:=1 to nValues do
    writeln(numCoin[i],' coins of value ',valCoin[i]/100:7:2);
end. {PayWages}
```

It is worth adding that such sets of coins exist for which the answer given by the above algorithm need not be unique or may even be incorrect. Unless each coin value is twice or more as large as the previous one, which is true in the above example, the optimal partitioning by the above algorithm cannot be guaranteed. If, for instance, there were coins for a quarter of one pound, as well as for 20, 10, and 5 pennies, our program would give the non-optimal partitioning of 40 pennies (25+10+5) instead of the optimal one of paying out two 20-penny coins. How would one tackle this kind of partitioning? And how, if some of the coin values were negative?

225A This is another case of a very easy problem. The only thing to watch out for is to centre the asterisks relative to the first line containing a single asterisk, and that this asterisk is displaced enough from the left edge.

```
program Rhombus(output);
{ Draws a large rhombus. }
  const
    width = 41;    { the height and the width of the rhombus }
    aster = '*';   { the rhombus is drawn using a '*' }
  var
    shift: integer; { the displacement of the first '*' in the first line }
    j: integer;

  procedure DrawLine(shift,nChars: integer);
    var j: integer;
  begin
    write(' ':shift);
    for j:=1 to nChars do write(aster);
    writeln;
  end; {DrawLine}

begin {Rhombus}
  shift:=(width+1) div 2;
  for j:=1 to width div 2 do DrawLine(shift−j, j*2−1);
  for j:=(width+1) div 2 downto 1 do DrawLine(shift−j, j*2−1);
end. {Rhombus}
```

Some competitors solved the problem by writing a sequence of 41 *writeln* statements. This solution was not particularly admired.

311A A line of numbers is represented by a table, containing space for 21 numbers. The algorithm to output the requested table may be roughly sketched as follows:

```
compose the first line
while the first number of the line equals 0 do
   output the line;
   compute the new line overwriting the old one
endwhile
```

Care must be taken when summing the three neighbour numbers to get a number in the next line. It is true that adding zero does not change the result, however, care must be taken not to slip too far at the edge of the table. The leftmost (first) element of the line is therefore computed as the sum of the first and the second element of the previous line, while the rightmost (last) one is the sum of the last two elements of the previous line.

The program terminates when the first (or the last) element of the line computed becomes nonzero. This termination criterion is proved as follows: each newly computed element is larger than or equal to the element of the old line at the same position; it is equal if zeros are added together, otherwise it is strictly larger. On each step, the boundary of positive elements moves one place away from the middle of the table: the table develops in a triangular shape. All numbers inside the triangle are positive. When the boundary reaches the start of the line, the program may terminate, as all elements of the line are positive.

Half of the additions are spared by computing only half of the table, since it is obviously symmetrical. There is also no need to store the other half of the table, but the first half must be correctly output.

```
program Table(output);
{ Outputs atable in which each element equals the sum of its three above neighbours.}
  const
    tabLen=10; { The table symmetrically spans the range from −tabLen to tabLen }
  var
    x,y: array [0..tabLen] of integer;           { the old and the new line of the table }
    i: integer;
    stop: boolean;

begin
  for i:=1 to tabLen do x[i]:=0;
  x[0]:=1;
  repeat
    stop:=x[tabLen]<>0;
    { first output the left half, then the right one }
    for i:=tabLen downto 1 do write(x[i]:6);
    for i:=0 to tabLen do write(x[i]:6);
    writeln;
    y[0]:=x[0]+2*x[1];                        { the middle must be computed separately,... }
                                       { ... since y[0]:=x[−1]+x[0]+x[1], where x[−1]=x[1]. }
    y[tabLen]:=x[tabLen−1]+x[tabLen];      { the edge element is computed separately }
```

```
    for i:=1 to tabLen−1 do
      y[i]:=x[i−1]+x[i]+x[i+1];
    x:=y;
  until stop;
end. {Table}
```

The program could be improved by avoiding adding zeros. Namely, when computing the k-th line, we know that only the elements in the range from 0 to k are nonzero. Half the additions would be spared at the price of making the program less readable.

When the table is long, copying $x{:=}y$ becomes a time consuming operation. Copying could be avoided by swapping the meaning of the two tables on each step. Computing in appropriate order we could compute the new line using a single additional variable, thus entirely avoiding the second table.

In this way or another the program could be improved almost indefinitely. Our first solution was entirely different from the one presented here. It is a question of preference as to whether it is worth investing this much effort in such a trivial problem — see a discussion on this topic in chapter 5.

321A The count-out to start the children's game of tag, or some other game, is fairly common among children. Although it is probably known to everybody, it is nevertheless worth describing in some detail:

1. n children are aligned in a circle;
2. assume that $1 \leq n \leq max$ and $m > 0$, where m is the number of words in the count-out, and max the maximum number of children; (consider what would happen if the above conditions did not hold);
3. the algorithm starts at the first child, and $n-1$ children must be eliminated; this is done as follows:
   - — the children are counted from 1 to m, (the already eliminated children are not counted); counting is done circularly, so that the first child follows the last one;
   - — the m-th child is eliminated;
4. the last remaining child is output as the result.

The program that follows uses a table of pointers *next* to manage the list of remaining children. When a child is eliminated, the pointer to it from the previous remaining children is changed to point to the successor of the eliminated, which is thus removed from the list of remaining children. The details are apparent from the program:

```
program CountOut(input,output);
{ Children's game count-out. }
  const
    max = 30;      { maximum number of children in the count-out }
  var
    m: integer;    { the length of the count-out (number of words) }
    n: integer;    { the actual number of children }
    p: integer;    { the current child }
    prev: integer; { the child previous to p }
    i,j: integer;
    next: array [1..max] of integer;
begin
  readln(n,m);
  if (n<1) or (n>max) or (m<=0) then
    writeln('?-Oh, my my, these children!')
  else begin
    next[n]:=1;
    for i:=1 to n-1 do next[i]:=i+1;              { link children into a circle }
    prev:=n; p:=next[prev];                          { now p is the first child }
    for i:=1 to n-1 do begin                      { n-1 children are removed }
      for j:=1 to m-1 do                              { first skip m-1 children }
        begin prev:=p; p:=next[p] end;
      next[prev]:=next[p];                               { p-th child falls off }
      p:=next[p];                       { next time start counting from p-th child on }
    end; {for}
    writeln('Number of children    ', n:1);
    writeln('Length of count-out ', m:1);
    writeln('Child to catch          ', p:1);
  end; {if}
end. {CountOut}
```

A different solution would be obtained by representing the set of remaining children by a table of Boolean values or a set, each entry denoting whether the child is still in the game or has been eliminated. Try writing it yourself.

Finally some words about the history of the problem: in literature count-out is also called the Josephus problem, after the Jewish historian Flavius Josephus (died approximately 95 AD). Many works have been written on this topic, especially since the 17th century on. You may find some interesting details on the Josephus problem in a work by W. Ahrens: *Matematische Unterhaltungen und Spiele*, Leipzig 1918 (Das Josephsspiel, pages 118–169) or in W. W. Rouse Ball, H. S. M. Coxeter: *Mathematical Recreations and Essays*, University of Toronto Press, Toronto 1974.

The problem may also be solved analytically: number the children from 0 to $n-1$, and denote the length of the count-out by m. Then the function f below computes the number of the child that remains.

$$f(n,m) = \begin{cases} 0 & \text{if } n = 1 \\ (f(n-1,m)+m) \textbf{ mod } n & \text{if } n > 1 \end{cases}$$

The following iterative program eases the understanding of the function:

```
f:=0;
for i:=2 to n do
  f:=(f+m) mod i;
```

You may find more facts about recursive functions in chapter C.

414A The solution is found by simple reasoning. First, it may be easily seen that the number A is smaller than B if it is not greater, so that:

$$A < B \Leftrightarrow \neg(A \geq B).$$

The operator $\geq$ is therefore often pronounced *not smaller than* instead of *greater than or equal to.* From this the formula for $A > B$ is immediately derived, namely:

$$A > B \Leftrightarrow B < A \Leftrightarrow \neg(B \geq A.)$$

To express equality, we use the fact that two numbers are equal, only if neither is smaller than the other, so:

$$A = B \Leftrightarrow (A \geq B) \wedge (B \geq A)$$

The numbers are different, only if they are not equal, so:

$$\begin{aligned} A \neq B &\Leftrightarrow \neg((A \geq B) \wedge (B \geq A)) \\ &\Leftrightarrow \neg(A \geq B) \vee \neg(B \geq A) \end{aligned}$$

which, in other words, tells us that the numbers are different, if either is smaller than the other.

The last is the easiest:

$$A \leq B \Leftrightarrow B \geq A.$$

Though simple, the problem is fairly instructive: have you ever tried to translate the Pascal **repeat** or **while** statement into FORTRAN or Basic, or either statement to the other without using the dreadful negation in the condition? Three quarters of never terminating loops are caused by improper negation and simplification of the conditions. So let us again look at the differently written De Morgan laws:

$$\neg(P \wedge Q) \Leftrightarrow \neg P \vee \neg Q$$
$$\neg(P \vee Q) \Leftrightarrow \neg P \wedge \neg Q.$$

Did you guess the latter correctly in the introduction to the problem 211A?

421A To write the requested program (called *TestChain*), we must first understand what the *Chain* program does. First it reads 101 integers, stores the first hundred into the table t and uses the last integer as the starting *index* into this table. If any of the first hundred integers lies outside the range from 0 to 100, the *Chain* program "aborts" (provided the table index range test is turned on) and therefore terminates abnormally. The same happens if the starting index is outside the range from 1 to 100. The *TestChain* program tests all data read if they lie within the corresponding range. If they do not, it announces the abnormal termination, otherwise it proceeds.

If the current index is within the correct range, it points to an element of the table. If the value of this element equals 0, the *Chain* program terminates, otherwise it uses this element as the index to the next element in the table. Since the table is of finite size, the only case the *Chain* program does not terminate is when the input to *Chain* contains a *cycle*. The *TestChain* program therefore simulates the execution of *Chain*, checking at the same time that each element of the table t has been visited for the first time (to do this it uses the table *seen*, setting $seen[i]$ to *true* when visiting $t[i]$). If an element is visited for the second time, it concludes that a cycle exists (its progression is not important), and outputs that the *Chain* program does not terminate.

The program requested:

```
program TestChain(input,output);
{ Tests whether Chain terminates for given data. }

  const
    max = 100;
  var
    k,i: integer;
    t: array [1..max] of integer;        { the data table }
    seen: array [1..max] of boolean;  { tells whether an element has been visited }
    testDone: boolean;

begin
  testDone:=false;
  for i:=1 to max do begin
    seen[i]:=false;
    read(t[i]);
    if ((t[i]<0) or (t[i]>max)) and not testDone then begin
      writeln('The Chain program terminates abnormally ',
              '(aborts, since a table element is out of allowed range).');
      testDone:=true;
    end; {if}
  end; {for}
```

```
  if not testDone then begin
    read(k);
    if (k<1) or (k>max) then begin
      writeln('The Chain program terminates abnormally ',
              '(aborts, since the starting index is out of allowed range).');
      testDone:=true;
    end; {if}
  end; {if}
  if not testDone then begin
    while (t[k]<>0) and not seen[k] do
      begin seen[k]:=true; k:=t[k] end;
    if t[k]=0 then writeln('The Chain program terminates.')
    else writeln('The Chain program does not terminate.');
  end; {if}
end. {TestChain}
```

The solution above is much more detailed than the one requested at the competition. The *TestChain* program would be much simpler if we assumed (as stated in the problem) that all data were in correct ranges.

Pascal compilers usually provide various tests to be executed during the execution time of the program (more precisely, the tests to check violation of the declarations are built into the translated program). For our case two kinds of tests are of interest:

a) the *integer range tests*, testing whether integer values lie in the range prescribed, and
b) the *index range tests*, testing that the index does not point outside the table.

If the test (b) is turned off, and the index is out of range, then the functioning of the *Chain* program depends on the values randomly occurring (from our point of view) in computer memory at given locations (if they exist at all). In this case, nothing can be predicted about the functioning of the *Chain* program.

If the test (b) is on, and the test (a) is not, the data could contain an invalid value of an element of the table; however, during execution that element would remain unvisited and would therefore not cause any problems.

Our program assumes that both tests are turned on.

424A In children's magazines one often encounters problems of the following kind: three pots are available, the first holding 8, the second 7, and the third 3 litres. The second and third pots are empty, while the first is full of water. The water must be divided in half only by pouring from one of the three pots to another, without spilling, of course. The solution requires no deep arithmetic knowledge. Instead of experimenting in the backyard and drenching our fingers, we may choose to experiment using a computer. Often an experiment in a simulated environment on a computer spares us work as well as time; such an experiment is safer than real experiments in nature, many times it is even the only way of performing it (the simulation of an accident in a nuclear power plant, the simulation of influence of the quantity of carbon dioxide and methane in the atmosphere on the climate in the next hundred years, etc.).

Let us return to the problem. The fact that the glasses are on a table, and not, for instance, beneath it, has no influence on pouring from one glass to another; this fact is therefore omitted from the data representation. Nor does it concern us that the liquid in the glasses is water and not something else. The conclusions above lead us to argue what in fact constitutes a **computer model**. The model is a representation (for instance, a code in a suitable programming language) of a state or event, where only the facts of interest are represented, while the non-essential details are left out.

So, we have to represent n glasses, numbered from 1 to n. Each glass has its own volume (the variable *vol*) and may contain some liquid, the volume of which we represent with the variable *cont*. The volume and the contents are represented by nonnegative real numbers.

The volume of a glass equal to zero may mean that the glass is missing, or that it is turned upside down; in neither case should that bother us. A very useful principle of programming says: *never impose unnecessary restrictions*, which is certainly true in our case. If a program correctly handles the boundary cases, it is usually easier to confirm that it works correctly in other cases.

Since the programming language Pascal does not enable us to restrict variables to nonnegative real values, the program itself must do that by properly initializing the variables, as well as the *Pour* procedure by maintaining the variable *cont* in the representation of the glasses nonnegative. Thus the data structure is represented as follows:

```
const
  n = 20;  { the maximum number of glasses }
type
  numGlass = 1..n;
  glasses = array [numGlass] of record vol,cont: real end;
```

When pouring water from one glass to another there are two possibilities:

1. there is enough space in the second glass to pour in the entire contents of the first glass; in this case the contents of the second glass becomes the sum of previous contents of both glasses, and the first glass becomes empty;
2. in the second glass there is not enough space for the entire contents of the first glass; in this case enough water is poured into the second glass to make it full, and the remainder left in the first glass.

If we attempt to pour the water from a glass back to itself, nothing happens (check what happens, if we forget to test whether i and j are equal in the program below—it is worth trying, you may become wizards):

```
procedure Pour(var g: glasses; i,j: numGlass);
{ Pours water from the i-th glass to the j-th glass. }
  var diff: real;

begin
  if i=j then {}                          { if pouring from a glass to itself do nothing }
  else begin
    diff:=g[j].vol-g[j].cont;
    if diff>=g[i].cont then                   { pour entire contents of the glass i }
      begin g[j].cont:=g[j].cont+g[i].cont; g[i].cont:=0 end
    else                                               { fill the glass j to the top }
      begin g[j].cont:=g[j].vol; g[i].cont:=g[i].cont-diff end;
  end; {if}
end; {Pour}
```

The problem is now solved. But here, as well as with most other problems which request a procedure or a part of a program to be written, doubt crawls in. Does the procedure perform the task required in the way we wish it to? We may observe the functioning of the program by supplying the environment for it, that is, the main program with the "user interface". To illustrate how you may build the environment for other problems, we give here an example for it:

```
program Pouring(input,output);
{ The program simulates pouring of water between glasses. }
  const  n = 20;  { the maximum number of glasses }
  type
    numGlass = 1..n;
    glasses = array [numGlass] of  record vol,cont: real end;
  var
    num: integer;  { the actual number of glasses }
    g: glasses;      { the glasses }

  procedure Initialize;
  { Sets the initial state of our model. }
    var h:integer;

  begin
    writeln('Pouring between glasses'); writeln;
    writeln('Several glasses are available; each of them may be full,');
    writeln('empty or partially filled. The liquid may be poured from');
    writeln('a glass to another to complement the contents of the latter.');
    writeln('First input the data about the glasses, then pour the liquid.');
    writeln('To exit, enter 0 when asked to input i or j.');
    writeln; writeln;
```

```
  repeat
    write('Enter the number of glasses: ');
    read(num);
    if (num<1) or (num>n) then writeln('?-Enter a number between 1 and ',n:1);
  until (num>=1) and (num<=n);
  for h:=1 to num do begin
    repeat
      write('Enter the volume of glass ',h:1,':');
      read(g[h].vol);
      write('Enter the contents of glass ',h:1,':');
      read(g[h].cont);
      if g[h].vol<0 then writeln('?-The volume may not be negative.');
      if g[h].cont<0 then writeln('?-The contents may not be negative.');
      if g[h].cont>g[h].vol then
        writeln('?-The contents may not be greater than the volume.');
    until (g[h].vol>=0) and (g[h].cont>=0) and (g[h].cont<=g[h].vol);
  end; {for}
end; {Initialize}

procedure PrintOut;
{ Outputs the state of glasses. }
  var j: integer;
begin
  writeln; writeln;
  write('Glass       ');
  for j:=1 to num do write(j:7);  writeln; write('Volume ');
  for j:=1 to num do write(g[j].vol:7:2);  writeln; write('Contents     ');
  for j:=1 to num do write(g[j].cont:7:2);  writeln;
end; {PrintOut}

procedure PourFromGlassToGlass;
{ The procedure performs pouring from a glass to another. }
  var
    i,j: integer;
    done: boolean;

  procedure Pour(var g: glasses; i,j: numGlass);
  { Pours liquid from the glass i to the glass j. }
    var diff: real;
  begin
    if i=j then {}                          { if pouring from a glass to itself do nothing }
    else begin
      diff:=g[j].vol-g[j].cont;
      if diff>=g[i].cont then                   { pour the entire contents of the glass i }
        begin g[j].cont:=g[j].cont+g[i].cont; g[i].cont:=0 end
      else  { fill the glass j to the top }
        begin g[j].cont:=g[j].vol; g[i].cont:=g[i].cont-diff end;
    end; {if}
  end; {Pour}
```

```
begin {PourFromGlassToGlass}
  done:=false;
  while not done do begin
    writeln('Pour from glass i to glass j:');
    repeat
      write('i = '); read(i);
      if i<>0 then begin write('j = '); read(j) end;
      if (i=0) or (j=0) then done:=true
      else if (i<1) or (i>num) or (j<1) or (j>num) then
        writeln('?-Enter a value between 1 and ', num:1)
      else Pour(g,i,j);
    until ((i>=1) and (i<=num) and (j>=1) and (j<=num)) or done;
    PrintOut;
  end {while};
  writeln; writeln('Remove the glasses!');
end; {PourFromGlassToGlass}

begin {Pouring}
  Initialize; PrintOut; PourFromGlassToGlass;
end. {Pouring}
```

Try improving the program above to pour by itself. As a problem, give it the starting distribution of water in glasses as well as the desired final one; the program should output whether it has found the solution and the sequence of pouring to achieve the desired result.

611A We assume that sequences *str1* and *str2* are equally long (you may try solving the case of sequences of different length yourself). We introduce the tables *notYet1* and *notYet2*, both n elements long. The i-th element of the table *notYet1* denotes whether the i-th element of the sequence *str1* has been dealt with or not, and equivalently for the table *notYet2*. The requested algorithm follows:

1. at the beginning, all elements in *str1* and *str2* must be considered, so all elements of the tables *notYet1* and *notYet2* are set to *true*; the variables *white* and *black* are set to 0;
2. we proceed to find equal elements at the same positions in strings *str1* and *str2* for each index value between 1 and n; if such a pair is found at the position i, the value of the variable *black* is incremented by 1, and the values of *notYet1*[i] and *notYet2*[i] set to mark that the pair of elements has been dealt with.
3. for each remaining element i of the sequence *str1* the sequence *str2* is searched to find a match at a different location j; if a match is found ($i \neq j$, *str1*[i]=*str2*[j]), then the variable *white* is incremented by 1, and the values

of *notYet1*[*i*] and *notYet2*[*j*] are set to mark that both elements have been dealt with.

4. The result (the values of the variables *black* and *white*) is output.

In addition to the description of the algorithm, we provide a program:

```
program Game(input,output);
{ A skeleton for the MEMO game. }
  const
    max = 100;
  type
    table = array [1..max] of integer;
  var
    str1,str2: table; { input sequences }
    ce,n: integer;
    black: integer;  { the number of equal elements at the same locations }
                     { in both sequences }
    white: integer;  { the number of other equal elements of both sequences }

  procedure Memo(str1,str2: table; var black,white: integer);
  { Returns the numbers of equal elements at the same positions of
    two sequences and the number of other equal elements. }
    var
      notYet1,notYet2: array [1..max] of boolean;
      { mark elements of str1 and str2 not yet dealt with }
      i,j: integer;

  begin
    black:=0; white:=0;
    for i:=1 to n do begin notYet1[i]:=true; notYet2[i]:=true end;
    for i:=1 to n do                   { look for equal elements at the same positions }
      if str1[i]=str2[i] then
        begin black:=black+1; notYet1[i]:=false; notYet2[i]:=false end;
    for i:=1 to n do                                  { look for other equal elements }
      for j:=1 to n do
        if notYet1[i] and notYet2[j] and (str1[i]=str2[j]) then
          begin white:=white+1; notYet1[i]:=false; notYet2[j]:=false end;
  end; {Memo}

begin {Game}
  read(n);
  for ce:=1 to n do read(str1[ce]);
  for ce:=1 to n do read(str2[ce]);
  Memo(str1,str2,black,white); writeln('Black: ',black:2,'    white: ',white:2);
end. {Game}
```

As an exercise, you may extend the *Game* program, so that you may play Memo with a computer. A hint: the computer should provide a sequence using a random number generator, and then ask you to guess the sequence by a series of trials. If you find it (that is, *black*=n) soon enough, you win, otherwise you lose. You may try writing the program for the contrary situation: you provide the sequence, the computer guesses...

612A

The solution requires no specific explanation.

```
program FloppyCola;
{ Placing bottles into boxes. }
  var x,y: integer;  { box compartment coordinates }
  function Sensor: integer; external;
  procedure Take; external;
  procedure Put(x,y: integer); external;
  procedure NewBox; external;
begin {FloppyCola}
{ initially an empty box is waiting }
  repeat
    for y:=1 to 3 do
      for x:=1 to 4 do begin
        repeat until Sensor=1;
        Take; Put(x,y);
      end; {for}
    NewBox;
  until false;
end. {FloppyCola}
```

713A

We may imagine that a point with the coordinates (x,y) travels inside a box of dimensions $xmax \times ymax$. At the edge of the box the point rebounds according to the law of rebound. The loop terminates when the point returns to its initial position with its initial direction. The motion may be simplified by reflecting the box over the entire plane. The path of the point then maps to the line $y = x$.

When the travelling point reaches the point (1,1) in any box, the condition is satisfied. The coordinates of the images of the point (1,1), where the point has its initial direction (that is, $dx = 1$, $dy = 1$), are $(2 \cdot n \cdot xmax + 1, 2 \cdot m \cdot ymax + 1)$. This may be proved as follows: when the box is reflected once (say, in the direction of the x-axis), a mirror copy of the box is obtained; by reflecting it again in the same direction, a displaced copy of the box is obtained, in which the point moves in the same direction as in the initial box. Such double reflection retains the direction of the moving point and may be repeated any number of times (n-times, n=0,1,2,...). The same is true for the double reflections along the vertical axis y. To determine the "final" coordinates of the moving point, we take into account that the starting position is (1,1).

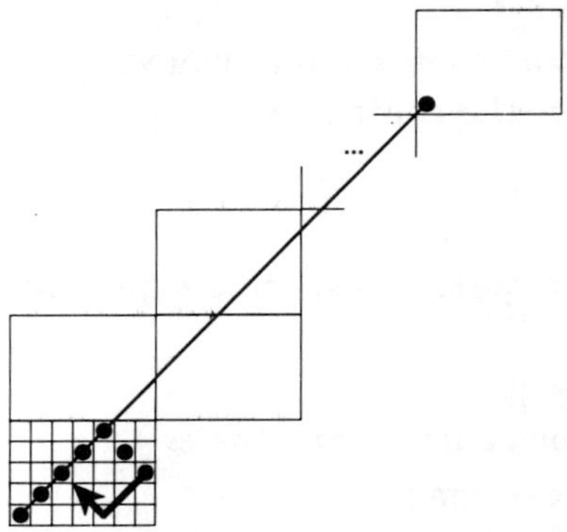

Figure A1: The path of the point

Since the point moves along the line $y = x$, integers m and n must be determined to satisfy the equation $2 \cdot n \cdot xmax + 1 = 2 \cdot m \cdot ymax + 1$, as the point must move for the same distance both in the x and the y direction. The equation simplifies to $n \cdot xmax = m \cdot ymax$. Since $xmax$ and $ymax$ are primes, the possible solutions for n are multiples of $ymax$, and the possible solutions for m the multiples of $xmax$. The minimum solution is therefore $n = ymax$ and $m = xmax$.

As the point starts to travel from the point (1,1) along the line $y = x$, it reaches the point $(2 \cdot ymax \cdot xmax + 1, 2 \cdot xmax \cdot ymax + 1)$ after exactly $2 \cdot xmax \cdot ymax + 1$ steps. The variable j whose value gets printed by the program counts precisely these steps. Therefore the program outputs 1427, since:

$2 \cdot xmax \cdot ymax + 1 = 2 \cdot 31 \cdot 23 + 1 = 1427.$

What would happen if $xmax$ and $ymax$ were not primes?

By the way: did you notice that the problem could be stated more simply as "add 1 to twice the number of the problem" to get the same result?

813A The motive of the problem originates in word-processing. When solving problems from this area, the text may be considered as a set of paragraphs, sentences, words, etc., or it may simply be considered as a sequence of letters or characters. The next four problems originate in this field. First, let us have a look at underlining, where the text is considered as a sequence of characters, since its structure bears no importance to the problem.

When writing this program, care must be taken to remove quotes from the text input, as well as from the line of underscores. The outline of the program follows:

```
while end of file not reached do
   while end of line not reached do
      read an input character;
      if the character equals '"', then invert the underlining mode,
      else output the character and, if necessary, record an underscore
   endwhile;
   terminate the input line;
   output the line with the recorded underscores
endwhile
```

A table is used to record which characters should be underlined. As the table size is limited it may be too short to record all data desired in the case of a long input line. In our case this results in characters at the end of the long line being output but not underlined even when they should have been. This kind of improper functioning of the program is a case of a soft failure of a program, mentioned in 3. paragraph of the part I.

The requested program:

```
program Underline(input,output);
{ The program underlines quoted parts of the text. }
  const
    max = 80;
  var
    line: packed array [1..max] of char;              { the line of underscores }
    inCh: char;                                   { the current character input }
    under: boolean;                         { the current character is underlined }
    i,length: integer;
begin {Underline}
  under:=false;
  while not eof do begin
    i:=0; length:=0;
    while not eoln do begin
      read(inCh);
      if inCh='"' then under:=not under
      else begin
        write(inCh); i:=i+1;
        if i>max then {}
        else if not under then line[i]:=' '
        else begin line[i]:='-'; length:=i end;
      end; {if}
    end; {while}
    writeln; readln;
    for i:=1 to length do write(line[i]);
    writeln;
  end; {while}
end. {Underline}
```

The Pascal standard requires that at the end of each line of a file of type *text* (even the last line), the *eoln* function returns *true*. To illustrate this point, let us devise a program to output the characters input, as well as the behaviour of the *eoln* and *eof* functions :

```
program TestReading(inp,output);
{ The program illustrates reading and functioning of eoln and eof functions. }
  var
    inp: text;         { the input file }
    c: char;           { the next character from input }
    el,ef: boolean;    { indicators of end of line and end of file }
begin
  reset(inp);
  writeln('char eoln  eof');
  writeln('---------------');
  while not eof(inp) do begin
    read(inp,c); ef:=eof(inp);
    if not ef then el:=eoln(inp)
    else el:=false;  { when eof=true the standard forbids calling the eoln function }
    writeln('"',c,'"',el,ef);
  end; {while}
end. {TestReading}
```

Suppose the input file *inp* consists of the following two lines:

```
ABC
12
```

If our compiler adheres to the standard, the program above must give the following output:

```
char eoln  eof
---------------
"A" FALSE FALSE
"B" FALSE FALSE
"C"  TRUE FALSE
" " FALSE FALSE
"1" FALSE FALSE
"2"  TRUE FALSE
" " FALSE  TRUE
```

All programs of our solutions assume that the reading from the files of type *text* behaves in this way. It is worth mentioning that some Pascal compilers violate this standard for some kinds of input files. A frequent violation is that at the end of the last line *eof* becomes *true*, while *eoln* remains *false*.

Particular difficulties in adhering to the standard occur in the case where the input file is an interactive terminal. When reading from a terminal it is, for instance, difficult to achieve that the variable *input*↑ as well as the values of the *eoln* and *eof* functions are defined, if, in the meantime, the user at the terminal keys in the first character of a line, or writes an empty line, or even terminates the input file. Different compilers have taken different approaches to solving this problem, and programs must be individually adapted for them.

Additional problems occur when reading numbers, since the *eoln* and *eof* functions reflect the state by characters. Spaces at the end of a line are especially annoying, since after reading the last number neither *eoln* is *true* nor can another number be read. An example of a program that reads numbers safely enough can be found in the solution 823E, while total safety may be achieved only by reading digits character by character and transforming them to their value using our own carefully devised program.

821A

This way of coding words is used to store vocabularies in a packed form. The most common use of the technique is made by the *spelling checker* programs. Such a program reads a word from the input file and tries to find it in the vocabulary. If the word is found, it proceeds to the next one. If, however, the word is not in the vocabulary, the program consults the user to find out what to do (insert the new word into the vocabulary, correct a typing mistake, etc.).

The output of a word is simple, the essence of the algorithm lies in the *ReadW* function which decodes the word during reading. Although this function could be coded as a procedure, we adhered to a frequent programming technique to promote a procedure to a function whose return value tells whether the call to the function has been successful or not. Prior to reading (with the exception of the first word), the table *word* contains the entire word previously read, and its length is known as well. If the first character of the new word is a digit between 0 and 9, the program behaves as if it has already read the corresponding number of characters by simply advancing the index to the correct character in the table *word*. If the digit 0 is read, the program simply skips it (so, in fact, it only wastes space). If the digit read is a 1, no space is saved, so it is better to write the correct letter instead. Nevertheless no harm is done if the program correctly handles such cases.

When the function reads the next character of a word, or the first character of the word which is not a digit, it places it into the word and proceeds to the next character. The reading ends when a terminator (terminal character) is read; in our case it may be a space, end of a line or end of the file. Other details are evident from the program:

```
program Vocabulary(input,output);
{ The program decodes alphabetically sorted coded words. }
  const
    maxW = 100;                              { the maximum word length }
  var
    word: packed array [1..maxW] of char;        { the decoded word }
    lengthW: integer;                        { the actual word length }
  procedure SkipSpaces;
  { Skips excess spaces and ends of line. }
    var lookOn: boolean;
  begin
    lookOn:=true;
    while not eof(input) and lookOn do
      if input↑<>' ' then lookOn:=false else get(input);
  end; {SkipSpaces}
  function ReadW: boolean;
  { Reads and decodes a word and tells whether the word could in fact be read. }
    var i: integer;
  begin
    ReadW:=not eof(input); lengthW:=0;
    if eof(input) then {}
    else if input↑ in ['0'..'9'] then begin
      i:=ord(input↑)-ord('0');
      if i>lengthW then write('error in word: ');
      lengthW:=i; get(input);
    end; {if}
    if not eof(input) then
      while input↑<>' ' do begin
        if lengthW<maxW then
          begin lengthW:=lengthW+1; word[lengthW]:=input↑ end;
        get(input);
      end; {while}
    SkipSpaces;
  end; {ReadW}
  procedure WriteW;
  { Outputs a word. }
    var i: integer;
  begin
    for i:=1 to lengthW do write(word[i]);  writeln;
  end; {WriteW}
begin {Vocabulary}
  SkipSpaces; lengthW:=0; while ReadW do WriteW;
end. {Vocabulary}
```

833A First, we define a word as a sequence of small and capital letters between a and z. For non-English languages this may mean that some special letters do not form parts of words (you may find more about character representation in computers in the solution 913B). Similarly, digits, dashes, and other special characters are not parts of words. A word must contain at least one letter; empty words are not allowed.

The characters not belonging to words terminate them (are terminators); in the same way a word is terminated by the end of a line or the end of file. The only exception is the carry-over, when a word is immediately followed by a dash, followed by perhaps some spaces and an end of line, and a word starting at the first character of the next line. In this case, the dash, spaces and end of line are discarded, and both parts of the word considered a single word. Of course it does not matter if the word is hyphenated two or more times.

Before writing the program we roughly describe the algorithm used:

```
initialize necessary variables;
while end of file not reached do
   while end of line not reached do
      input a character;
      if the character is a letter then
         increment the letter counter;
         if the letter starts a new word, increment the word counter
         mark there is no carry-over;
      else if the character is a space, mark end of word
      else if the character is a dash, mark possible carry-over
         (possible carry-over is actually a carry-over if the dash is
         followed only with spaces and end of line)
      else mark end of word, mark no carry-over
   endwhile;
   if possible carry-over marked then
      mark carry-over
endwhile;
output the number of words and their average length
```

The details may be observed from the program:

```
program CountWords(input,output);
{ Counts words in a text taking care of carry-over. }
  var
    nLetters: integer;                  { the number of letters read from the file }
    nWords: integer;                    { the number of words read from the file }
    inWord: boolean;                    { indicates that a word is being read }
    carryOver: boolean;                 { indicates possible carry-over }
    ch: char;
```

```
begin {CountWords}
  nLetters:=0; nWords:=0; inWord:=false; carryOver:=false;
  while not eof do begin
    while not eoln do begin
      read(ch);
      if ch in ['A'..'Z','a'..'z'] then
        begin
          carryOver:=false; nLetters:=nLetters+1;
          if not inWord then
            begin nWords:=nWords+1; inWord:=true end;
        end
      else if ch=' ' then inWord:=false
      else if (ch='-') and inWord then
        begin inWord:=false; carryOver:=true end
      else begin inWord:=false; carryOver:=false end;
    end; {while}
    inWord:=carryOver; carryOver:=false;
    if not eof then readln;
  end; {while}
  writeln('Number of words ',nWords:1);
  write('Average word length is ');
  if nWords=0 then writeln('not defined.')
  else writeln(nLetters/nWords:4:1, ' letters.');
end. {CountWords}
```

913A The characters received from the computer are forwarded to the printer. The spaces are not sent immediately. Instead, the program waits until a nonblank character is received and counts the spaces (little memory is required to do that); if the character received marks end of line, the program "forgets" the spaces counted; if any printable character is received, the program first sends all spaces received (and counted) prior to it, followed by the character itself. Instead of a detailed algorithm, we present a program, simple enough to require no additional explanation:

```
program Truncate(input,output);
{ Truncates blanks at ends of lines. }
  var
    endLn: char;        { the end of line character }
    ch: char;           { the current character }
    nSpaces: integer;   { counts spaces }
    i: integer;

  procedure Receive(var ch: char); external;
  procedure Transmit(ch: char); external;
```

```
begin {Truncate}
  endLn:=chr(13); nSpaces:=0;
  repeat
    Receive(ch);
    if ch=' ' then nSpaces:=nSpaces+1
    else if ch=endLn then begin Transmit(ch); nSpaces:=0 end
    else begin
      for i:=1 to nSpaces do Transmit(' ');
      nSpaces:=0; Transmit(ch);
    end; {if}
  until false;
end. {Truncate}
```

Are you surprised at the number 13 as the argument to the *chr* function? It is the ASCII code for the ⟨CR⟩ character. You may find more about ASCII codes in solution 931B. Furthermore it is worth noting that the character read at end of line by standard Pascal is a space and not the *chr*(13) (see explanation in the solution 813A). Since the problem specifies that the end of a line is represented by a special character, the most appropriate has been chosen.

The problem originates in a useful box connected between a computer and a printer. The box may contain a very simple microcomputer in a single chip, having a limited memory of approximately 1000 characters. Besides truncation, such a box might be capable of translating printer commands, switching among several printers, or similar.

914A

The input data to the program *Bla* were:
2 3 4 9 0 7 8 10 6 5

The program treats each number as a pointer to the next number in the table b. In this way, individual elements of the table b are linked into a chain which starts at $b[1]$ and ends when the pointer to the next element in the table equals 0. If any pointer points to a subsequent element of the table (when $b[i] = i+1$), the two elements form a sequence. Several elements form a sequence when all adjacent pairs form sequences. The *Bla* program outputs the element sequences as well as isolated elements. To denote sequences the following notation is used:

$$x - y,$$

denoting elements from x to y.

The solution above was obtained the following way: since $b[1] = 2$, $b[2] = 3$, $b[3] = 4$, $b[4] = 9$, $b[9] = 6$, $b[6] = 7$, $b[7] = 8$, $b[8] = 10$, $b[10] = 5$ in $b[5] = 0$, the *Bla* program finds a sequence 1–4, an isolated element 9, another sequence 6–8, and finally two isolated elements 10 and 5.

The problem arises from a real problem; an example is the management of free disk blocks: files may be randomly dispersed all over the disk, leaving larger or smaller free (unoccupied) spaces between them. When a file is deleted, it may be necessary to join several free spaces into a single one (three in the worst case: one before the deleted file, one at the space of the file deleted, and one following it). This would of course be impossible, if it were not known where on disk the free space lay.

As an exercise you could try writing a *CounterBla* program, which reconstructs the input data to the *Bla* program when given its results as input.

1014A The *Waster* program is a real waster. It repeatedly adds things added dozens of times before, and uses tons of memory to keep trace of it. If care is taken to print the results as they are computed, old partial results may be discarded (and space saved), and since the partial result computed may be used to compute the next result, a lot of work is saved. Let us first consider the requested program; it is simple enough and requires no extra explanation:

```
program Swift(output);
{ Prints the first m elements of a sequence. }
  const
    m = 1000;  { the number of the elements to print }
  var
    c,sum: real;
    n: integer;
begin
  writeln(1, 0.0:10:3); writeln(2, 0.0:10:3); sum:=0;
  for n:=3 to m do
    begin c:=n+sum/n; writeln(n, c:10:3); sum:=sum+c end;
end. {Swift}
```

Let us now consider the space and time complexities of both programs. *Swift* uses three variables, independently of the value of m, while *Waster* requires an additional table of size m, which may be a substantial waste for large m.

It is usually assumed that the time spent by a program is proportional to the number of operations it performs. In our case, we only deal with addition and division (the implicit additions and subtractions performed to control the loops are ignored). In each repetition of the loop

```
for n:=3 to m do ...
```

the *Waster* program performs n additions and one division, altogether

$$4+5+\cdots+m+(m+1)=\frac{(m+1)\cdot(m+2)}{2}-6$$

operations (to prove that, the well known anecdote about Gauss should be remembered; see E. T. Bell: *Men of Mathematics*, Simon and Schuster, New York 1965). In our case for $m = 1000$ it performs $1001 \cdot 501 - 6 = 501495$ operations. On the contrary, in each repetition of the loop

```
for n:=3 to m do ...
```

the *Swift* program performs two additions and one division, altogether $3 \cdot (m-2)$, in our case 2994 operations (we have ignored the fact that the division may be several times slower than addition).

Compared to *Waster* the *Swift* program uses 150 times less time and more than 300 times less space for variables. This is an enviable achievement.

You may find more about complexity of algorithms in the introduction to Chapter D. The *Waster* program has quadratic time complexity while *Swift* has linear; *Waster* has linear space complexity while *Swift* has constant.

1114A

The program works incorrectly when the longest subsequence appears at the end of input data. An example for that is, say, ten equal numbers.

The program is corrected by inserting the statement

```
if d>dmax then dmax:=d;
```

immediately before the *writeln* statement.

It is interesting to note that the problem originated from an error in a solution in this book. When the error was discovered, it reminded us of the following rule of programming: *always double-check the initial and termination conditions of the program*, otherwise an error is sure to creep in.

1121A

The program inputs an integer and outputs the corresponding bar code. Since the bar code must end with a black strip of appropriate width, the binary representation must be of even length (a leading zero must be added if necessary, for instance, 4 is written in binary as 0100).

```
program BarCode(input);
  const
    WHITE = 0;  BLACK = 1;
    THIN = 0;  WIDE = 1;
  type
    widthT  = THIN..WIDE;
    colourT  = WHITE..BLACK;
  var n: integer;

  procedure DrawBar(colour: colourT; width: widthT); external;
```

```
procedure PrintBarCode(n: integer);
{ Prints the bar code corresponding to the positive integer "n". }
  var
    i,k: integer;
    bits: array [1..32] of 0..1; { the binary representation of the number n }
    width: widthT;               { the width of the current strip }
    colour: colourT;             { the colour of the current strip }
 begin {PrintBarCode}
  k:=0;
  while n>0 do begin k:=k+1; bits[k]:=n mod 2; n:=n div 2 end;
  if odd(k) then begin k:=k+1; bits[k]:=0 end;
  colour:=BLACK; width:=WIDE; DrawBar(colour,width);
  for i:=k downto 1 do begin
    if bits[i]=1 then width:=1-width;
    colour:=1-colour; DrawBar(colour,width);
  end; {for}
 end; {PrintBarCode}
begin
 readln(n); PrintBarCode(n);
end. {BarCode}
```

In fact, the above statements

```
width:=1-width; and colour:=1-colour;
```

should more correctly read

```
width:=WIDE+THIN-width; and colour:=WHITE+BLACK-colour.
```

In that case, the values of the constants *THIN*, *WIDE*, *WHITE*, and *BLACK* could be arbitrarily chosen, and the program would still work correctly, while in the original case it would not. This is the easiest way to alternate between two distinct values of a variable. How would this be most easily done for three values? And how for more?

Chapter B

Computational Problems

The common feature of problems collected in this chapter is that they compute something or prove a numerical property. Therefore we will first present some concepts, which will be met often in the solutions.

The problems dealing with integers often involve checking whether an integer, say a ($a \neq 0$), evenly divides another integer, say b. In Pascal this is done in the following way:

```
if (b mod a) = 0 then ···
```

since a evenly divides b if and only if the remainder of the division of b by a equals 0. When $a = 2$, the *odd* logical function, which checks whether its argument is odd, may be used as well:

```
if not odd(b) then ···
```

The corresponding tests in other programming languages follow:

```
IF INT(b/a)*a = b THEN ···      (Basic)
IF (B/A*A .EQ. B) ···           (FORTRAN)
IF REMAINDER :a :b = 0 ···      (Logo)
```

Other problems require the determination of digits of the decimal or binary notation of a number. So let us examine how the digits of a number are obtained in a given number system.

A decimal numeral is an abbreviation, as we usually write 12 734 instead of $1 \cdot 10^4 + 2 \cdot 10^3 + 7 \cdot 10^2 + 3 \cdot 10^1 + 4 \cdot 10^0$. The first, leftmost digit of the numeral (1 in our case) is called the *most significant* or the *leading* digit, while the last, rightmost digit (4 in our case) is called the *least significant* or the *trailing* digit. The notation above clearly shows how the trailing digit of the notation is obtained: it equals the remainder of the division of the number (call it n) by 10, which is written in Pascal as n **mod** 10. If the number is divided by 10, (n **div** 10), the quotient obtained comprises the remaining digits of the number shifted right by one place. The remainder of the repeated division by 10 then gives the next digit. This procedure is repeated until the quotient equals 0. In this way, all digits can be computed in the reverse order. Since the remainder of division by 10 lies in the range between 0 and 9, all digits lie in this range. The number 10 is thus of special importance for the decimal system, and is thus called the **base** of the decimal system. In the binary system, the role of the base is played by the number 2. There are two digits, 0 and 1, and the rest is the same as above: a binary numeral is a shorthand notation for a long sum of powers of the base 2, for instance, 10011 shortens $1 \cdot 2^4 + 0 \cdot 2^3 + 0 \cdot 2^2 + 1 \cdot 2^1 + 1 \cdot 2^0$. Binary digits are usually called *bits*.

The decimals (the digits of the fractional part) of a non-integer number are computed in a similar way, except that they are shifted in the opposite direction: instead of being divided, the fraction must be multiplied by the base. Formerly, the digit was obtained as the remainder of the division, here it is the integer part of the product, in Pascal for example $trunc(10 * n)$.

It is not difficult to deduce from the above how the number is determined from its digits: the corresponding sum of powers must be computed. This is **never** done by explicitly computing the powers. In mathematics, an easier way is known, called the *Horner algorithm*. It proceeds as follows (m is the number of its digits, and $c[k]$ for $k = 0, 1, \ldots, m-1$ are the digits of the number, ordered from the least to the most significant):

```
n:=0;
for k:=m-1 downto 0 do n:=10*n+c[k];
```

The result of this computation is the integer n, which has as its digits exactly the given values $c[m-1]$,...,$c[1]$, $c[0]$. Try writing the algorithm for the fractional part of the number, assuming that the decimal digits are stored in the array $f[1..m]$.

It may be easily seen that this algorithm complements the method previously described for computing the digits of a number; it is therefore sometimes called the *inverse Horner algorithm*.

Several times the notion of a four-digit number is mentioned in the solutions. In most cases it means all numbers in the range from 0 to 9999; those which may be written using four decimal digits at most. By analogy this definition is extended to other numbers of places as well as for other bases; problem 834B deals with ten-bit binary numbers (note that the n-digit binary numbers are usually called n-bit numbers). According to the above definition, all three-digit numbers are four-digit as well. To avoid this, the notion of the *exactly* four-digit number is sometimes defined; these are the numbers in the range from 1000 to 9999. This notion is extended analogously as above. In the problems, it is usually evident from the problem itself whether it deals with the n-digit or the exactly n-digit numbers.

Finally, a frequent misconception in expressing and thinking should be commented on. It is often said that the computer calculates using binary *numbers*, while humans use decimal. In fact, it is the *numeral* which is binary or decimal, that is, the notation (character string, or magnetic and electrical record in the computer memory) used to represent a number. A *number* is an abstract notion, representing the value of the matching numeral. All algorithms for the basic arithmetic operations taught in primary schools deal with numerals; that is why one must specifically familiarize oneself with the binary multiplication (as we will in solutions 824B and 214C). Mathematically speaking, any operation is a function, which from a pair of numbers (that is, *values*) determines the third (again a *value*). Likewise, in computer science the algorithms for the basic arithmetic operations themselves are usually of no interest. Instead, the basic interest lies in the algorithms, which are specific ways of writing mathematical functions and consequently deal with numbers. Therefore programs, being in fact the algorithms coded in a programming language, also deal with numbers (the type *integer* is therefore a subset of the set of *integral numbers*). The programs convert the numbers to numerals (of the type **packed array** ... **of** *char* in Pascal) only when they must print them out.

To summarize: in computation, numbers (neither binary nor numerals) are used, but numerals are output. It is therefore nonsense to say that a procedure returns a hexadecimal address of something, since (at least in a computer) an address is a number and not a numeral; the procedure therefore simply returns an address. In a similar way, it is nonsense to say that a computer calculates using binary numbers; it only performs binary algorithms on numbers, or better, on binary notation of numbers.

111B The condition $x^2 \leq 1$ holds if and only if $|x| \leq 1$, which is equivalent to $-1 \leq x \leq 1$. So, the algorithm terminates when first testing this condition, if $|x| \leq 1$. Otherwise, if $|x| > 1$, the variable x attains the value $2/x$. Denote this new value by x_1 to avoid confusion. Its absolute value is less than or equal to 1 if and only if $|x| \geq 2$. In this case the algorithm terminates after the second step. If, however, $|x| < 2$ (and also $|x| > 1$), then $1 < |x_1| < 2$. This means that the next value $x_2 := 2/x_1$ again falls into the range between 1 and 2 in absolute value. The same holds for x_3, x_4, etc. In this case the algorithm never terminates. The set of numbers for which the algorithm terminates is depicted in Figure B1.

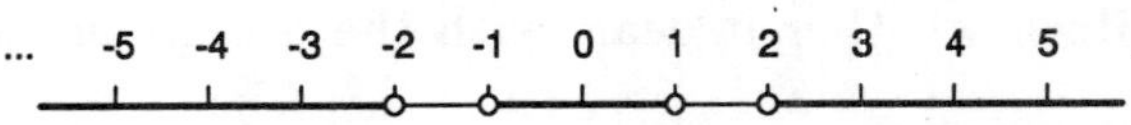

Figure B1: The set of numbers for which the algorithm terminates

411B

a) By tracing the flowchart it is easily verified that in this case the algorithm terminates, and that at the end $k = 4$.

b,c) The algorithm terminates when n equals 1. This may even happen in the first step, in which case k equals 0 at the end. Assume now that $n \neq 1$. Its value changes only if it is evenly divisible by p. In this case it is divided by p, and k increased by 1. So the variable k counts how many times n can be evenly divided by p. This happens several times if n is evenly divisible by a higher power of the number p. The algorithm terminates if and only if in some step n becomes equal to 1, which happens if and only if $n = p^r$, that is, a power of p. In this case k ends with the value of $k = r = \log|n|/\log|p| = \log_{|p|}|n|$.

413B The most evident algorithm is to determine the number of divisors for each of the numbers $1, 2, \ldots, n$. The number with most divisors is stored in *kmax* and the number of its divisors in *dmax*. The divisors of the number k are most easily found by testing, for any number between 1 and k, whether it evenly divides k. The work may even be reduced. Consider: if a number p evenly divides k, then so does k/p. If $p < \sqrt{k}$, then $k/p > \sqrt{k}$. If, however, $p > \sqrt{k}$, then $k/p < \sqrt{k}$. Therefore, it is sufficient to find all divisors of k in the range from 1 to $\sqrt{k}$ and count each twice. At the end, the divisor $\sqrt{k}$ must be counted, if k is a square. Naturally, there is no need to compute the square root, the loop should terminate when $p^2 \geq k$. The program follows:

```
program Divisors(input,output);
{ Determines, which number between 1 and n has most divisors. }
  var
    n: integer;
    kmax,dmax: integer;        { the number with most, that is dmax divisors }
    k,d: integer;              { the current number and the number of its divisors }
    p: integer;                { a divisor of k }
```

```
begin {Divisors}
  readln(n);
  kmax:=1; dmax:=1;
  for k:=2 to n do begin
  { Find the number of divisors of k. }
    d:=2; p:=2;
    while sqr(p)<k do begin
      if (k mod p) = 0 then d:=d+2;
      p:=p+1;
    end; {while}
    if sqr(p)=k then d:=d+1;
  { Has k most divisors so far ? }
    if d>dmax then begin dmax:=d; kmax:=k end;
  end; {for}
  writeln('In the range from 1 to ',n:1,' the number ',kmax:1,' has most divisors. ');
end. {Divisors}
```

Similarly as in problem 1123B we may use a table.

If a number k has more divisors than all smaller numbers, then k is called a **maximally divisible number**. The program above therefore finds the largest maximally divisible number not larger than n.

If $F(n)$ denotes the number of divisors of n, it may be observed that the primes are the minima of this function. The maximally divisible numbers, on the other side, are the peaks of the function F in the following sense: the value of the function F at a maximally divisible number is greater than at any smaller number. Let us consider a method for fast determination of most maximally divisible numbers representable on a computer.

For any integer n there is a unique way to decompose it into primes, that is, to write it as a product

$$n = p_1^{k_1} \cdot p_2^{k_2} \cdot \ldots \cdot p_r^{k_r},$$

where $1 < p_1 < p_2 < \cdots < p_r$ are prime numbers.

The number of divisors of the number n is then easy to compute from the decomposition. Each divisor is a product of some of the primes of the decomposition, and in this product each prime p_j may appear zero or up to k_j times, giving $(k_j + 1)$ different possibilities for a divisor. The number of all divisors (including 1 and the number itself) is thus

$$F(n) = (k_1 + 1) \cdot (k_2 + 1) \cdot \ldots \cdot (k_r + 1).$$

Since a maximally divisible number is the smallest number where $F(n)$ reaches a maximum, the following must be true:

$$k_1 \geq k_2 \geq \cdots \geq k_r,$$

and $p_1, p_2, \ldots, p_r$ must be the smallest successive primes, namely

$$p_1 = 2, \quad p_2 = 3, \quad p_3 = 5, \quad p_4 = 7, \quad \text{etc.}$$

since for given values of k_i the number n must be as small as possible. All interesting combinations of the exponents of k_1, k_2, k_3,... are easily produced, and then tested to see if they are maximally divisible. Using this method, all 65 maximally divisible numbers smaller than 10^9 are computed in a few moments, while the program above labours hard to investigate the numbers up to 10^5.

Finally some questions. Which numbers have an odd number of divisors? Is it possible to find a number with a prescribed number of divisors? Are there infinitely many maximally divisible numbers, as there are primes? Which is the smallest maximally divisible number divisible by 7?

415B Recalling from the introduction the algorithm to compute the digits of the binary notation of a number, it is easily seen that the part of the program from the problem counts the number of ones in the binary notation of a number. The smallest number with ten ones is:

$$1111111111_{(2)} = 2^{10} - 1 = 1023.$$

425B See solution 415B.

512B The *Hamming* program counts the number of places at which the binary notations of the numbers x and y differ. This number is usually called the Hamming distance of the numbers x and y.

a) Example:

$$\begin{aligned} x &= 76 = \mathbf{01001100}_{(2)} \\ y &= 154 = \mathbf{10011010}_{(2)} \\ & \qquad\quad \uparrow\uparrow\ \uparrow\ \uparrow\uparrow \end{aligned}$$

We obtain 5.

b) There are many possibilities for the *AntiHamming* program, since for a given number x and the distance d several numbers y exist at the Hamming distance d from x. Our solution finds the number y whose binary notation differs from the notation of x in the lowest (least significant) d bits and equals x in others.

```
program AntiHamming(input,output);
{ Determines a number y at Hamming distance d from the number x. }
  var
    x,y,d: integer;
    i,twoToI: integer;

begin {AntiHamming}
  readln(x,d);
{ Loop through all binary places of x and form the value y }
{ by inverting the digits of x at the lower d binary places. }
  i:=0; twoToI:=1; y:=0;
  while (x<>0) or (i<d) do begin
    if odd(x) = (i>=d) then y:=y+twoToI;
    i:=i+1; twoToI:=twoToI*2; x:=x div 2;
  end; {while}
  writeln('The result is: ',y);
end. {AntiHamming}
```

It should be added that the value of the input d should be less than the number of bits necessary to represent integers. Thus, for personal computers, we might require that $d < 16$. You could try solving the problem for larger values yourself.

515B

The problem is most easily solved by testing, for each number between 1 and n, whether its square is a palindrome. At first sight this is not easy, since it is fairly difficult to determine the leading digit of a number, at least with the means provided by the programming languages. (The trailing digit of x is obtained by the expression $x \mod 10$). It is easiest to invert the number and compare the result to the original number. In the program below, the inverse Horner algorithm to compute the digits of the original is combined with the Horner algorithm to compute its inverse. With the first algorithm we are getting the digits of x starting with the least significant, and using the obtained sequence as input to the Horner algorithm, we get the number whose most significant digits are precisely the least significant digits of x, that is the number with digits of x in the reverse order.

```
program Palindrome(input,output);
{ Determines all palindromic squares of numbers between 1 and n. }
  var
    n,m: integer;
    x,a,b: integer;

begin {Palindrome}
  readln(n);
  for m:=1 to n do begin
    x:=sqr(m); a:=x; b:=0;
```

```
  { The digits of x are transferred to b in inverse order. }
   while a>0 do begin b:=10*b + a mod 10; a:=a div 10 end;
   if b=x then writeln(m,x);
  end; {for}
end. {Palindrome}
```

522B For $a \geq 10$ the first **while** loop determines the largest number k of the form $k = 10 \cdot 2^d$ satisfying $k \leq a < 2k$. If $a < 10$ (possibly negative), then k remains equal to 10.

First, let us examine the easier case when $a < 10$. The second loop does not execute at all in this case; the program outputs 0 if and only if $a = 0$.

Now let $a \geq 10$. The second **while** loop first subtracts $k = 10 \cdot 2^d$ from a, and then divides k by 2. In the next pass it subtracts $k = 10 \cdot 2^{d-1}$, if only $a \geq k$. If necessary it then subtracts $10 \cdot 2^{d-2}$ and so on. What is going on is most easily seen by writing the number a as:

$$a = 10 \cdot a_1 + a_0, \quad \text{where} \quad 0 \leq a_0 < 10.$$

If a_1 is represented in binary by $a_1 = b_k b_{k-1} \ldots b_2 b_{1\,(2)}$, then after the first pass of the loop a becomes equal to $b_{k-1} \ldots b_2 b_{1\,(2)} \cdot 10 + a_0$. In the next pass it becomes $a = b_{k-2} \ldots b_2 b_{1\,(2)} \cdot 10 + a_0$ and so on. The **while** loop repeats until a becomes smaller than 10, that is, equal to a_0. At the end, this value is printed. Therefore, 0 is printed if and only if a is evenly divisible by 10. To summarize: the program outputs 0 if and only if $a \geq 0$ and a **mod** $10 = 0$.

The program in the problem presents a very efficient algorithm for the binary division by the divisor 10. For a general divisor the algorithm is as follows:

```
{ The inputs are a and b, a is the dividend, b is the divisor }
 q:=0; r:=a; k:=b; m:=1;
 while k<r do begin k:=k*2; m:=m*2 end;
 while r>=b do begin
   if r>=k then begin r:=r-k; q:=q+m end;
   k:=k div 2; m:=m div 2;
 end; {while}
{ the quotient is q, the remainder is r }
```

It is worth mentioning that the program uses only multiplication and division by 2, which is implemented by a single place left or right shift of the binary notation. Each loop executes approximately $\log q$ times, which makes the algorithm suitable for use in cases where the computer does not provide an instruction for division. When dealing with signed numbers, the signs of the quotient and the remainder must be processed separately. An almost identical algorithm is used to implement integer division in the processing units of most computers, except that it is implemented by a microprogram or circuitry there. Similar problems are dealt with in problems 824B, 112C, and 214C.

613B A long integer might be represented in Pascal as follows:

```
const
  base = 10; base1 = 9; { base1 = base-1 }
  nPlaces = 20;          { maximal number of digits }
type
  longInteger =
    record
      sign: (plus,minus);
      digit: array [1..nPlaces] of 0..base1;
    end;
```

The least significant digit of the number x (of the type *longInteger*) may be stored at the start, that is, in $x.digit[1]$; the next in $x.digit[2]$, and so on.

There are two cases of the algorithm for addition:

a) *The addition of equally signed numbers.* In this case the sign of the sum equals the sign of the summands, and the digits are computed as follows:

```
carry:=0;
for i:=1 to nPlaces do begin
  a:=x.digit[i] + y.digit[i] + carry;
  carry:=a div base; sum.digit[i]:=a mod base;
end; {for}
```

If at the end the value of the variable *carry* is nonzero, the **range overflow** occurs, the result is in our case a 21-digit number.

b) *The addition of numbers of opposite sign.* In this case the sum carries the sign of the summand greater in absolute value. The latter is determined by finding the highest digits of both summands which differ; the larger digit determines the number greater in absolute value. If the numbers are equal in absolute value, the result is zero, and has the sign, say, *plus*. The digits of the sum are determined by the elementary subtraction algorithm as follows (the number x is greater in absolute value than y):

```
carry:=0;
for i:=1 to nPlaces do begin
  a:=base + x.digit[i] – (y.digit[i] + carry);
  carry:=1 – a div base; sum.digit[i]:=a mod base;
end; {for}
```

To subtract long integers the sign of the subtrahend is inverted and the algorithm for addition used.

The sole reason that the value of the constant *base* above is chosen to be 10 is that the above algorithms for the addition in fact represent the ones taught in the primary school. Any value not greater than half of the largest integer (*maxInt* in Pascal) is appropriate. On a 16-bit computer, 10000 can well be chosen as the base, or — with some additional effort — even 32768= *maxInt* + 1. In the latter case, instead of a value greater than the base, a carry over to the next place in the array *digit* is signified by a negative value. Correct values of the digits can still be reconstructed. If the multiplication was necessary, it would be desirable to choose for the base a value whose square would not exceed the largest integer. Why?

The proposed notation of the sign is only one of alternatives. In various cases it may be more suitable to represent negative numbers in the complementary form, as they are commonly represented in computers. In the *complementary* form, the sign is not represented separately. If numbers in the range from 0 to n may be represented using the unsigned notation, then, for the complementary notation, the numbers in the range from 0 to n **div** 2 represent nonnegative numbers, and the numbers in the range from (n **div** 2) + 1 to n represent negative numbers. When performing computation, no special care need be taken about the sign, the addition and subtraction are performed as if only positive numbers were engaged. Special care must be taken only to detect overflow: the result is incorrect, if both summands were equally signed, while the sum has a different sign, or if the subtrahend and minuend differ in sign, and the difference differs in sign from the subtrahend. You will find more about number notation in the book by D. E. Knuth: *The Art of Computer Programming*, Vol. 2, Addison-Wesley, Reading 1981.

In mathematics, this way of writing numbers is called *positional notation* using the given base. There are other ways of representing numbers. Here, only one will be mentioned, the so-called *modular notation*. Consider the first n primes: $2, 3, 5, \ldots, p_n$. Denote by r_i the remainder of the division of the number by p_i, $i = 1, 2, \ldots, n$. Number theory (the Chinese remainder theorem) then states that all numbers between 0 and the product of all the primes involved, $m := 2 \cdot 3 \cdot 5 \cdot \ldots \cdot p_n$ are uniquely determined by the set of the remainders r_i. Computing with the remainders is easy; two numbers are added (subtracted, multiplied) by adding (subtracting, multiplying) the remainders at the same positions, and the notation of the result is obtained by taking the remainders of these sums (differences, products) in division by appropriate primes. With this notation it is, however, far more difficult to implement division and therefore the printout of the number as well.

614B The number n which appears in the statement of the problem seems to be out of the context of determining the lucky numbers smaller than 1000. We will keep it to generalize the problem: by choosing $n = 1000$ in the algorithm, the lucky numbers smaller than 1000 are determined, by choosing other values, the lucky numbers from some other interval are computed. In this way, n may be given as input.

The sequence of numbers will be stored in the table *num*. In each deletion, the numbers deleted will be physically removed from the sequence. Let the variable k contain the number from the sequence in turn for deleting — each k-th number must be deleted, that is, the elements *num*[k], *num*[$2k$], etc.

The number *remain* contains the number of remaining elements of the sequence. We start with the sequence with each other element removed, so there are $(n+1)$ **div** 2 elements in the sequence at the beginning. In this way the first step is skipped, saving half of the space required for the table, as well as a significant amount of work. When each k-th number is deleted from the table, (*remain* − *remain* **div** k) numbers remain in the table. Since the new value of the *remain* may be predicted prior to deleting the unlucky numbers from the table, the **while** loop in the program below might be replaced by an appropriate **for** loop. We avoided this to conform to the rules of good programming practice. The *Reverse* function in the program "reverses" the given number. The method used to do this is explained in detail in the solution 515B.

```
program LuckyNumbers(input,output);
{ Determines the lucky numbers in the interval from 1 to n, n<=1000. }
  const
    max = 500;          { half of the interval }
  var
    num: array [1..max] of integer;
    n,i,p,k: integer;
    index: integer;     { the index of the next element }
    remain: integer;    { the length of the sequence }

begin {LuckyNumbers}
  readln(n); if n>2*max then n:=2*max;
  remain:=(n+1) div 2;
  for i:=1 to remain do num[i]:=2*i-1;
  if remain=1 then num[2]:=3;
  index:=2;
  while num[index]<=remain do begin
    k:=num[index]; i:=k; p:=k+1;
    while p<=remain do begin
    { Delete unlucky numbers and squeeze the table. }
      num[i]:=num[p];
      i:=i+1; p:=p+1; if (p mod k) = 0 then p:=p+1;
    end; {while}
    remain:=i-1; index:=index+1;
  end; {while}
```

```
  writeln('Lucky numbers:');
  for i:=1 to remain do begin
    write(num[i]:4);
    if i mod 15 = 0 then writeln;
  end; {for}
  writeln;
end. {LuckyNumbers}
```

621B The division will be performed "manually", as we were taught in primary school. The integer part of the quotient x/y equals x **div** y. The digits of the fraction are obtained by repeatedly multiplying the remainder of the division by 10; the integer part of the quotient represents the next digit of the fraction. This procedure is repeated for each digit to be computed.

```
program Division(input,output);
{ Computes the quotient x/y to m places using the "manual" method. }
  var x,y,m,i: integer;

begin
  write('Input the numbers x and y    : '); readln(x,y);
  write('Input the number of places m: '); readln(m);
  write('The quotient equals : ', x div y:5, '.');
  for i:=1 to m do begin
    if i mod 50 = 0 then { 50 digits in a line }
      begin writeln; write(' ':19) end;
    x:=(x mod y)*10;  write(x div y:1);
  end; {for}
  writeln;
end. {Division}
```

711B The algorithm is simple: the starting element $a_0 = a$ of the sequence is input, and then the following elements $a_1, a_2, \ldots, a_k$ computed until an element equal to 1 is reached. The shortcoming of this algorithm is that there is no guarantee that an arbitrary starting element indeed generates a sequence containing 1. Since we cannot prove this, the number of repetitions is limited by the constant 10000, which may be increased if necessary.

```
program Sequence(input,output);
{ Which element of the sequence equals 1? }
  const kMax = 10000;
  var a,k: integer;
```

```
  function Reverse(num: integer): integer;
  { The result is the number with the reversed order of digits. }
    var new: integer;
  begin
    new:=0;
    while num<>0 do
      begin new:=10*new + num mod 10; num:=num div 10 end;
    Reverse:=new;
  end; {Reverse}

begin {Sequence}
  write('Starting element: '); readln(a);
  k:=0;
  while (a<>1) and (k<kMax) do
    begin a:=Reverse(a+4); k:=k+1 end;
  if a=1 then
    writeln(k:5, '-th element of the sequence equals 1.')
  else
    writeln('Among the first ',kMax:6,' elements none equal 1.');
end. {Sequence}
```

With a simple modification to the program above you may easily verify that for the starting elements smaller than 1000 the sequence fairly quickly reaches 1, while for slightly larger starting values (1011 to begin with) the first 10000 elements of the sequence are all different from 1. A more detailed survey of the sequence shows that after some starting elements the sequence runs into a cycle: a set of elements start to repeat, not necessarily from the initial element on but from a later one.

Similar sequences are frequently encountered; such series are produced by some generators of "random" numbers. In the latter case, it is important to determine the length of their cycle; the longer the cycle, the better the generator is. How can one determine whether the elements of the sequence start to repeat? The first idea, to store the successive elements and compare the current one to them, not only uses a lot of memory, it is computationally extremely demanding as well — try estimating its space and time complexity (you may find more about complexity in the introduction to Chapter D). There is an easy way to determine the cycle. Along with the elements of the sequence a_n, the sequence b is computed, whose elements are $b_n = a_k$, $k = n$ **div** 2. Thus the next a_k is computed at each step, while b_n is changed at every second step only. When the sequence b enters the cycle, a is certain to be already cycling in it, and it catches b before it reaches the point of entrance into the cycle. Extending the program above is an easy exercise, and it is also easy to compute the length of the cycle. It is, however, much more difficult to find the exact start of a cycle.

724B First, let us find out what the *Mac* function does. At the start of the k-th pass of the **while** loop, the value of the variable x equals 2^{k-1}. The condition $odd(a+b)$ holds if and only if one of the numbers a and b is even and the other is odd, which means that the last digits of their binary notations are different. On each step, a and b get halved, so the above condition holds each time their binary digits at the same positions are different. Since powers of 2 are added to c, the k-th digit of c is 0, if the digits at that position in a and b are different, and is 1 otherwise. Denoting by a_k, b_k and c_k the k-th binary digits of the numbers a, b and $c = Mac(a, b)$, the relation is as follows:

a_k:	0 0 1 1
b_k:	0 1 0 1
c_k:	0 1 1 0

Tracing the execution of the program, the following values are obtained at the k-th binary place:

a_k	0 0 1 1
b_k	0 1 0 1
new $a_k = Mac(a,b)_k$	0 1 1 0
new $b_k = Mac(a,b)_k$	0 0 1 1
new $a_k = Mac(b,a)_k$	0 1 0 1

It is easily seen that in all cases the k-th binary digit of the new value of the variable a equals the digit of the old value of the variable b, and conversely, b has the same digit as a had before. The values of the variables a and b are interchanged.

The majority of experienced programmers would immediately substitute *Xor* for *Mac*, since the function indeed computes the exclusive disjunction (see solution 211A) bit by bit. Its truth table is in the first table above. It is easily seen that it is independent of the order of the operands. If Pascal provided an appropriate arithmetic operator, say **xor**, the above interchange of values would be written as

```
a:=a xor b; b:=a xor b; a:=a xor b;
```

The values of the variables a and b may also be interchanged using only addition and subtraction:

```
a:=a+b; b:=a-b; a:=a-b;
```

When programming in an assembly language, one of the above ways is used to interchange the values of two processor registers without accessing memory, and without using an additional register, if the processor provides no swap instruction. In Pascal and similar programming languages this solution is not only mysterious but also slower than the usual interchange with the use of an auxiliary variable:

```
t:=a; a:=b; b:=t;
```

Some programming languages even provide a special command for the interchange, for instance

```
a:=:b
```

Also, most processors provide a special instruction for it.

731B Since solution 621B deals with a similar problem, you may find it useful to peek at it. The fraction will be constructed digit by digit, as the division proceeds when performed manually. Let us denote the remainder of the current division by p (at start $p = 1$). Then the next digit q and the next remainder r are obtained from the equation:

$$10p = mq + r$$

where m denotes the denominator of the fraction. Let us prove that q is indeed a digit, that it lies between 0 and 9. Since r is the remainder in the division by m, $0 \leq r < m$, and since p is the remainder of the previous division, $0 \leq p < m$. From that

$$0 \leq 10p < 10m$$
$$0 \leq mq + r < 10m$$
$$0 \leq q + r/m < 10$$

so that $0 \leq q \leq 9$, which shows that q is indeed the next decimal digit.

Since the course of the division in the subsequent steps depends only on the remainder in the current step, and there are m possible values of the remainder $(0, 1, \ldots, m-1)$, the current remainder repeats after at most m steps. If the division terminates evenly after several steps, we assume that the remainder 0 repeats from there on.

All these observations lead us to the requested program. In addition to the digits (the quotients), the remainders must be stored, as it is evident only after the first repetition of the remainder from which point the remainders repeat. In solution 711B you will find a discussion of an algorithm to determine when the remainders start to repeat which is more economic with memory. In our case, the simplest solution described works well enough.

```
program Fractions(input,output);
{ Computes the decimal notation of fractions. }
  const
    mDenom = 1000;      { the maximum denominator }
    mLine = 70;         { the length of the printed line }
  type
    table = array [0..mDenom] of integer;
```

```
var
  dig,rem: table;          { the digits and the remainders in division }
  denom: integer;          { the denominator of the fraction, m from text }
  rem10: integer;          { remainder*10 }
  d: integer;              { the length of the written part of the line }
  i,j,k: integer;

begin {Fractions}
  write('Input the fraction denominator: '); read(denom);
  i:=0; rem[0]:=1 mod denom; dig[0]:=1 div denom;
  repeat                   { compute denominators up to the first repetition }
    rem10:=10*rem[i];
    i:=i+1; dig[i]:=rem10 div denom; rem[i]:=rem10 mod denom;
    j:=0; while rem[j]<>rem[i] do j:=j+1;
  until j<i;
  write(' 1/',denom:4,' = ',dig[0]:1,'.'); d:=12;                      { output }
  for k:=1 to j do begin write(dig[k]:1); d:=d+1 end;     { the non-periodic part }
  write('('); d:=d+1;
  for k:=j+1 to i do begin                                    { the periodic part }
    write(dig[k]:1); d:=d+1;
    if d>mLine then begin writeln; write(' ':12); d:=12 end;
  end; {for}
  writeln(')');
end. {Fractions}
```

824B The program gives no output, since the value of the variable f equals 0 in any execution of the last **if** statement. For each k between 1 and 1984 the following computation takes place: in the **while** loop, the well known binary multiplication of the numbers a and b is performed (this may be formally proved by mathematical induction on a, but is slightly more difficult to guess, see 214C). The value of the variable f after the loop terminates therefore equals k^2. The **for** loop now subtracts from f the value of the sum:

$$1+3+5+\cdots+(2k-1) = 2\cdot(1+2+\cdots+k)-k = \\ = 2\cdot(1/2)\cdot k\cdot(k+1)-k = k^2$$

Finally therefore $f = 0$.

The numbers involved in computations are always less than or equal to 1984×1985, which is large enough to cause overflow on a 16-bit computer, while there is no problem when a larger integer range is used (can you tell how large the range must be?). This was the reason for overflow on the small computer used in the problem.

834B The program gives no output. In the first loop (**while** $f\ldots$) it fills the table with the reverse binary notation of the index, and reverses the order of the bits in the second (**for** $i\ldots$). Thus, the elements of the table are numbers equal to the indices. Let us consider the loops in more detail.

The table is filled with numbers with ten binary digits (bits). The reverse of 0 is of course 0, since its notation does not contain a one, while the reverse of 1 is 512 (binary 1000000000). It is easy to prove that the reverse of twice a number equals half the reverse of the number itself.

Consider the notations of the first four numbers (00, 01, 10, and 11). Then it may be easily seen that the notations of the next four are obtained by preceding the first four by a 1 (obtaining 100, 101, 110 and 111), that is, by adding 4 to these notations. The next eight numbers are then obtained by adding 8, that is, putting a one to the fourth place from the right. From the above we see how the reverses of consecutive numbers are computed. Given the reverses of the first four numbers, the reverses of the next four are obtained by adding the reverse of 4 to the first four. The reverses of the next eight are then computed by adding to the first eight the reverse of 8, which equals half of the reverse of 4. In this way the table is filled in the first loop.

In the second loop, the program reverses the bit order in the most straightforward way: bits are transferred one by one from the original to the reverse by first shifting the reverse one bit left, transferring the rightmost bit of the original to the reverse and finally shifting the original bits right. The rightmost bit of the number a is obtained by the expression a **mod** 2, bits are shifted left by multiplying by 2, and right by dividing by 2 (the rightmost bit is lost in division).

Reversing the bit order is comparatively rare in computer use. That is why most processors provide no appropriate instruction for it, and the bits must be in fact reversed by a program. In addition to the bit-by-bit solution, a table may be used. This is the most effective solution for short numbers, up to 8 bits long (more about this in solutions 931B and 1123B). The table for 8-bit numbers may be used also to reverse the numbers with lengths which are multiples of 8. The algorithm is easy, so it is left for you to consider. You may find a hint in solution 224D.

931B Before we begin, some remarks are due. Characters (letters, digits, etc.) are represented in a computer by small integers, called the character **codes**. It depends on the computer system which code represents a particular character.

Today most computers use the ASCII coding. (ASCII is an abbreviation which has become a computer jargon word; it means the American Standard Code for the Information Interchange). In its basic version, the character codes are seven bits long (numbers between 0 and 127), it is therefore called seven-bit character coding. The characters with codes between 32 and 126 are *printable*, and they include the space, the upper- and lower-case letters, the decimal digits, some punctuation marks and other special characters, 95 in total.

The rest of the characters, with codes between 0 and 31 and the code 127, are called the *control* characters. They are used to control, format, and separate data during transmission. The control characters are designated by a two- or three-character label, usually the acronym of its English name. For instance, the characters with codes 10 (LF, line feed) and 13 (CR, carriage return) are frequently encountered. The character CR moves the printing position (the printing head of a typewriter) to the left edge of the paper, the character LF advances the paper for a single line; the joint effect of both characters is to move to the start of a new line. A new page is started by the ASCII character with the code 12 (FF, form feed), the character with the code 7 (BEL, bell) is used to sound an audible signal. Also frequently encountered is the character with the code 27 (ESC, escape), starting a sequence of characters which do not form part of the text, but are a command to the receiver (an *escape sequence*). For instance, the sequence ⟨ESC⟩[2J erases the screen of certain terminals, while the sequence ⟨ESC⟩E starts bold printout on certain printers. In both cases the label of the control character has been surrounded by angle brackets to delimit it from other text.

Under most circumstances seven bit codes suffice; only occasionally are they preceded by the eighth parity bit. This bit is chosen in such a way as to make the number of ones in the binary notation of the character code even (or odd on some computers). In this way the characters are secured when recorded on a magnetic tape (more about that in solution 113B) or during transmission over a telephone line. The line may often be disturbed, which may cause an error in the character transmitted. If the disturbance is short, most probably a single bit is inverted, and thus the parity changes. The errors during transmission may thus be discovered by the receiver and adequately reacted to.

ASCII coding forms the base of international as well as British and other national standards; in the latter case some special characters (e.g. brackets and braces) are substituted by specific national characters. An eight-bit extension of the ASCII coding exists, which has been adopted recently; the majority of computer vendors still do not conform to it and use a proprietary coding instead. One of the extensions contains line drawing characters in the upper half, the other italicized characters of the lower half. The sixteen-bit standard is in preparation, which will, among others, perhaps accommodate even the 9000 most used Chinese technical characters.

Let us now solve our problem! The parity bit may be determined by counting ones in the character code. The character codes with an odd number of ones are preceded by the parity bit by adding 128 to the code, while the parity bit of the codes with the even number of ones is already correct. The *ParChar* function below provides the character code with the correct parity bit. The solution under the item (**a**) is obtained if this function is called for each input character.

Since characters usually repeat in text, we may avoid computing the parity bit each time by using a (parity) table. In it, characters with proper parity bit added are stored. In this way the corresponding call to the *ParChar* function is replaced by a much faster operation of indexing into a table; we obtain the solution of the item (**b**).

```
program AddParityBit(input,output);
{ Copies a text, adding the parity bits to the characters. }
 var
   ch: char;
   parTab: array [char] of char

 function ParChar(ch: char): char;
 { Precedes the character by the parity bit. }
   var
     code: integer;     { character code }
     even: boolean;     { is the number of ones even }
 begin
   even:=true; code:=ord(ch);
   while code<>0 do begin
     if odd(code) then even:=not even;
     code:=code div 2;
   end; {while}
   if even then ParChar:=ch else ParChar:=chr(128+ord(ch));
 end; {ParChar}

begin {AddParityBit}
 for ch:=chr(0) to chr(127) do  parTab[ch]:=ParChar(ch);       { parity table }
 while not eof do                                              { copy }
   begin read(ch); write(parTab[ch]) end;
end. {AddParityBit}
```

The parity bit is found here by counting ones among the bits. You could try to compute the parity table in a way similar to how the program from solution 834B fills the table of reverse numbers in its first loop. A hint might be appropriate: if the parities of the first four codes (00, 01, 10, and 11) are known, the next four have inverse parities: the parity of 101 is inverse to the parity of 01. Try estimating which way of computing is faster. To measure that, count the numbers of additions and multiplications or divisions by 2, as well as indexing into a table. You can assume that all these operations have the same duration.

The functions are frequently substituted by tables. This substitution is particularly appropriate for functions over a small interval of integers. Some examples are conversion of letters to upper case, partitioning of the characters into classes (letters, digits, separators, etc.), tabulation of a trigonometric function by degrees, etc. In this book, other solutions were frequently improved by using a table; in solving problem 1123B the use of a table will allow us to conceive an entirely new and considerably faster solution; a table was used to improve solution 623B.

1012B

We have met the determination of digits of a number several times so far. The largest number composed of a given set of digits is that in which the digits occur in a descending order from the leading one onwards, and in the smallest they are ordered in the reverse fashion. The digits of the number have thus to be ordered. For this purpose the insertion sort is used in our solution (see the introduction to Chapter D). The program requested thus poses no difficulties: first, the digits of the number are determined, sorted, the largest and the smallest numbers computed from them, and subtracted. This procedure is repeated until the difference repeats.

```
program StrangeSequence(input,output);
{ Determines when the elements of a strange sequence repeat. }
  const
    nPlaces = 4;           { the number of decimal places in the number }

  var
    oldDif,                { the previous difference }
    newDif: integer;       { the current difference }
    digit: array [0..nPlaces] of integer;  { the digits of the number }
    nRep: integer;         { the repetition counter }

  procedure ComputeDigits(newDif: integer);
  { Computes the digits of the number newDif. }
    var i: integer;
  begin
    for i:=nPlaces downto 1 do begin
      digit[i]:=newDif mod 10;
      newDif:=newDif div 10
    end; {for}
  end; {ComputeDigits}

  procedure SortDigits;
  { Sorts the digits using the insertion sort. }
    var i,j, t: integer;
```

```
  begin
    for i:=2 to nPlaces do begin
      t:=digit[i]; digit[0]:=t; j:=i;
      while digit[j-1]<t do begin digit[j]:=digit[j-1]; j:=j-1 end;
      digit[j]:=t;
    end; {for}
  end; {SortDigits}

  function Smallest: integer;
  { Compute the smallest number from the given digits. }
    var i,t: integer;
  begin
    t:=0; for i:=nPlaces downto 1 do t:=10*t+digit[i];
    Smallest:=t;
  end; {Smallest}

  function Largest: integer;
  { Computes the largest number from the given digits. }
    var i,t: integer;
  begin
    t:=0; for i:=1 to nPlaces do t:=10*t+digit[i];
    Largest:=t;
  end; {Largest}

begin {StrangeSequence}
  nRep:=0;
  write('Input the starting number: '); readln(newDif);
  repeat
    writeln(nRep:10,newDif:10); nRep:=nRep+1;
    oldDif:=newDif; ComputeDigits(newDif); SortDigits; newDif:=Largest-Smallest;
  until newDif=oldDif;
end. {StrangeSequence}
```

1032B The example from the problem shows us the way to prove the statement in it, as well as how to solve the problem, so let us examine it in detail. We immediately observe that the element D appears only in the right half of the sets. If it is removed from these sets, we observe that in this half of the sequence exactly the same sets as in the left half appear, but in the reverse order.

Before programming, let us prove the statement. It is most easily proved by mathematical induction on the set size n (you will find more about the mathematical induction principle in the introduction to Chapter C). When $n = 0$ there is nothing to prove, since the only subset of the empty set is the empty set itself. Suppose now that at a chosen number n the subsets of a n-element set have been arranged in the order required. Add a new element to the set. Then the left half of the sequence is evident: it is identical to the arrangement of the sets in the case of n elements. The right half is constructed by arranging the elements from the left half in the reverse order with the new element added. At the joint, the last set in the left half differs from the first set in the right half only in the newly added element; the same holds for the first and the last set in the sequence. It is easy to see that the same is true inside the right half, as the difference of two consecutive sets equals that in the left half. So, if the induction hypothesis holds for the sets with n elements, it also holds for the sets with $n+1$ elements; since it holds for $n = 0$, it holds for all nonnegative integers.

```
program OrderedSubsets(input,output);
{ Outputs the sequence of subsets in which two consecutive }
{ sets in it differ in a single element. }
  const
    mElem = 10;                 { the maximum number of set elements }
    mSubset = 1024;             { the maximum number of subsets }
  type
    element = 1..mElem;         { the elements }
    elSet = set of element;     { the subsets }
  var
    nSubset: integer;           { the number of subsets produced }
    subset: array [0..mSubset] of elSet;  { the subsets }
    nElem: element;             { the number of elements }
    elem: element;              { the added element }
    i,k: integer;
begin {OrderedSubsets}
  write('Input the number of elements: '); readln(nElem);
{ Construct the subset sequence. }
  nSubset:=2; subset[0]:=[ ]; subset[1]:=[1];
  for elem:=2 to nElem do begin
    k:=2*nSubset-1;
    for i:=0 to nSubset-1 do subset[k-i]:=subset[i]+[elem];
    nSubset:=2*nSubset;
  end; {for}
{ Print the arrangement. }
  for i:=0 to nSubset-1 do begin
    write('{');
    for elem:=1 to nElem do
      if elem in subset[i] then
        write(chr(ord('A')+elem-1));
    writeln('}');
  end; {for}
end. {OrderedSubsets}
```

It is worth noting that in a computer a set of small integers from 0 to $n-1$ may be represented by an n-bit integer M. Using this notation, a 1 (a "bit set") at the k-th bit in the binary notation of M means that the number k is an element of the set represented by M. Pascal sets are usually represented in this way. Can you think of a way to compute the set union or intersection of the sets represented in this way? How would you determine whether an element is in the set; how would you add an element to the set? Clearly, bit operations should be used, but which? The program above could be written to use the binary notation of integers instead of sets. Closely connected to such a solution is the function f from solution 1133B. So try solving the puzzle posed there.

The above set ordering in fact originates in a special arrangement of n-bit integers, conforming to the following two rules:

— the arrangement comprises all numbers between 0 and $2^n - 1$;
— the binary notations of two consecutive numbers in the arrangement differ in a single bit only.

This arrangement is called the *Gray coding*. If the following requirement is added:

— the binary notations of the first and the last number differ in a single bit as well,

the coding is called the *cyclic Gray coding*. Because of the reflective pattern by which the coding is formed, it is sometimes called also the *reflected binary coding*.

The Gray coding was invented by the American electronics engineer Frank Gray, who did important research in electric signal transmission for teletype and television. The coding may be adapted for other number bases as well: in this generalization, all n-digit numbers occur, and each pair of consecutive numbers differs in a single digit, where the digits differ by 1.

The cyclic Gray coding is used to mark sequences of positions or angles in robots, printers, measuring equipment and similar devices. The numbers ordered in the above arrangement, are drawn on a tablet or disk, the ones by black, the zeros by white or transparent squares. The tablet moves or rotates past light sensors that detect the state of the tablet and thus its position. The first requirement above ensures that it is always possible to detect a change in the position, since the labels of different positions are all different, and therefore the readings of the sensors also differ for different positions.

The second requirement ensures the stability and uniqueness of the measurement. Let us observe what would happen when reading data encoded in a binary code in which several bits may change from one position to the next (when changing from 3 to 4 in standard binary code all three lowest bits change). Due to a slight inaccuracy in light sensor placement or due to a dust particle on the coding tablet, one of the bits might change a moment earlier than the others. The sensors would in this case detect two or even three changes when moving from code 011 to 100—for instance, from 011 to 010, then from 010 to 000 and finally from 000 to 100. Only after the last change could an error be detected, too late to be corrected — the measuring device would have lost its position. The Gray code guarantees that measurement is not susceptible to slight errors in the measuring device fabrication.

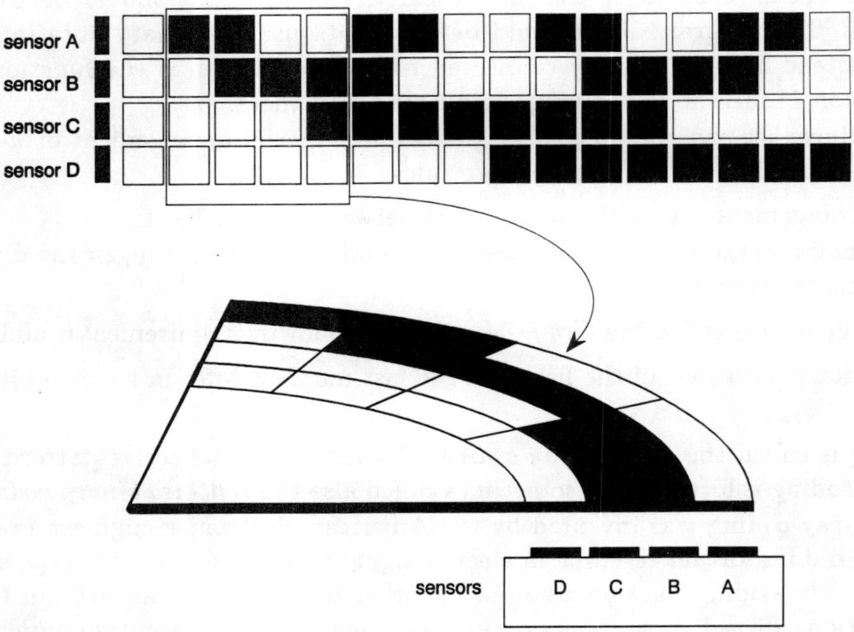

Figure B2: The Gray coding of position

Usually, decoding of the sensor readings is translated to the more common standard binary code by an electronic circuit. Closely related to such a circuit is the function g from the solution 1133B, while the function f from that solution shows how a circuit translates the standard binary coding to Gray code.

The Gray code may also be interpreted from the graph theory standpoint. As known, the n-dimensional cube has exactly 2^n vertices (the zero-dimensional cube is a point, the one-dimensional one is a line segment, the two-dimensional one is a square, and the three-dimensional one is the ordinary cube). To label the vertices of a cube, one of them is positioned at the origin of the coordinate system with its sides parallel to the coordinate axes and the coordinate system unit chosen equal to its side. The labels of the vertices are then obtained by combining the vertex coordinates into a binary number. The Gray code then defines a path through the vertices of the cube; the first rule guarantees that it is the Hamilton path (see problem 823E), the second that the path only passes the cube sides and not its diagonals, as you may easily confirm for yourself.

There is another interesting relationship of the Gray code, which leads us to the well known Hanoi towers game. To play it, n coins of different sizes, initially stacked one upon another at the position A, must be moved to the position B, using a third position C as an auxiliary stacking post. Let us assume that the three positions form vertices of a triangle. In no move may a larger coin be stacked upon a smaller one; initially the coins are stacked with the smaller ones upon the larger. To analyse the game, number the coins from 1 to n top-to-bottom. If playing with a single coin, the solution is easy: move the first coin from position A to position B, in short notation: 1: A–B; in the case of two coins, the moves are: 1 :A–C, 2 :A–B, 1 :C–B. In general, the game can be finished in $2^n - 1$ moves. When moving correctly, the odd numbered coins rotate in one direction, and even numbered ones in the opposite direction. The direction depends on the total number of coins: when n is odd, the odd numbered coins travel in the direction A–B–C, when it is even they travel in the opposite direction. If we do not allow duplicate moves, the sequence of moves is thus given in advance by the above rules: the coin number and position precisely determine the next move. Arranging the consecutive positions of coins in the Gray ordering, the sequence of moves is precisely determined without even moving a coin: the number of the coin to be moved equals the number of the bit that changes in transition to the next state in the Gray ordering.

1111B The background of the problem is the local optimization method to determine (local) extrema of functions. The idea of the algorithm is described precisely enough in the problem itself. Further analysis, however, forces us to give some details.

The fact that the edge lies higher than the other terrain, by itself does not simplify the problem in any way. Its proper role is achieved only if the ball may not start on the edge. Our solution assumes this additional restriction.

To ease testing of the program, the terrain are randomly generated, and the roll-down followed from various starting points. The variation of the terrain height depends on a factor near the call to the *Random* function in the *Terrain* procedure. Other details may be seen from the program below.

```
program Ball(input,output);
{ Rolls a ball down the terrain from a given }
{ start-point in the direction of the steepest descent. }
  const
    m = 20;
  var
    height: array [1..m,1..m] of integer;  { the terrain height }
  function Random: real; external;
```

```
procedure MakeTerrain;
{ Randomly generates the terrain relief. }
  var
    x,y: integer;
begin
  for x:=1 to m do begin height[x,1]:=100; height[x,m]:=100 end;
  for y:=1 to m do begin height[1,y]:=100; height[m,y]:=100 end;
  for x:=2 to m-1 do for y:=2 to m-1 do
    height[x,y]:=trunc(15*Random) + (5*abs(x-7)+7*abs(y-16)) div 3;
end; {MakeTerrain}

procedure PrintTerrain;
{ Outputs the terrain relief. }
  var
    x,y: integer;
begin
  for y:=1 to m do begin
    for x:=1 to m do write(height[x,y]:3);
    writeln;
  end; {for}
end; {PrintTerrain}

function Direction(x,y: integer; var dx,dy: integer): boolean;
{ Determines the direction of the move from the point (x,y). }
  const
    sqrt2 = 1.414;
  var
    u,v: integer;
    dv,ds,slope: real;
begin
  dx:=0; dy:=0; slope:=0;
  for u:=-1 to 1 do for v:=-1 to 1 do begin
    dv:=height[x,y]-height[x+u,y+v];
    ds:=abs(u)+abs(v);
    if ds>1 then ds:= sqrt2;
    if dv>slope*ds then
      begin dx:=u; dy:=v; slope:=dv/ds end;
  end; {for}
  Direction:=(dx<>0) or (dy<>0);
end; {Direction}

function Point(var x,y: integer): boolean;
{ Reads the coordinates of the starting point. }
begin
  write('x = '); readln(x);
  write('y = '); readln(y); writeln;
  Point:=(1<x) and (x<m) and (1<y) and (y<m);
end; {Point}
```

```
procedure RollDown;
{ Rolls the ball down to the bottom. }
  var
    x,y: integer;      { the current ball position }
    dx,dy: integer;    { the move direction }
    step: integer;
begin
  while Point(x,y) do begin
    writeln('Starting point  (',x:4,',',y:4,')');
    step:=0;
    while Direction(x,y,dx,dy) do begin
      writeln(step:5,x:4,y:4,height[x,y]:6,dx:3,dy:3);
      x:=x+dx; y:=y+dy; step:=step+1;
    end; {while}
    writeln(step:5,x:4,y:4,height[x,y]:6);
  end; {while}
end; {RollDown}

begin {Ball}
  MakeTerrain;
  PrintTerrain;
  RollDown;
end. {Ball}
```

To avoid squaring and taking the square root when computing the length ds of the move in the *Direction* function, we observed that for u, v from the set $\{-1, 0, 1\}$ the following equality holds

$$ds^2 = u^2 + v^2 = |u| + |v|$$

and that the value of ds^2 may only be 0, 1, or 2. The statements

```
ds:=abs(u)+abs(v); if ds>1 then ds:=sqrt2
```

could be equivalently substituted by the statement

```
ds:=len[abs(u)+abs(v)]
```

provided the table *len* would be initialized with proper values

```
len[0]:=0; len[1]:=1; len[2]:=1.414;
```

From this problem another interesting one arises. Suppose the ball is exchanged by a rain-drop. Could you write a program to simulate the falling rain, and at the end show where on the terrain the puddles form? How could you speed up the drifting of a large number of rain-drops down to the valley? (See the hint at the end of solution 931B.)

1113B We have already met the notion of the parity bit: in solution 931B the characters were supplied with the transverse parity bit. When writing the characters on a tape, the corresponding longitudinal parity bits are written in addition to the transverse ones. When the tape is read, the parity bits are computed anew and compared to the ones read. If a computed transverse parity bit differs from the one read, the character is certainly incorrect. Otherwise the character may either be correct or contain an even number of incorrect bits. The situation with the longitudinal parity bits is analogous.

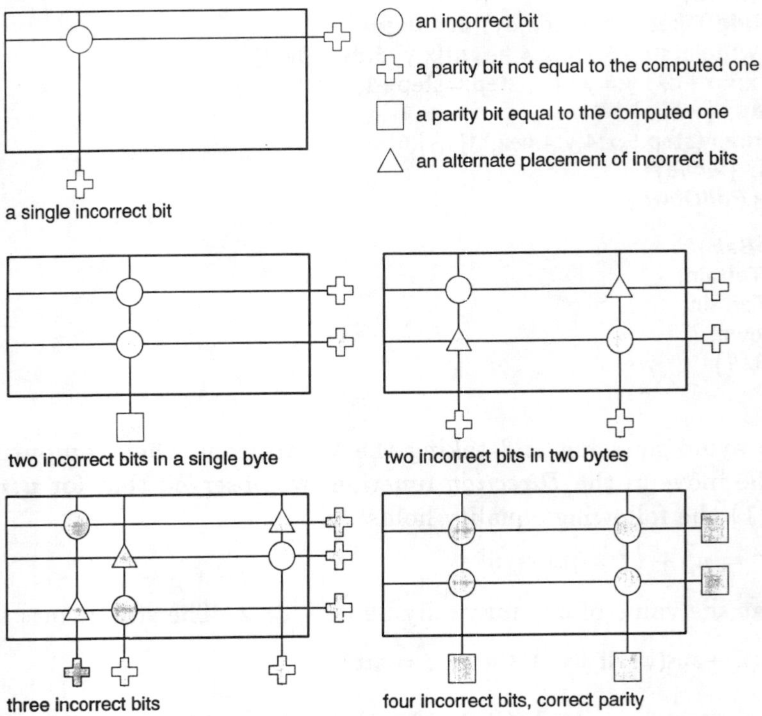

Figure B3: Errors in a block

Consider now the block from the problem in more detail. Suppose that during writing, an error occurred in a *single* bit of the block. In this case, both the corresponding transverse and longitudinal bits are incorrect. The transverse determines the incorrect character, while the longitudinal bit tells which bit in it is incorrect. The error may therefore be exactly located, the incorrect bit inverted and the error recovered.

If *two* bits are incorrect three cases must be distinguished. First, both incorrect bits may appear in the same character. In this case, the transverse parity bit of the incorrect character is correct, and two longitudinal bits are incorrect. The error may thus be detected, but not located and so not recovered. Similar to this is the case if two bits of the same row are incorrect. In the third case, when the incorrect bits appear in different characters as well as in different rows, both the two incorrect characters and rows may be located; the error however still cannot be recovered, since it cannot be decided which of the diagonal pairs of bits is incorrect.

In the case of *three* incorrect bits the situation is similar, but there are six possible arrangements of incorrect bits; some particulars should nevertheless be pointed out. If two incorrect bits are in the same character or row, the corresponding transverse or longitudinal parity bit is correct, a single parity bit can be detected for that direction. If the incorrect bits lie in three vertices of a rectangle, a single incorrect parity bit is detected in either direction; it seems that a single bit is incorrect, namely the fourth vertex of the rectangle. The procedure therefore reacts incorrectly, and by recovering destroys an additional bit.

In the case of *four* incorrect bits, it may happen that the error is not even discovered. This happens when the incorrect bits lie at the vertices of a rectangle. In this case there are two incorrect bits both in two characters and in two rows, so that all parity bits are correct. A similar arrangement may be found for all *larger even numbers* of errors, so that in these cases the error may skip unnoticed (try to find a similar arrangement of six bits). In the case of odd numbers of incorrect bits, one bit always stays out of such an arrangement, so that due to this extra bit an error is always detected. As in the case of three bits the procedure may seemingly find a single incorrect bit and by correcting it introduce an additional error into the block.

To summarize: at most a single erroneous bit may be detected and recovered. Two incorrect bits may only be detected, but not recovered. Three or a larger odd number of bits may be discovered, but they may seem to the procedure as a single one; in recovering it a further error is introduced into the block. Four or a larger even number of incorrect bits may slip by unnoticed.

```
const
  mTrans = 9;             { the number of bits in the extended character }
  mLong = 257;         { the length of the block including the parity character }

type
  bitT = 0..1;
  charT = packed array [1..mTrans] of bitT;
  blockT = packed array [1..mLong] of charT;
  errorT = (NOERROR,RECOVERED,IRRECOVERABLE);
```

```
procedure ECC(var block: blockT; var error: errorT);
{ Recover an error in the block if possible and if at all necessary. }
  var
    ixLong,ixTran: integer;  { indices of the row and character containing the error }
    parityTran: bitT;        { computed transverse parity }
    parityLong: charT;       { computed longitudinal parity }
    t,l: integer;            { transverse and longitudinal counter }

begin
  error:= NOERROR;  ixLong:= 0;  ixTran:= 0;
  for t:= 1 to mTrans do parityLong[t]:= 0;
  for l:= 1 to mLong do begin                              { compute parity bits }
    parityTran:= 0;
    for t:= 1 to mTrans do begin
      parityTran:=    (parityTran   +block[l,t]) mod 2;
      parityLong[t]:= (parityLong[t]+block[l,t]) mod 2;
    end; {for}
    if parityTran=0 then begin                       { error: even transverse parity }
      if ixTran=0 then ixTran:= l else error:= IRRECOVERABLE;
    end; {if}
  end; {for}
  for t:= 1 to mTrans do
    if parityLong[t]=0 then begin                  { error: even longitudinal parity }
      if ixLong=0 then ixLong:= t else error:= IRRECOVERABLE;
    end; {if}
  if error=IRRECOVERABLE then {}
  else if (ixTran=0)<>(ixLong=0) then error:= IRRECOVERABLE
  else if (ixTran<>0) { and (ixLong<>0) } then begin
    block[ixTran,ixLong]:= 1-block[ixTran,ixLong];
    error:= RECOVERED;
  end; {if}
end; {ECC}
```

ECC is the acronym for the term error correcting code, which marks the computer storage devices (disk and magnetic tape units, memories) that use a similar algorithm to the one above to process parity errors. The algorithm is fairly frequently used although it has its deficiencies. The main reason for its use in spite of the risk of missing some of the errors or introducing additional ones is that the probability that more than one error occurs in a block is far smaller than the probability of a single one.

1123B The first solution is easily devised: it is modelled after the definition of the friendly numbers. Introducing the constant N=30 000, the solution reads:

```
for a:=1 to N do
  for b:=1 to a do
    if (S(a)=b) and (S(b)=a) then
      writeln('A friendly pair ',a,b);
```

However, this solution is useless. Let us analyse it in more detail: $1+2+\cdots+N = \frac{1}{2}N(N+1)$ pairs have to be tested, and in our case that means approximately 450 million pairs. For each pair, the sum of divisors must be computed twice, amounting to about 900 million sums, and since a day is approximately 90 000 seconds long, that means approximately a day of computation, provided 10 000 sums of divisors are computed per second. This would require at least a Cray, if not something faster. So let us try finding a better solution.

To do that, we transcribe the two conditions from the problem into a single one: a and $S(a)$ are friendly numbers if and only if $S(S(a)) = a$. Then, a single loop suffices:

```
for a:=1 to N do begin
  b:=S(a);
  if b<=a then
    if S(b)=a then
      writeln('A friendly pair ',a,b);
end;
```

Instead of computing $N(N+1)$ sums only $2N$ are needed. Computing 10 000 sums in a second, that is, with a Cray (or something more powerful), we would be through in few seconds. An almost reasonable solution, but since we have no Cray available let us try something else. The most time-consuming operation of testing is the computation of the sum S. The sum must be computed for each number from 1 to N, and for some it is computed twice or even more times (in the conditional). A new idea arises from this: store all the sums in a table, and instead of $2N$ only N sums have to be computed.

This improvement leads us to another program. As we observed, the most time-consuming operation is the computation of the sum of divisors of a number. If it is computed separately for each number, the algorithm is as follows:

```
S:=1; p:=2; q:=a div p;
while p<q do begin
  if (a mod p)=0 then S:=S+p+q;
  p:=p+1; q:=a div p;
end;
if sqr(p)=a then S:=S+q;
```

Compare this algorithm to the one in solution 413B. As we will see at the end, this algorithm may be slightly improved.

To compute each sum $2\sqrt{a}$ divisions are needed, making the total number of divisions approximately equal to $2(1 + \sqrt{2} + \sqrt{3} + \cdots + \sqrt{N})$, which is approximately $\frac{4}{3}N\sqrt{N}$. (*Remark*: the derivations of the estimates in this solution require knowledge of powerful mathematical tools and are therefore omitted here. You may find more about this in the first part of the "bible" of programming, the book by D. E. Knuth: *The Art of Computer Programming*, Vol. 1, Addison-Wesley, Reading 1968.)

But *all* sums will be needed, so there is no need to compute a sum at once. Can you already see how we shall proceed? Of course: for each number a between 1 and $N/2$, a will be added to the sums of all multiples of a except to the sum of the number itself. The more sharp-sighted among you will immediately discover the close relation of this algorithm to the well known sieve of Eratosthenes.

Since among N numbers there are N divisible by 1, $N/2$ divisible by 2, $N/3$ divisible by 3, and so forth, this algorithm is much faster: the above $\frac{4}{3}N\sqrt{N}$ divisions are replaced by $N(1 + 1/2 + 1/3 + \cdots + 1/(N \textbf{ div } 2))$, that is, approximately $N \log N$ repetitions of the inner loop, each of which requires three operations taking the same time as the addition (indexing, addition and loop control). By introducing the table, the time required to run the program (its time complexity) was reduced. On the other hand the memory requirements (its space complexity) grew significantly. (You may find more about complexity of algorithms in the introduction to Chapter D.

```
program FriendlyNumbers(output);
{ Computes pairs of friendly numbers. }
  const N = 30000;
  type sum = array [1..N] of integer;
  var
    s: sum;                                    { the table of sums of divisors }
    divisor,multiple: integer;
begin                                          { Compute the table of sums. }
  for divisor:=1 to N do s[divisor]:= 1;
  for divisor:=2 to N div 2 do begin
    multiple:=2*divisor;
    while multiple<=N do begin
      s[multiple]:=s[multiple]+divisor; multiple:=multiple+divisor;
    end; {while}
  end; {for}
  for divisor:= 1 to N do                      { Determine the friendly pairs. }
    if s[divisor]<=divisor then
      if s[s[divisor]]=divisor then writeln(divisor,s[divisor]);
end. {FriendlyNumbers}
```

Instead of using Pascal to code the algorithm, we might use an assembly language. Various experiments show that we might expect the program to run three times as fast as the Pascal program. Had the initial program been coded in assembly language, it would still be much slower than the program above.

On a MicroVAX II computer the initial program would execute for about three weeks (for justifiable reasons we did not try it; instead, the run time was estimated based on other measurements). The second version executed in a little more than two minutes and a half, and the third in four and a half seconds. If coded in an assembly language, the first would still execute for a week, the second would terminate in a minute and the third in a second and a half.

Let us now reconsider our path to the program above. First, a new, faster algorithm enabled us to speed up the program dramatically. The next considerable saving in the program execution time was obtained by choosing a different and more suitable data structure, which, in turn, enabled us to devise a faster algorithm. Finally, some speed-up could be achieved by coding the algorithm in an assembly language instead of using Pascal; however, the saving would be minor to all others. So, when a program is found to run too slow:

— the **first** thing to do is to try finding *another, faster algorithm* and *better suited data structures*,

— and **later** resort to *translating to assembly language*, if this is at all necessary after the first step.

Nowadays, manual translation to assembly language is rarely performed. In large program systems it usually suffices that *a few dozen key lines* of code are written in assembly to achieve all that is needed. Although the effect is almost as if the whole program had been written in assembly language, a lot of work is saved.

Similar estimations of algorithm requirements are frequently conducted, as it is usually important to know how long it will take to compute the solution of the problem. As long as we deal with problems of small size, we are usually satisfied with the first solution we think of. If in the above case we were interested in the friendly numbers smaller than 100, the first solution shown would be chosen. To solve the problem, an hour, say, would be required to find and program it, and, say, a minute to compute the answer. The reasoning leading to the last solution would take at least half an hour more, and it would save us at most one minute. For small problems the execution time is negligible relative to the time required to develop the program. When the size of the problem grows, the execution time becomes the primary factor, and the ratio of the execution and development time radically changes. This could be observed in the case above, when a little thought shortened the execution time from a few weeks to several seconds.

Considering the discussion about time complexity in the introduction to Chapter D, and the above discussion about the solutions to our problem, can you tell what are the time complexities of the second and the third algorithm for finding the friendly pairs? For the primitive operations take the arithmetic ones, and not, for example, the computations of the sum of divisors. The former are independent of the values of their operands while the latter are not (as may be deduced from the solution).

Finally, a more elegant way to compute the sum of divisors deserves to be mentioned. In this way the best solution of the problem can be achieved if we give up storing the sums in a table. As we know, any integer may be uniquely decomposed as a product of powers of prime numbers if the primes are sorted by size (see also solution 413B). For instance, $360 = 2^3 \cdot 3^2 \cdot 5^1$. Denote by a our integer, and write its decomposition: $a = p_1^{w_1} \cdot p_2^{w_2} \cdot \ldots \cdot p_n^{w_n}$. The divisors of a are then exactly the numbers of the form $p_1^{v_1} \cdot p_2^{v_2} \cdot \ldots \cdot p_n^{v_n}$, where $0 \leq v_i \leq w_i$. In the example above, the following are some of the divisors $1 = 2^0 \cdot 3^0 \cdot 5^0$, $2 = 2^1 \cdot 3^0 \cdot 5^0$, $3 = 2^0 \cdot 3^1 \cdot 5^0$, and so on. When the divisors in the sum are arranged in an appropriate order and the common factors taken out, the following formula is obtained for the sum:

$$S(a) = (1 + p_1 + p_1^2 + \cdots + p_1^{w_1}) \cdot (1 + p_2 + p_2^2 + \cdots + p_2^{w_2}) \cdot \ldots$$
$$\ldots \cdot (1 + p_n + p_n^2 + \cdots + p_n^{w_n}) - a$$

Using the rule to add the geometric series,

$$1 + x + x^2 + x^3 + \ldots + x^n = \frac{x^{(n+1)} - 1}{x - 1}$$

the above formula simplifies to

$$S(a) = \frac{p_1^{(w_1+1)} - 1}{p_1 - 1} \cdot \frac{p_2^{(w_2+1)} - 1}{p_2 - 1} \cdot \ldots \cdot \frac{p_n^{(w_n+1)} - 1}{p_n - 1} - a.$$

In each denominator, the prime divisors of the number appear alone, while in the numerator they appear in the power in which they occur in the decomposition of the number, increased by 1. In a similar way the divisors of a number were counted in solution 413B. The sum of the divisors of a may therefore be computed in the following way:

```
S:=1; n:=a; p:=2;
while n>1 do begin
  if (n mod p)=0 then begin
    f:=p;
    while (n mod p)=0 do begin n:=n div p; f:=f*p end;
    S:=S*(f-1) div (p-1);
  end; {if}
  p:=p+1;
end; {while}
S:=S-a;
```

To determine the friendly numbers our second program would be used.

Some remarks are still necessary. Each time the condition in the **if** statement is true, the number p is a prime. You should be able to prove this yourself.

The meaning of f is also clear: it is the power of p, by which it occurs in the decomposition of a, increased by 1. At the end of the outer **while** loop, S contains the sum of all the divisors of a, including the number itself.

1133B The function f forms its value based on the binary notation of its argument. It sequentially examines each bit from the least to the most significant, adding one to the result, if the current bit differs from the previous one, or zero otherwise. The function g also produces its result bit by bit by adding to it the value of the variable m, which at start equals 0, and then changes at each one in its argument.

```
function g(n: integer): integer;
{ The inverse to the function f. }
  var i,r,m: integer;
begin
  r:=0; m:=0;
  for i:=0 to 14 do begin
    if odd(n) then m:=1-m;
    r:=2*r+m; n:=n div 2;
  end; {for}
  g:=r;
end; {g}
```

The function f relates to the Gray code from solution 1032B in a secret way. Can you discover the relation of the output of the program below to the output of the program in solution 1032B?

```
program Puzzle(input,output);
{ Output of the ordered subsets. }
  var
    nElem: integer;    { the number of elements }
    nSubsets: integer; { the number of subsets }
    value: integer;    { the value of the function f }
    bit: integer;      { the bit counter }
    i: integer;
    ...
  { THE DECLARATION OF THE FUNCTION f FROM THE PROBLEM }
    ...
begin {Puzzle}
  write('The number of elements: '); readln(nElem);
{ nSubsets:=2**nElem - 1 }
  nSubsets:=1; for i:=1 to nElem do nSubsets:=2*nSubsets;
  nSubsets:=nSubsets-1;
```

```
{ Output the subsets }
  for i:=0 to nSubsets do begin
    value:=f(i);
  { Output the bits set in f(i) }
    for bit:=14 downto 0 do begin
      if odd(value) then write(chr(ord('A')+bit));
      value:=value div 2;
    end; {for}
    writeln;
  end; {for}
end. {Puzzle}
```

1134B Most problems with the addition of real numbers on a computer originate in the following characteristics of the computer arithmetic:

— if a small number is added to a large one (by absolute value), the latter may not even change;
— if two almost equal numbers are subtracted, several places of precision may be lost.

The result of adding several real numbers may therefore depend on the order of the computation. Suppose that six decimal places are used with no rounding. Then, for example

$$(999990 + 0.5) + 0.5 = 999990$$

but

$$999990 + (0.5 + 0.5) = 999991.$$

Therefore, a more precise result is obtained if the sum of several small numbers is added to a large number instead of adding each of these small numbers separately.

In the continuation we will assume that a sequence of positive real numbers is given. When *adding* these numbers by *adding the current element to the partial sum*, a more precise result is obtained if the numbers are sorted increasingly. The algorithm must therefore first sort the numbers and then add them.

If the number of the elements in the sequence becomes large (several hundred approximately equal numbers), the partial sum may become much larger than the elements alone—the computation becomes very inaccurate. In this case, more precise results are obtained by performing the addition in "balanced" groups, as described in the next program. To make the solution simpler, the sequence is assumed to be stored in a table.

```
const
  n = 10000000;
var
  a: array [1..n] of real;
  newThresh,threshold,sum: real;
  nElem,elem,group: integer;
begin
...
{ the numbers are in the table a }
  nElem:=n;
  newThresh:=a[1];
  while nElem>1 do begin
    threshold:=2*newThresh;
    elem:=1; group:=0;
    while elem<=nElem do begin
      sum:=0;
      while (elem<=nElem) and (sum<threshold) do
        begin sum:=sum+a[elem]; elem:=elem+1 end;
      group:=group+1; a[group]:=sum;
      if sum>newThresh then newThresh:=sum;
    end; {while}
    nElem:=group;
  end; {while}
{ the sum is in a[1] }
...
end.
```

Another way to solve the problem is to increase the precision of the computation. In some programming languages, for instance FORTRAN, this possibility is built into the language — the real numbers with double number of places (DOUBLE PRECISION). Some languages, for example Logo or Lisp, allow the user to choose an arbitrary number of places to be used in computations. If the language does not provide such a feature, more precise addition of real numbers may be implemented by a program. If the data are on a file, double precision is probably the most effective solution.

As mentioned before, too much precision may be lost even when adding several hundred numbers. This frequently happens when the inner product of two vectors is computed or when matrices are multiplied. In both cases, a double precision variable is almost always used to hold the sum.

Using double precision does not solve all problems. When the set of numbers to be added becomes sufficiently large, the problem recurs in the same form. Consider the case of a real computer. Ordinary real computation is usually precise to approximately six, and the double precision computation to fifteen, decimal places. For the problem to reappear in the case of double precision computation, at least 10^9 summands would be involved (this is the ratio of the precision of the computation). Such a number of summands is not met in any real problem; if it were, new problems of overflowing the range of the exponent of a real number would probably appear first.

When would the problem of item (b) be encountered? It would be fairly extraordinary to have to add millions of numbers stored on a file. It is much more usual that the numbers to be added are continuously received (as, for example, measurements of the temperature each minute). In this case the data received in a longer interval cannot be stored, so the above described algorithms using a table, or their derivatives cannot be used either. As a rule, summing all such data has no meaning, since it can only be used to compute the average value of the data. Frequently, it is most interesting to determine the average value in a limited interval in the past. Solution 1023F deals with a related problem.

More information may be derived from the distribution of the values measured into ranks: the interval of the possible measurements is divided into n subintervals, and for each subinterval the number of data falling in it counted. If the number of the subintervals is sufficiently large, such *spectrum* may tell a lot about the value measured.

Even if the problem posed in the question is far from being real, it leads into the area at the boundary between computer science and mathematics, which studies numerical algorithms. *Numerical mathematics* studies the design, choice and the analysis of such algorithms.

An important property of a good numerical algorithm is its insusceptibility to changes in input data. If the data slightly change (perhaps due to the rounding error caused by the translation to internal computer representation) the solution should change only slightly as well. Such algorithms are called *stable*. Stable algorithms exist for many numerical problems (our addition problem certainly is one, as well as the solution of a system of linear equations). However, problems exist for which no stable algorithm exists to solve them; one such well known problem is the determination of the zeros of a polynomial. Experience, additional knowledge, as well as knowledge of numerical algorithms must be applied to choose an appropriate algorithm in such cases.

Inherently unstable problems exist. Nonlinear systems of differential equations are an example of such problems. Some such systems for instance describe the turbulent flow of liquids. In this cases, minimal changes in the starting state may cause essentially different future of the system. In recent years, a number of interesting experimental results in this area were presented. To understand the character of such systems, one uses the picture of their Mandelbrot or Julia sets, so frequently seen on the covers of computer magazines today.

Chapter C

Recursive Functions

Most problems in this chapter use **recursion** in one way or another. In programming, recursion means that a subprogram (a procedure or a function) invokes itself. In mathematics, a **recursive definition** defines a function in terms of its values at some other argument. In general, a recursive definition must contain at least two parts: a *termination criterion*, defining the function value for certain argument values in absolute terms, as well as the *recursive definition*, which defines the value of the function in other cases by using the function itself with different arguments. At first sight, the recursive definitions define the function in terms of itself, however, when viewed in more detail, they express an algorithm to compute the function value from precisely defined values (given by the termination criterion).

In programs, recursive subprograms with side effects are often encountered, unlike the functions in pure mathematical sense. In this case the conduct of recursive functions may be much more complicated. There are several cases of recursive subprograms with side effects in this book, for instance 115H, 733C, 732G, 933G, etc.

To understand the functioning of recursive subprograms properly, it is important to understand the notion of the **local variables**. In the pure sense of recursive functions, the sole local variables of a recursive function are its arguments, while in programs other local variables may be declared. It should be stressed that local variables of each *incarnation of a recursive subprogram* are independent of each other, and must therefore occupy independent memory space.

Some algorithms are easily expressed recursively, especially when the data call for it (a number of good examples may be found throughout this book; for instance in problems 115H, 224D, 514D, 524D, 525E, 721C, 732G, 733C, 933G). Modern computers and compilers usually provide good support for recursive algorithms, yet the latter are still more wasteful relative to the iterative (the algorithms using loops). This wastefulness becomes exceedingly evident if one is not aware of the exact meaning of recursion (and, for example, one uses large local variables without reason).

Not all programming languages support recursion, an example of a non-recursive language is FORTRAN. In such languages, one must implement recursive algorithms by "manually" handling the stack of local data. You can find more about this in solution 115H.

Recursion is equivalent in expressive power to loops: any iterative algorithm may be expressed by a recursive algorithm without loops, and any recursive algorithm may be expressed solely using loops and auxiliary memory (a **stack**); in this way it actually executes on most computers. In spite of this equivalence, it is reasonable to use both methods in programs to make full use of the expressive power of each of them. In special cases, some compilers take care to remove some recursive calls or to replace them by loops. Other compilers discover groups of mutually recursive subprograms and take special care when translating recursive programs. Lisp or Logo usually handle separately the tail recursion when a subprogram calls itself in the last statement of its body. This is a very usual feature in recursive subprograms.

In general, recursion should be used with caution in practical programs. The algorithms which are recursive in nature may be coded recursively, but be aware that the subprogram call alone may be time and space consuming. Also, take care to avoid unnecessary local variables and arguments; an example of avoiding local variables is in solution 732G. The algorithms not recursive in nature should be coded non-recursively. The typical examples of the *misuse of recursive definitions* are the computation of Fibonacci numbers (solution 323C), bisection or binary tree search, the *Invert* procedure from solution 224D and most of the arithmetical problems in this chapter. The typical examples where recursion should be used are various searches with descents — backtracking (problems 721C, 733C), parsing and compiling of languages (problem 115H) or traversal of recursive data structures (for example, ordered traversal and output of a binary tree, solution 732G).

Perhaps it is worth noting that recursive functions over nonnegative integers are as powerful in expressive power as any other known way to describe algorithms (Turing machines, Markov algorithms, semi-Thue systems, Post-production systems, etc.). A problem is (intuitively) *computable*, if an algorithm exists to solve it. The famous Church's thesis claims that a problem is computable if it is computable as a recursive function over nonnegative integers (or — due to equivalence — computable on a Turing machine). Well known (and simple) problems exist which are *not computable*, one such problem is described in problem 315C. To prove such statements Church's thesis must be adopted. The fact that recursive functions may express all algorithms forms the base of the programming language Lisp, which, in its purest form, provides neither variables (except for the arguments) nor loops.

The principle of **mathematical induction** is found in mathematical texts on integers. It is a principle for proving a statement, which first requires proof that the statement to be proved holds in some basic cases (most frequently for the integer 0); and then proof that if the statement holds for the integer n (the **induction hypothesis**), then it holds for the integer $n+1$. In the solutions that follow, this or another form of the induction will be frequently used. A generalization of classical mathematical induction is described in solution 112C and used elsewhere.

Induction is a natural way of thinking about recursive algorithms. The validity of a statement about a recursive algorithm is proved by first proving that the statement is true when the termination criterion holds (the basic case) and then showing that the statement holds in the cases when the recursive call is used.

112C

a) When studying simple recursively defined functions, it is usually convenient to manually compute some cases, as they frequently intuitively clarify the definition. Let us try it for our case:

$$f(2,5) = 2 \cdot f(2,4)$$

As the second argument is odd we have used the last line of the definition. $f(2,4)$ is computed according to the middle line, (since the second argument is even):

$$f(2,4) = (f(2,2))^2$$

We continue:

$$f(2,2) = (f(2,1))^2$$
$$f(2,1) = 2 \cdot f(2,0)$$
$$f(2,0) = 1$$

Writing together we obtain:

$$\begin{aligned}
f(2,5) &= 2 \cdot f(2,4) = \\
&= 2 \cdot (f(2,2))^2 = \\
&= 2 \cdot ((f(2,1))^2)^2 = \\
&= 2 \cdot ((2 \cdot f(2,0))^2)^2 = \\
&= 2 \cdot ((2 \cdot 1)^2)^2 = \\
&= 2 \cdot (2^2)^2 = 2 \cdot 4^2 = 2 \cdot 16 = 32
\end{aligned}$$

b) This computation leads us to guess that $f(a,n) = a^n$. If the computation above does not suffice, another example might assist us to guess. With our level of knowledge guessing cannot be avoided; however, methods exist which in some cases greatly help the guessing. To validate our guess, mathematical induction on n will be used to prove that f equals

$$f(a,n) = a^n$$

for any number a and any nonnegative integer n. The statement may be proved for all nonnegative integers n by induction, if we prove (1) that the equality holds for $n = 0$, and (2) that for any positive m the statement holds for $n = m$, if it holds for all $n < m$.

1) First, let us see if the statement holds for $n = 0$. $f(a,0)$ by definition equals 1, and a^0 as well, so the statement is true for $n = 0$.

2) Now, choose an arbitrary positive integer m and assume that for any $n < m$ the statement is true that

$$f(a,n) = a^n$$

2.1) Let us analyse the case when m is even in $f(a,m)$. In this case, $f(a,m)$ is computed according to the second line of the definition of f, therefore

$$f(a,m) = \left(f\left(a, \frac{m}{2}\right)\right)^2$$

But $m/2 < m$ $(m > 0)$, therefore the induction hypothesis may be used for $m/2$, so

$$f(a,m) = \left(f\left(a, \frac{m}{2}\right)\right)^2 = \left(a^{\frac{m}{2}}\right)^2 = a^m$$

and the formula holds for m.

2.2) Now consider the case when m is odd. Then, $f(a,m)$ is computed according to the last line of the definition of f. Since $m-1 < m$ and considering the induction hypothesis for $m-1$ we obtain

$$f(a,m) = a \cdot f(a,m-1) = a \cdot a^{m-1} = a^m$$

The statement holds in this case as well. Using mathematical induction we have proved that $f(a,n) = a^n$ for any nonnegative n. This form of mathematical induction may seem uncommon. It is more usual to prove that a statement holds for m if it holds for $m - 1$. However, it is easy to prove that this generalized principle of induction is equivalent to the usual one. The usual inference from $m - 1$ to m would not work in our case, since $m/2$ occurs in the induction step.

The function f defines a fairly effective algorithm to compute powers. It is easily expressed without recursion as follows

```
f:=1;
while n>0 do
  if odd(n) then begin f:=f*a; n:=n-1 end
  else begin f:=sqr(f); n:=n div 2 end;
```

This algorithm is appropriate to implement the computation of powers in a language not supporting it (e. g. standard Pascal), but it works only for the nonnegative integers. It may easily be adapted by considering the case of negative powers separately. In the next solution a similar algorithm for multiplication appears, and there we will compute the number of operations necessary to compute f.

The algorithm of the function f is suitable to compute powers in general, but it does not always use the least number of multiplications. An example is $n = 15$. According to this (binary) algorithm,

$$a^{15} = a \cdot \left(a \cdot \left(a \cdot a^2\right)^2\right)^2$$

using 6 multiplications; computing

$$a^{15} = a^3 \cdot \left(\left(a^3\right)^2\right)^2$$

uses 5 multiplications if performed carefully (a^3 is computed only once). The question of determining the least number of multiplications needed to compute a^n for a given n is yet unsolved in general. As mentioned earlier, the algorithm is equivalent to the multiplication algorithm from problem 214C. Therefore, the multiplication algorithm using the minimum number of additions is as yet unknown. As an exercise, it is interesting to compute for all n between 1 and 1000 how a^n should be computed to use the minimum number of multiplications. You may find help at this as well as an extensive discussion of the known theory in D. E. Knuth: *The Art of Computer Programming*, Vol. 2, Addison-Wesley, Reading 1980.

214C

a) The values of $f(5,3)$ and $g(3,5)$ are computed as in solution 112C, but more succinctly:

$$\begin{aligned}f(5,3) &= f(5,2)+5= \\ &= (f(5,1)+5)+5= \\ &= ((f(5,0)+5)+5)+5= \\ &= ((0+5)+5)+5=15 \\ g(3,5) &= g(6,2)+3= \\ &= g(12,1)+3= \\ &= (g(24,0)+12)+3= \\ &= (0+12)+3=15\end{aligned}$$

b) Again it is easy to guess that the value of $f(a,b)$ and $g(a,b)$ equals the product ab. We confirm this guess by proving it using mathematical induction on the second argument of both functions, on b.

1) First, consider $f(a,0)$. By definition, $f(a,0)=0$, and so does the product $a\cdot 0=0$, the statement holds for $b=0$. The same is true for g.

2.f) Choose an arbitrary positive m and assume that the statement holds for all b less than m. Let us then prove that

$$f(a,m)=g(a,m)=am$$

holds as well. Again consider f first. By definition of f, $f(a,m)=f(a,m-1)+a$, and $m-1<m$, so by the induction hypothesis

$$f(a,m)=f(a,m-1)+a=a(m-1)+a=am$$

The statement holds for $b=m$.

2.g) Two separate cases must be considered for the function g. First, let us consider the case when m is an even number. Then, by definition of g, considering the induction hypothesis and observing that $m/2<m$ we obtain

$$g(a,m)=g\left(2a,\frac{m}{2}\right)=(2a)\frac{m}{2}=am$$

Similarly we obtain in the case when m is an even number

$$g(a,m)=g\left(2a,\frac{m-1}{2}\right)+a=(2a)\left(\frac{m-1}{2}\right)+a=am$$

All cases are thus exhausted, so we have proved by induction that for any a and nonnegative b

$$f(a,b)=g(a,b)=ab$$

c) Finally, we must analyse the number of calls of the functions f and g. The value of $f(a,b)$ is computed by decrementing b by 1 and calling f again. The function is called last when b becomes 0, so to compute the value of $f(a,b)$ f is called exactly b times.

When the value of g is computed, it is called each time with an argument of value less than or equal to $b/2$. The computation terminates when the second argument becomes 0. The consecutive values of the second argument are therefore less than or equal to the following numbers

$$b, \frac{b}{2}, \frac{b}{4}, \frac{b}{8}, \ldots, \frac{b}{2^n}$$

where n is the number of calls. Since odd arguments are always decremented by 1 the division is always even, so in the above sequence only the integer part (*trunc*) of the quotient needs to be considered. Therefore, the smallest such n must be found that

$$\mathrm{trunc}\left(\frac{b}{2^n}\right) = 0$$

The integer part of a number equals 0 if the number is less than 1, so

$$\mathrm{trunc}\left(\frac{b}{2^n}\right) = 0, \quad \frac{b}{2^n} < 1$$

$$b < 2^n$$

we take logarithms of both sides

$$\log b < n \cdot \log 2$$

$$\frac{\log b}{\log 2} = \log_2 b < n$$

The previous element of the sequence must be greater than or equal to 1, otherwise the sequence would have ended with it; so according to a similar argument

$$n \le \log_2 b + 1 = \frac{\log b}{\log 2} + 1$$

The number of steps therefore satisfies the inequality

$$\log_2 b < n \le \log_2 b + 1$$

We may conclude that the number of steps equals the binary logarithm of b (precisely to a step). Since the logarithmic function increases much more slowly than the linear one, we may assume that the function g is much more effective than the function f.

The function f shows us how the multiplication of nonnegative integers may be implemented when the computer does not provide this operation (many microprocessors do not provide integer multiplication in their instruction set), since in the definition of f only addition is necessary. But we have discovered that f is not particularly effective, g is better. Luckily, the division and multiplication in the definition of g are only fictitious. The only divisions and multiplications are by 2, which in binary notation denote a shift for a binary place left (the multiplication) or right (the division). In fact, the function g expresses the actual algorithm for multiplication in a computer; if the computer does not provide the multiplication instruction, the algorithm is implemented in the operating system, otherwise in circuitry or by a microprogram. Only the fastest computers use slightly improved algorithms, which are always implemented in special circuitry.

It is interesting to note that the algorithm g for integer multiplication was known in old Egypt almost 4000 years ago, and that it was widely used among peasants in Russia in the nineteenth century.

A remark is due here about the language used. In computer science, it is common to consider a function as a rule (instructions) or even an algorithm according to which the function value is computed from its arguments. This way of thinking was common in mathematics up to the middle of the nineteenth century. In contemporary mathematics, however, a function is usually considered as a graph (that is, a set of pairs (argument, function value)). In strict mathematical meaning, then, the functions f and g are the same, they are only defined differently. Computer science and the areas of mathematics related to it (for instance, lambda calculus) keep to the convention that the function is defined by its functioning and not solely by its graph. As a rule this convention is observed throughout this book.

222C The problem states that the program computes the zero of the function presented in it, which may be easily confirmed by inspecting the program. Intentionally, the problem is posed to make the direct tracing of the program impractical due to the large numbers occurring during execution. Let us observe several consecutive values of the function f

$$f(1) = 2m$$
$$f(2) = 2^2m - 2^2$$
$$f(3) = 2^3m - 2^3 - 2^3$$
$$f(4) = 2^4m - 2^4 - 2^4 - 2^4$$

so we guess

$$f(n) = 2^nm - (n-1)\cdot 2^n = 2^n\cdot(m-(n-1))$$

and prove by induction.

The case for $n = 1$ is computed above: $f(1) = 2^1 \cdot (m - (1 - 1)) = 2m$, the statement is true in this case.

Choose an arbitrary $k > 1$ and assume that the statement is true for all n less than k. Let us prove that the statement holds for k; first, by definition of the function f

$$f(k) = 2 \cdot f(k-1) - 2^k$$

then, by the induction hypothesis

$$f(k) = 2 \cdot \left(2^{k-1} \cdot (m - (k-2))\right) - 2^k = 2^k \cdot (m - (k-1))$$

The statement is proved for all nonnegative integers n, and the zero of the function f is now easily determined. Obviously, $f(n) = 0$ if and only if $n = m + 1$; in our case the program outputs the number 22.

The problem originates from the following simple problem: a colony of m bacteria that multiplies by doubling their number each day, is attacked by a virus. The virus destroys the attacked bacterium and divides into two new viruses. For how long will the attacked colony of bacteria survive?

313C a) As in problems 112C and 214C, the values of $s(15324)$ and $p(15324)$ are easily computed, especially if the details about the number systems are looked up in the introduction to Chapter B.

$$\begin{aligned} s(15324) &= s(1532) + 4 = \\ &= s(153) + 2 + 4 = \\ &= s(15) + 3 + 2 + 4 = \\ &= s(1) + 5 + 3 + 2 + 4 = \\ &= 1 + 5 + 3 + 2 + 4 = 15 \end{aligned}$$

$$p(15324) = p(s(15324)) = p(15) = p(s(15)) = p(6) = 6$$

b) From the above it is clear that $s(n)$ computes the sum of the digits of the decimal notation of the number n (its argument). The statement may be quickly and intuitively verified:

1) The sum of digits of a single-digit number (a number less than 10) equals the number itself.
2) The sum of digits of a number of more places is obtained by adding the last digit to the sum of the remaining digits. n **mod** 10 equals the last digit of the decimal notation, while the result of the integer division n **div** 10 equals the number with the last digit removed.

The formulation above is somewhat loose. Even if the subject is clear from the context, the reasoning resembles a proof by "waving hands", which usually does not work in books. At the competition such verification was accepted, as the problem does not require a formal proof, and strict formulation takes some time to devise. Nevertheless we will make the effort of proving the statement by the mathematical induction.

We immediately notice that the usual method of induction on n ($n = 1, 2, 3, \ldots$) does not work in this case, since the value of the function s does not depend directly on the number n but on its decimal notation. A natural way of induction is implied by the above intuitive reasoning: the induction on the *number of digits* in the decimal notation of the number n.

The number n is written as a sequence of decimal digits

$$a_{m-1}a_{m-2}\ldots\ a_2a_1a_0$$

or longer:

$$n = a_{m-1} \cdot 10^{m-1} + a_{m-2} \cdot 10^{m-2} + \cdots\ + a_1 \cdot 10 + a_0$$

where m denotes the number of digits in the decimal notation of n, and a_i are the digits of the notation, $0 \leq a_i < 10$. We must prove that

$$s(n) = a_0 + a_1 + \cdots\ + a_{m-1}$$

or

$$(\dagger)\quad s\left(\sum_{i=0}^{m-1} a_i \cdot 10^i\right) = \sum_{i=0}^{m-1} a_i$$

is true for any nonnegative integer m, that is, for the decimal notation of any length.

The case $m = 1$ involves single digit numbers, for which the statement holds.

$$s(n) = s(a_0) = a_0, \quad \text{since} \quad a_0 < 10.$$

Now, assume (†) holds for some $m \geq 1$, and observe how $s(n)$ is computed, when n has $m + 1$ decimal digits.

$$n = \sum_{i=0}^{m} a_i \cdot 10^i = a_0 + 10 \cdot \sum_{i=0}^{m-1} a_{i+1} \cdot 10^i.$$

Since n is obviously greater than 9, we obtain

$$s(n) = n \textbf{ mod } 10 + s(n \textbf{ div } 10) = a_0 + s\left(\sum_{i=0}^{m-1} a_i \cdot 10^i\right)$$

According to the induction hypothesis, (†) holds for the first term, so that we get

$$s(n) = \sum_{i=0}^{m} a_i.$$

c) According to the definition of p the statement certainly holds for nonnegative integers less than 10. For $n > 9$, the value of $s(n)$ is computed first, and its result is the new argument to the function p. What does this mean? Can we still tell what is the remainder of the division by 9 of the previous forgotten argument? We proceed to show the function s preserves this information, in other words

(‡) $s(n)$ **mod** $9 = n$ **mod** 9

If this is true, our problem is solved, since successive use of the function s (by the last rule to compute p) reduces its argument until it falls in the range from 0 to 9, where the statement is already true.

Let us now prove that 9 evenly divides the difference $n - s(n)$. This is true if and only if (‡) holds. This difference is rewritten as in (b) to obtain:

$$n - s(n) = \sum_{i=0}^{m-1} a_i \cdot 10^i - \sum_{i=0}^{m-1} a_i = \sum_{i=0}^{m-1} \left(a_i \cdot 10^i - a_i\right) =$$

$$= \sum_{i=0}^{m-1} \left(a_i \cdot \left(10^i - 1\right)\right) = \sum_{i=1}^{m-1} \left(a_i \cdot 9 \cdot \left(1 + 10 + \ldots + 10^{i-1}\right)\right)$$

The sum obtained at the end is indeed evenly divisible by 9, which proves the statement of the problem.

315C

This problem leads us to the lesser known realm of theoretical computer science. In computer science so far we are used to dealing with problems for which a program or an algorithm had to be written. This time we deal with the problem-solving algorithms themselves. In computer science as well as in other sciences thoroughly practical problems exist, for which there is no algorithm to solve; therefore, the programs to solve them cannot be written either. To study algorithms, simple formal mechanisms exist to represent the intuitive notion of the algorithm, some of which have been listed in the introduction to this chapter (the Turing machine, recursive functions, and similar), and which are all equivalent. The Turing machine is well described in the text by D. Harel: *The Science of Computing*, Addison-Wesley, Reading 1987, where the topic of this problem is discussed in more detail. A more advanced reader may find more on this topic in the book by J. E. Hopcroft, J. D. Ullman: *Introduction to Automata Theory, Languages and Computation*, Addison-Wesley, Reading 1979, which treats the basic problems of computer science quite theoretically.

One of the problems for which there is no solution in the algorithmic form is the termination problem (of a Turing machine), as described here.

The suggestion in the text of the problem hints at how the problem should be solved: a program with logically contradictory behaviour cannot exist. Let us then try to create circumstances under which the action of the program T would cause a *logical contradiction*. Suppose that the program from the problem exists and denote it by T. Rewrite it as a function, whose arguments are an arbitrary program and some data for it, and which returns *true*, if the program terminates for the data given, and *false*, if not. Using T write the following procedure:

```
procedure Q(prog);
  begin
    while T(prog,prog) do;
    write('OK');
  end;
```

The data to Q are an arbitrary program *prog*, and Q may terminate for this data or not. The programs having programs as input are nothing unusual, compilers are an example of them. We may assume that *prog* is coded in an appropriate programming language and stored in a file read by Q. The function T then finds out, whether *prog* terminates if it inputs itself as its data. This is a reasonable question; even compilers may compile their own code (you may find more about the benefits of this procedure in problem 1124H). So it is reasonable to ask what happens, if we try to compute $Q(Q)$.

Let us now examine whether the computation of $Q(Q)$ terminates. If it does, then it may only happen if $T(Q,Q) =$ *false*, which, according to the definition of T, means that Q does not terminate. If, on the other hand, the computation of $Q(Q)$ does not terminate, this can only happen if $T(Q,Q) =$ *true*, which, according to the definition of T, means that Q terminates. Both possibilities lead us into contradiction. So we must conclude that the program Q cannot exist. Since in Q anything exists except T we conclude that T cannot exist.

The logical contradiction described is only one of many forms of the *liar's paradox*, known already in ancient times: "Everything I say is a lie" (is this statement a lie?). The famous paradox by which B. Russell at the start of this century shook the foundations of the then young set theory is also of this kind (see: R. R. Stoll, *Set Theory and Logic*, Freeman, San Francisco 1961, p. 127). Our example is similar to the barber puzzle: "In some city there lives a barber, who shaves exactly those citizens that do not shave themselves. Who shaves the barber?" We might say that we have composed a procedure Q, which terminates for all data (programs) that themselves do not terminate.

The problems similar to the described termination problem, are called **incomputable**. Sometimes problems are encountered for which it is not evident whether they may be solved (they are computable) or not. When this cannot be proved directly, one often tries to transform the problem into a known incomputable problem, among which the termination problem is probably the best known.

323C

a) First, let us compute $f(5)$ as we used to do in previous similar problems.

$$\begin{aligned} f(5) &= f(4) + f(3) = \\ &= f(3) + f(2) + f(3) = \\ &= f(2) + f(1) + f(2) + f(3) = \\ &= f(1) + f(0) + f(1) + f(2) + f(3) = \\ &= 1 + 0 + 1 + f(1) + f(0) + f(3) = \\ &= 1 + 0 + 1 + 1 + 0 + f(2) + f(1) = \\ &= 1 + 0 + 1 + 1 + 0 + f(1) + f(0) + f(1) = \\ &= 1 + 0 + 1 + 1 + 0 + 1 + 0 + 1 = 5 \end{aligned}$$

During this clumsy and lengthy computation we soon observe that the function value must be computed more times for the same value of its argument. It would therefore be much easier to build the value of the function f from the bottom to the top, using a simple table.

n	0	1	2	3	4	5	6	7	$\cdots$
$f(n)$	0	1	1	2	3	5	8	13	$\cdots$

The numbers may be readily recognized as the starting elements of the Fibonacci sequence. The function f is indeed the recursive definition of this interesting sequence possessing many unusual and interesting properties. The general form of the element of the Fibonacci sequence is the following:

$$f(n) = \frac{\varphi^n - (-\varphi)^{-n}}{\sqrt{5}}, \quad \varphi = \frac{1}{2}(\sqrt{5} + 1)$$

This formula is easily proved; nevertheless, the proof will be omitted here. You may find it in D. I. A. Cohen: *Basic Techniques of Combinatorial Theory*, John Wiley, New York 1987, p. 63. Already at first sight, it is interesting that the value of this strange and seemingly fully irrational expression is an integer for any nonnegative integer k. The key number φ in the formula is known as the *golden ratio*.

Let us now compute $g(5)$.

$$g(5) = h(0,1,5) = h(1,1,4) = h(1,2,3) = h(2,3,2) = h(3,5,1) = 5$$

It seems that the function g computes the elements of the Fibonacci sequence as well (we will prove this in item (c)), but is much more effective at this than the function f. The function h simulates the bottom-up way of computation which we found easier and faster when computing $f(5)$. But h needs no table, it only remembers the last two elements of the sequence needed to compute the next one. This function is more general as well, since it generates other sequences for other argument values.

b) We must prove that

$$h(a,b,e) + h(c,d,e) = h(a+c, b+d, e)$$

when a, b, c, d, and e are arbitrary nonnegative integers. The sharp-sight method (looking into the definition of the function h) tells us that the mathematical induction on e should be used.

The statement obviously holds for $e = 0$ and $e = 1$ for *arbitrary* nonnegative integers a, b, c, and d.

Let k be an arbitrary integer greater than 1. Suppose that the statement is true for all nonnegative integers a, b, c, and d, if $e = k$. Let us then prove that it is true for $e = k + 1$.

$$\begin{aligned} h(a,b,k+1) + h(c,d,k+1) &= h(b, a+b, k) + h(d, c+d, k) = \\ &= h(b+d, a+b+c+d, k) \end{aligned}$$

since, by induction hypothesis, the statement holds for $e = k$. But

$$h(a+c, b+d, k+1) = h(b+d, a+c+b+d, k)$$

The statement is proved.

c) Let us now prove that for any nonnegative integer n

$$f(n) = g(n) = h(0,1,n)$$

Again, the induction is used.

Directly from the definitions of f and h we see that the equality holds for $n = 0$ and $n = 1$. Assume now that k is an integer greater than 1, and assume that the statement is true for all $n < k$. Similarly to the proof in the previous item we prove that it holds for $n = k$. In the proof, we use the definition of the function f, the induction hypothesis, and the statement of item (b), respectively.

$$\begin{aligned} f(k) &= f(k-1) + f(k-2) = \\ &= h(0,1,k-1) + h(0,1,k-2) = \\ &= h(1,1,k-2) + h(0,1,k-2) = h(1,2,k-2) \end{aligned}$$

Now transform the function g

$$g(k) = h(0,1,k) = h(1,1,k-1) = h(1,2,k-2)$$

The results obtained are equal, therefore the values of the functions $f(n)$ and $g(n)$ are equal.

The function f represents the usual definition of the Fibonacci numbers; we have seen that it is rather ineffective as a computational procedure. Computing the Fibonacci numbers according to this definition is an excellent example in which recursion should **not** be used to program. We have already shown how the value of f can be computed iteratively; here we show how a similar definition, which is not that easy to compute iteratively, could be dealt with by a "learning" algorithm.

```
var
  known: array [0..max] of boolean;
  val: array [0..max] of integer;
  ii: integer;

function f(n: integer): integer;
{ Computes the n-th element of the Fibonacci sequence. }
begin
  if n>max then f:=f(n-1) + f(n-2)
  else if known[n] then f:=val[n]
  else begin val[n]:=f(n-1) + f(n-2); known[n]:=true; f:=val[n] end;
end; {f}

begin
{ Initial values }
  for ii:=2 to max do known[ii]:=false;
  known[0]:=true; val[0]:=0;
  known[1]:=true; val[1]:=1;
{ the use of the function f follows }
  ...
end.
```

It is much more difficult to handle definitions like

$$f(n) = \begin{cases} 0 & \text{if } n = 0 \\ 13 & \text{if } n = 7 \\ f(n-1) + f(n-2) & \text{otherwise} \end{cases}$$

which precisely defines the function f, but is not suitable as an algorithm to compute its values. This is the so-called boundary problem for a difference equation and must be solved as a system of linear equations or with the sharp-sight method by letting $f(n) = \varphi^n$. The learning algorithm is of no use in this case.

325C

See solution 315C.

721C

This program requires a computer with $maxInt > 10^5$. The solution using 16-bit integers ($maxInt = 32767$) would be much more complicated.

Let us denote the number $2n$ by m. The easiest solution would be to test for all even five-digit numbers m (between inclusive 10 000 and 99 999) whether they have the required property, whether in the numbers m and $n = m/2$ all decimal digits occur. This method is called the *brute force* method and is usually appropriate to solve small problems.

We will choose another way by which all solutions are obtained much faster. The number m is constructed digit by digit, starting from the leading digit (the ten thousands digit), and appending the subsequent ones. All the way, the repeated digits will be avoided in m and checked not to occur in n. How can we do that? Suppose that m has been constructed up to the third digit, say:

$$m = 413\text{XY}$$

Then we know

$$n = 206\text{VW}$$

The next digit X of m may be chosen from the set $\{5, 7, 8, 9\}$. If, for instance, we choose X=9, then m =4139Y and n =2069W. This choice is therefore not good, since the digit 9 is repeated.

This idea is implemented by a procedure which has for its first argument the starting portion of the number m, and for the second argument the set of available digits. It works recursively.

```
program AllDigits(output);
{ Determines all five digit numbers n, such that n and 2*n }
{ contain all 10 decimal digits, each one exactly once. }
{ The algorithm used: backtracking. }
  type digitSet = set of 0..9;

  procedure TryStart
    (m: integer;              { the start of the number 2*n }
     freeDigits: digitSet);   { the set of free digits }
  { Recursive descent }
    var i,j: integer;
```

```
  begin {TryStart}
    if m>10000 then
      begin if not odd(m) then writeln(m div 2,m) end
    else begin
      for i:=0 to 9 do
        if i in freeDigits then begin
          j:=((10*m+i) div 2) mod 10;
          if j in (freeDigits-[i]) then
            TryStart(10*m+i,freeDigits-[i,j]);
        end; {if,for}
    end; {if}
  end; {TryStart}

begin {AllDigits}
  TryStart(0,[0..9]);
end. {AllDigits}
```

The idea used in the above program is the same as the one used to solve the well-known *eight queens problem*—how should eight queens be positioned on a chessboard without attacking each other? The method is called *backtracking* and may be coded without recursion (see for example N. Wirth, *Algorithms+Data Structures=Programs*, Prentice-Hall, Englewood Cliffs 1976).

As shown by experiment, the easiest solution, using the brute force method, would take approximately twenty times more time to run than the program above.

This is one of many cases showing that a more thorough reflection leads to a much better solution. Yet this also shows how things are not done in practice. The problem posed by the exercise is precisely defined, above all, its size is fixed (in the sense of the discussion in the introduction to Chapter D). Also, the problem has no obvious generalizations (except perhaps the analogous problem for other number systems). Therefore, if the program occurred in practice, (and it would probably only occur as a puzzle), we would tackle it with a *throw-away program* (see Section 5). Relative to the time necessary to develop the program, its execution time is negligible even on the most primitive computers. The program would therefore be developed with the least effort, using the sequential search method, even if it were to consume twenty times more time. Also, we would feel more sure that the result obtained is correct.

As an interesting point we give the same algorithm written in Prolog:

```
solution( M, N ) :-
  properPair( M, N,  0, 0,  [0,1,2,3,4,5,6,7,8,9] ).

properPair( M, N,  M, N,  [ ] ).
```

```
properPair( M, N,  HeadM, HeadN,  FreeDigits ) :-
  element( DigitM, FreeDigits, FreeDigits1 ),
  NewHeadM is 10*HeadM+DigitM, NewHeadN is NewHeadM/2,
  DigitN is NewHeadN-10*HeadN,
  element( DigitN, FreeDigits1, FreeDigits2 ),
  properPair( M, N,  NewHeadM, NewHeadN,  FreeDigits2 ).

element( A, [A|SetNoA], SetNoA ).
element( A, [HeadNoA|Set], [HeadNoA|SetNoA]) :-
  element( A, Set, SetNoA ).
```

The program requires some explanation. A program in Prolog is composed of statements, which are separated by points. The name of a statement (its first word) is called a *predicate*, which may be followed by arguments in parentheses. For instance, *solution* is a predicate with two arguments. The statements in Prolog may be **facts**, which define basic relations between definite objects, or **rules**, which relate objects using other rules. The program above contains no fact; a fact is for instance

```
nonnegativeInteger( 0 ).
```

which states that 0 is a nonnegative integer. An example of a rule, according to which other nonnegative integers are obtained follows

```
nonnegativeInteger( X ) :- Y is X-1, nonnegativeInteger( Y ).
```

stating that X is a nonnegative integer, if its predecessor is a nonnegative integer.

Besides definite objects (for instance, the number 0), **variables** may appear in rules. In a program they denote a place where any appropriate object may appear. For example: in the fact about nonnegative integers a precisely definite object appears: the number 0. In the rule about nonnegative integers, the X and Y variables appear, denoting the number itself and its predecessor.

Some words are due about the lexical tokens of Prolog. The names of its variables start with a capital letter while other names start with a lower case one. The word *is* in Prolog sometimes means assignment (the same as the symbol := in Pascal) and sometimes comparison (the symbol = in Pascal), more on this later. The symbol :- in Prolog stands for "if", while the commas between predicates at the right of this symbol denote conjunction (cf. 211A). A Prolog list is written by separating its components by commas and putting them between brackets. The notation $[A|B]$ is a short way to write a list, whose first element is A, while the remaining ones form the list B. Finally, [ ] denotes an empty list.

All this said, there is one worrying point: nowhere can it be seen how the *execution* of the program flows. At first sight, the program above specifies only the relations among the objects treated. The execution procedure itself is in fact hidden in the Prolog understanding of the program. The divide and conquer method is used to execute. The *goal* is designated to Prolog: a predicate to be satisfied; in our case the question to Prolog is *solution*(M, N). Prolog then discovers that to satisfy the designated goal, a *partial goal* must be satisfied first; in our case this is

```
properPair(M,N, 0,0, [0,1,2,3,4,5,6,7,8,9] ).
```

To do that, Prolog considers all rules and facts about this predicate and tries to use them one after another. In our example, it tries first to use the first *properPair* rule, but fails, since the list of digits above is non-empty (more about this later). Therefore, it searches on, and tries to use the second rule about a proper pair. The latter may be satisfied only by first satisfying all the predicates at the right of the symbol :–, which now become the new partial goals. The procedure then recursively repeats for each of the partial goals until either all of them are satisfied and a solution is found, or a goal is found that cannot be satisfied.

In the first case, Prolog outputs the solution; if the solution is not suitable, Prolog may be directed to continue as if no solution was found. In the other case, when Prolog finds no way forward, it *backtracks* and tries to satisfy the preceding goals again, but in a different way; this happened when the first *properPair* rule was used the first time. For example, if Prolog finds out that with the digit *DigitM* the goals cannot be satisfied, it tries to use another. The *backtracking*, the characteristic we alone have programmed in our Pascal solution, is built into Prolog. This is one of the characteristics of Prolog program execution.

The other characteristic is the treatment of Prolog variables. They differ significantly from variables in other languages; they play a similar role to the variables in algebra. Prior to dividing a goal into partial goals, Prolog arranges — *unifies*— the variables: compares or assigns their values or remembers that two variables mean the same. Examples: satisfying the goal *solution*, Prolog first tries to use the first rule for *properPair*, and fails after trying to unify the lists of digits (which is the full list of digits in the goal and the empty list in the rule). Therefore it uses the second rule, in which *HeadM* and *HeadN* attain the value 0, and *FreeDigits* becomes the list of all digits. The M and N variables remain undefined, Prolog just remembers they mean the same as in the *solution* predicate. For the same reasons the *is* operator sometimes denotes assignment (when the variable at its left is undefined) and sometimes comparison (when both variables are defined). Similarly, the *element* predicate at one place chooses a new digit *DigitM* from the specified list of digits (since this variable is undefined), and elsewhere tests whether the digit *DigitN* is in the list (since its value has been previously defined).

After all is said and done, is it still necessary to explain the program in detail? Probably not, but let us compare it to the Pascal solution. The *properPair* predicate corresponds to the *TryStart* procedure of the Pascal solution. It specifies which pair *HeadM*, *HeadN* of numbers still satisfies the requirements of the exercise for the unused digits from the *FreeDigits* list. The first rule of this predicate specifies when a pair of numbers represents the final solution, and the second how this solution is constructed. The *element* predicate combines two set operations: it tests whether a digit is the element of a set (**in** in Pascal), and it removes a digit from the set (the set difference in Pascal). The *solution* predicate specifies the source of solving: the initial list of digits and the initial value of the pair *HeadM*, *HeadN*. The second rule of the *properPair* predicate is central to the program, as it tells how a new proper pair *NewHeadM*, *NewHeadN* is constructed from the old proper pair *HeadM*, *HeadN*: first, a digit *DigitM* is chosen and removed from the set *FreeDigits* of free digits, appended to the end of the number *HeadM* obtaining the number *NewHeadM*, the new number *NewHeadN* is computed, its last digit *DigitN* extracted, tested to belong to the list of free digits and removed from it, and finally the new pair is tested to comply to the requirement of the exercise.

Since programs written in Prolog are usually interpreted, it was expected that the execution time would be fairly long. In our case it was approximately 45 times longer than in the case of our Pascal solution.

Finally, we mention a title of a book in which more on Prolog and its use can be found: I. Bratko: *Prolog Programming for Artificial Intelligence*, (2nd edition) Addison-Wesley, Reading 1990.

733C

This problem was not a particularly lucky choice as a competition problem, since it is — especially the question (**b**) — a research project. The idea for the problem originates in biochemistry, or rather, in a computer scientist's naive imagination of a problem in biochemistry.

Proteins are composed of 20 amino acids in total; all their variety stems from the sequence in which these amino acids appear in the molecule of a protein. The molecules of proteins are composed from ten to several thousand amino acids. In large molecules, the order of the amino acids is difficult to determine. Therefore, using various enzymes biochemists split the molecule into smaller parts — peptides, separate them, and determine the sequence of amino acids in each of the peptides. Several enzymes are available, which split the molecules in various ways. From the sequences of the amino acids in all peptides obtained in two or more divisions, the sequence of the amino acids in the original molecule may be constructed. The question (**a**) in the problem therefore represents an idealized problem, and the question (**b**) a (perhaps) realistic problem of the analysis of a molecule of a protein. Actually, the enzymes act differently from tearing paper; a particular enzyme splits the molecule at the points where a particular sequence of amino acids appears. This slightly simplifies the work in combining the peptides.

It is interesting to mention that nowadays genetic engineers know better methods to determine the sequence of amino acids; instead of analyzing the molecule itself, these methods are based on the analysis of the sequence of nucleic acids in the DNA where the genetic code for the synthesis of the molecule is stored. Today, it is particularly fancy to use computers in biochemistry to determine the spatial and functional structure of the molecule analyzed.

But let us return to the problem of the torn line of text. To start, let us limit ourselves to question (a), question (b) will only be tackled briefly at the end. Let us try to imagine how the torn paper problem would be dealt with manually. Since the heaps of the torn pieces are separated, for each heap a line would be reserved. The pieces of paper would be inserted into it, ensuring that the portions of the text composed so far would coincide. In the middle of lining up the arrangement of the pieces on the table would look as follows:

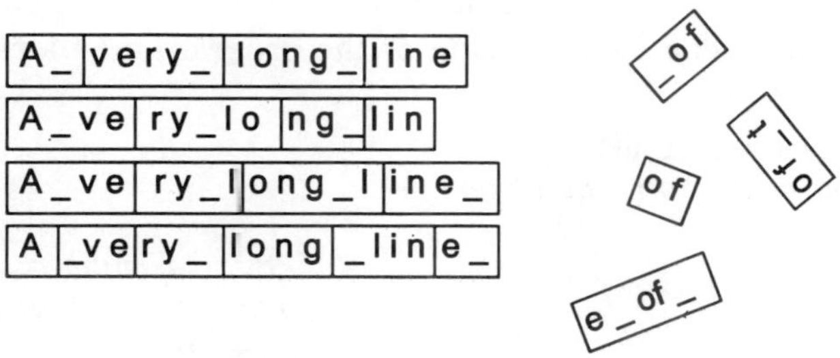

Figure C1: The text composition

A new piece would be appended to one of the shorter lines so that the text on it would coincide with the text of the longer lines. It is most appropriate to extend the shortest line, since in this case the most information is available to choose the next piece appended— the entire text from the end of the shortest and up to the end of the longest line.

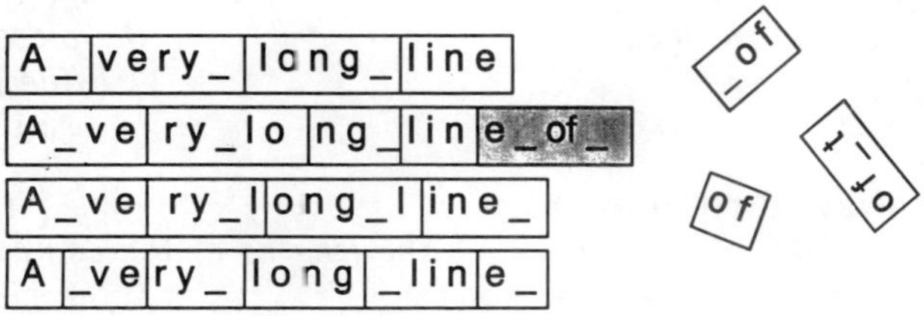

Figure C2: The addition of a new piece

Naturally, it may happen that at some point an incorrect piece is added. This is discovered when adding cannot be continued from some point, since no available pieces suit. In this case, a portion of the text lined up must be undone up to a point where there are more possibilities available to continue, and use another possibility there. This means that *backtracking* must be used in the algorithm (as in solution 721C). But prior to dealing with the searching procedure let us design the data structure.

Since the text lined up is the same for all lines, it suffices that their text is stored in a single string, and the length of each composed portion of a line is stored separately. Since the exact lengths of the pieces of text cannot be determined in advance, all pieces of the torn text are aligned in a single string, and described by the index of the start of a piece and its length. These data are stored in a two-dimensional table, indexed by the number of the line (copy) and the number of the piece. A separate table will indicate whether a piece has been used in the composition so far. The basic version of the program may already be designed:

```
program Compose(inp,output);
{ Reconstruction of the torn line of text. }
  const
    txtM = 200;                          { the maximum composed line length }
    strM = 4000;                  { the maximum length of all pieces together }
    copM = 20;                              { the maximum number of copies }
    heaM = 100;                   { the maximum number of pieces in a heap }

  type
    pieT =          { the description of a piece of text: its length and start }
      record ll,ss: integer; end;
    heaT = array [1..heaM] of pieT;                { the piece description table }

  var
  { the input data }
    str: packed array [1..strM] of char;                  { the piece strings read }
    strL: integer;                          { the total length of all pieces read }
    copL: integer;                                      { the number of copies }
    pieL: array [1..copM] of integer;           { the number of pieces in a heap }
    hea: array [1..copM] of heaT;                   { the piece description table }
    length: integer;                                    { the length of the text }

  { work data }
    txt: packed array [1..txtM] of char;                     { the composed text }
    txtL: array [1..copM] of integer;    { the lengths of the composed parts of lines }
    used: array [1..copM, 1..heaM] of boolean;          { the piece has been used }
    inp: text;                                        { the input file with data }
```

```
procedure ReadData;
{ Reads input data. }
  var
    copC,pieC: integer;                          { the copy and piece counters }
    separ: char;                            { the separator between text pieces }
begin
  readln(inp,copL); strL:=0;                              { the number of copies }
  for copC:=1 to copL do begin
    readln(inp,pieL[copC]); length:=0;          { the number of pieces in a copy }
    for pieC:=1 to pieL[copC] do begin
      read(inp,separ); hea[copC,pieC].ss:=strL+1;             { the text of a piece }
      while inp↑<>separ do
        begin strL:=strL+1; str[strL]:=inp↑; get(inp) end;
      readln(inp); hea[copC,pieC].ll:=strL-hea[copC,pieC].ss+1;
      length:=length+hea[copC,pieC].ll;                 { compute the total length }
    end; {for}
  end; {for}
end; {ReadData}

procedure Initialize;
{ Initializes the search. }
  var copC,pieC: integer;
begin
  for copC:=1 to copL do txtL[copC]:=0;                     { all lines are empty }
  for copC:=1 to copL do                                      { no piece is used }
    for pieC:=1 to pieL[copC] do used[copC,pieC]:=false;
end; {Initialize}

function Suits(var dsc1,dsc2: pieT): boolean;
{ Compares the piece described by dsc1 (in str) }
{ to the piece described by dsc2 (in txt). }
  var
    i1,i2: integer;
    done: boolean;
begin
  i1:=dsc1.ss; i2:=dsc2.ss;
  repeat
    done:=true;
    if i2>=dsc2.ss+dsc2.ll then Suits:=true                         { end of dsc2 }
    else if i1>=dsc1.ss+dsc1.ll then Suits:=true                     { end of dsc1 }
    else if str[i1]<>txt[i2] then Suits:=false               { different characters }
    else begin done:=false; i1:=i1+1; i2:=i2+1 end;              { equal characters }
  until done;
end; {Suits}

procedure Append(min,max,pieC: integer; var nmin,nmax: integer);
{ Appends the piece (min,pieC) and recomputes the numbers of the shortest }
{ and the longest line. The piece is appended to the currently shortest line. }
  var jj,kk: integer;
```

```
begin
  used[min,pieC]:=true;                              { the piece is now used }
  nmin:=min; nmax:=max;
  with hea[min,pieC] do begin
    if txtL[min]+ll>txtL[max] then begin
      nmax:=min; kk:=txtL[min];                                { update max }
      for jj:=ss to ss+ll-1 do                              { append to txt }
        begin kk:=kk+1; txt[kk]:=str[jj] end;
    end; {if}
    txtL[min]:=txtL[min]+ll;                            { update the length }
  end; {with}
  for jj:=1 to copL do                              { the new shortest line }
    if txtL[jj]<txtL[nmin] then nmin:=jj;
end; {Append}

procedure Remove(copC,pieC: integer);
{ Removes the last appended piece (copC,pieC). }
begin
  txtL[copC]:=txtL[copC]-hea[copC,pieC].ll;             { update the length }
  used[copC,pieC]:=false;                         { the piece is no more used }
end; {Remove}

procedure TryPiece(min,max: integer);
{ Recursively tries to append a new piece, min is the index of the shortest }
{ line, max is the index of the longest line. To choose pieces, the text of the }
{ max-th line from the end of the min-th on is used. }
  var
    pattern: pieT;                           { the pattern looked for in txt }
    pieC: integer;             { the index of the tried piece of the minimum line }
    newmin,newmax: integer;
    ii: integer;
begin
  if txtL[min]>=length then
    begin                                             { output the solution }
      for ii:=1 to txtL[max] do write(txt[ii]);
      writeln;
    end
  else begin
    pattern.ss:=txtL[min]+1; pattern.ll:=txtL[max]-txtL[min];
    for pieC:=1 to pieL[min] do                    { try pieces not yet used }
      if used[min,pieC] then {}                                 { which suit }
      else if Suits(hea[min,pieC],pattern) then begin
        Append(min,max,pieC,newmin,newmax);
        TryPiece(newmin,newmax);
        Remove(min,pieC);
      end; {if,for}
  end; {if}
end; {TryPiece}
```

```
begin {Compose}
  reset(inp); ReadData; Initialize; TryPiece(1,1);
end. {Compose}
```

The program might be improved in various ways. To begin with, the determination of the shortest and the longest line might be organized by using a heap (see solutions 622D and 1021H). The next deficiency shows up if several pieces are equal in a copy. In this case we obtain as many equal solutions as there are permutations of the equal pieces. The problem may be avoided by skipping any unused piece equal to any of the previous ones. The next improvement is possible when the composed portions of all lines are of the same length (as is the case initially). Then, using a simpler search through the available pieces, pieces with a common start would be chosen from each copy.

A more serious deficiency of the algorithm described shows up, if all copies are cut at the same point or at several such points. Then, the permutations of the portions between common cuts appear as solutions. There are many permutations, and so the computation tends to be very long. The existence of such separate portions means that there is not enough information to compose the line. Therefore, it would be best to output the separate portions of the line separately and leave the choice to someone who understands the text and may guess the correct solution.

In any case, the requirement of the problem that a *very* long line is involved means that the composition is practically impossible. Experiments with the program above and its modifications have shown that the problem becomes practically unsolvable if the number of copies is less than six and the number of pieces in the line exceeds 30.

To solve the problem in item (b), we only propose some ideas. If some characters at the joints are missing, or even some pieces are missing, the problem may be regarded as in the previous case, if a "wildcard character" is used, which may be appended to the start or to the end of any piece and suits any character. This means that the pieces are not appended at the end of a string, but that some "wildcard characters" may appear between the end of the string and the piece appended. The number of combinations tested by the algorithm in this case is even more tremendous, so that additional restrictions must be imposed for the solution of any practical problem. One cannot even talk about *all* solutions to the problem, since there are always infinitely many of them. Therefore it is important that the solutions are computed in such an order as to obtain the most probable (or any) solutions first.

The first possibility we think of is to count characters in each copy and compute their frequencies. If we assume that at least one copy is complete, we may deduce from the frequencies of the characters in particular copies which characters are replaced by the "wildcard character". Even if no heap is complete, we may probably assume that no character is missing in all copies at the same time. This additionally aids in reducing the number of possibilities.

The second change, reaching much deeper into the algorithm, would be to join strings of pieces instead of joining pieces independently. The strings of pieces should be prepared in advance so that the pieces within a string would be joined confidently (there would be great probability that they fit together). When joining strings one has more information to test suitability of a string joint so that the wildcard characters bother us less.

Chapter D

Reordering

A suitable ordering of data often enables us to devise a more efficient algorithm for a given problem. The ordering may be achieved in various ways:

- the ordering is provided outside the program when preparing data. The data are input in the prescribed order. In these cases, the input is usually intermingled with the verification of ordering;
- the data are reordered in the prescribed way prior to using the algorithm;
- the ordering is provided and maintained by the algorithm used to solve the problem.

Also, ordering is very important in program output.

Most frequently linear ordering is encountered (the ordering of numbers, alphabetical ordering, etc.). In some algorithms (e.g. the Critical Path Method), however, partial ordering suffices (the topological sort, see for example, N. Wirth, *Algorithms+Data Structures=Programs*, Prentice-Hall, Englewood Cliffs 1976, pp. 182–189). Suppose that n items of data of the ordered type *element* are stored in the table *tab*.

```
const nmax = 100;
type table = array [1..nmax] of element;
var tab: table; n: integer;
```

How could the elements of such a table be ordered (sorted, rearranged) in the ascending order?

As a rule, the sorting algorithms one devises oneself are of quadratic complexity, i.e., the sorting time increases proportionally to the square of the table length. (You may find more about the complexity of algorithms later on in this introduction.) The best known such algorithm is the *bubble sort*; perhaps the shortest is the *insertion sort*:

```
for i:=2 to n do begin
  s:=tab[i]; tab[0]:=s; j:=i;
  while tab[j-1]>s do begin tab[j]:=tab[j-1]; j:=j-1 end;
  tab[j]:=s;
end; {for}
```

Here, the table *tab* must be extended by the "sentinel" *tab*[0], that is

```
type table = array [0..nmax] of element;
```

The actual table still starts at *tab*[1]. The use of the sentinel only allows a simplification of the algorithm—the **while** statement certainly terminates.

As long as the table is short (a few dozen elements), these algorithms work quite well. For longer tables they become tediously slow.

Extensive literature exists on sorting (see N. Wirth: *Algorithms+Data Structures=Programs*, Prentice-Hall, Englewood Cliffs 1976, A. V. Aho, J. E. Hopcroft, J. D. Ullman: *The Design and Analysis of Computer Algorithms*, Addison-Wesley, Reading 1974 and elsewhere). For longer tables the *heap sort* algorithm is more suitable; its time complexity is of the order $n \log n$:

```
procedure Sort(var tab: table; n: integer);
{ Sorts the first n elements of the table tab
  in ascending order using the heap sort method. }
  label 14;
  var
    d,top,father,son: integer;
    cur: element;
begin
  d:=n; top:=1 + d div 2;
  while d>1 do begin
    if top>1 then begin top:=top-1; cur:=tab[top] end
    else begin cur:=tab[d]; tab[d]:=tab[1]; d:=d-1 end;
    father:=top; son:=2*father;
    while son <= d do begin
      if son<d then if tab[son+1] >= tab[son] then son:=son+1;
      if cur >= tab[son] then goto 14;
      tab[father]:=tab[son]; father:=son; son:=2*father;
    end; {while}
14: tab[father]:=cur;
  end; {while}
end; {Sort}
```

The **goto** statement may be avoided by the following modification:

```
if cur >= tab[son] then son:=d+1
else begin tab[father]:=tab[son]; father:=son; son:=2*father end;
```

The *Sort* procedure will be used in solution 622D.

The complexity of the heap sort reaches the lowest bound of complexity of the algorithms for sorting by comparison. On average it is slightly less efficient than Hoare's *quick sort*, which is, however, quadratic in the worst cases. Even more efficient algorithms exist which observe the contents of the data. The *radix sort* (also called the *bin sort*) works in this way.

On some occasions, sorting is misused. For table searching, hashing is much more efficient (N. Wirth: *Algorithms+Data Structures=Programs*, Prentice-Hall, Englewood Cliffs 1976, pp. 264–274).

The lesson learned from various problems in this book (most notably problems 1014A, 1123B and perhaps 721C) is that various methods for solving problems are of varying quality, that with the increasing size of the problems their **time** or **space complexity** rises with different speed. Neither complexity will be defined precisely here. Serious complexity analysis requires a knowledge of mathematics beyond the scope of this book. (You can find more about the analysis of algorithms in the book by A. V. Aho, J. E. Hopcroft, J. D. Ullman: *The Design and Analysis of Computer Algorithms*, Addison-Wesley, Reading 1974 as well as in the book by Knuth mentioned earlier.) Nevertheless, we can say a few words about time complexity using our limited knowledge.

Denote by N the size of a problem, which limits the quantity of the input data to an algorithm. In solution 1123B for example, N denotes the upper boundary of the numbers among which the friendly pairs are looked for. The size of the matrix could be considered to be the size of the problem in problem 1111B about the ball rolling down the terrain, while in problem 1021H about the passionate dicers the number of players would serve that purpose. The execution time depends on N. Denote this dependence by $f(N)$. The execution time does not depend exclusively on the choice of the method, it is influenced by other environmental data as well. If, for instance, another computer is used, the execution for the same size of problem requires the same number of basic operations (in our case arithmetic operations: additions, multiplications and divisions), but takes a different amount of time. If, for example, all operations of one computer are three times slower than those of the other, the execution takes three times more for the same size of problem. Therefore, the execution time itself is not a good measure of time complexity. In addition to the choice of computer, the execution time is influenced by the choice of programming language, the choice of primitive operations (for the primitive operations one may take the arithmetic operations as well as the bit operations needed to perform the arithmetic ones) and so on. Only when all effects of such influences are removed from the dependence above is a precise measure of the time complexity of a method obtained. Still, the execution time is the only parameter that can be empirically measured, and is therefore usually used to demonstrate the performance of a method, always specifying the precise environment in which it was measured. Two methods are of the *same time complexity*, if the ratio of the execution times of both methods is independent of the problem size in any environment in which they are run. If this ratio grows or diminishes as the problem size increases or decreases, one of the methods is more time complex than the other.

Let us illustrate this by an example: when comparing the bubble sort, the insertion sort, the heap sort and the quick sort (see elsewhere in this introduction), the following execution times were measured (in seconds on a MicroVAX II computer):

The number of integers sorted	10	50	100	500	1000	5000	10000
1 The bubble sort	0.01	0.05	0.22	5.69	21.76	552.98	2143.63
2 The insertion sort	0.00	0.03	0.13	1.91	8.83	411.68	933.98
3 The heap sort	0.00	0.02	0.03	0.22	0.44	3.61	6.88
4 The quick sort	0.00	0.02	0.13	0.13	0.31	2.23	4.28
The ratio 1:2	–	1.67	1.69	2.97	2.46	1.34	2.29
The ratio 2:3	–	1.50	4.33	8.68	20.07	114.04	135.75

The last two lines represent the ratios of the execution times of the bubble sort to the insertion sort, and of the insertion sort to the heap sort. The first line is more or less constant (relative to the precision of the measurement, the differences are more or less accidental in nature) and confirms the hypothesis that the bubble sort and the insertion sort have the same time complexity. The second line, on the other hand, shows that the heap sort has lower time complexity than the insertion sort. This is indeed proved by the theoretical analyses of the algorithms, which show that their time complexities are as follows:

the bubble sort	proportional to N^2
the insertion sort	proportional to N^2
the heap sort	proportional to $N \log N$
the quick sort	proportional to $N \log N$

The proportionality here is not direct. In mathematics, if it is discovered that a quantity is approximately proportional to $f(N)$ (or to a function of a lower order), it is referred to as of order $O(f(N))$. The precise definition of this notion again goes beyond the scope of this book. Therefore, the heap sort method is of order $O(N \log N)$.

215D

In the theory of sorting algorithms, the maximal non-decreasing or non-increasing subsequences are called **runs**. A subsequence is maximal, if it is not a subsequence of another subsequence of the same kind. In the statement of the problem, all (non-decreasing) runs of the specified sequence are listed. A non-decreasing sequence is 9,9,10 as well, but it is not a run, since it is contained in the subsequence 7,9,9,10,11.

The algorithm for determining the longest non-decreasing run is evident from the following Pascal program.

```
program Runs(input,output);
{ Determines the longest non-decreasing run. }
  var
    newEl,oldEl: real;  { the current and the previous element }
    d: integer;         { the length of the current run }
    dMax: integer;      { the length of the longest run }
begin
  if eof then dMax:=0
  else begin
    readln(oldEl); d:=1; dMax:=1;
    while not eof do begin
      readln(newEl);
      if newEl>=oldEl then d:=d+1
      else begin
        if d>dMax then dMax:=d;
        d:=1;
      end; {if}
      oldEl:=newEl;
    end; {while}
    if d>dMax then dMax:=d;
  end; {if}
  writeln('The longest run is ',dMax:3,' elements long.');
end. {Runs}
```

224D

Two solutions of the problem will be considered:

a) Using the *Swap* procedure, a circular right shift of one place may be accomplished by taking the last element of the table and swapping it $n-1$ times with the preceding element of the table. For instance:

$$\begin{array}{cccccccc}
1 & 2 & 3 & 4 & 5 & 6 & \underline{7} & \underline{8} \\
1 & 2 & 3 & 4 & 5 & \underline{6} & \underline{8} & 7 \\
1 & 2 & 3 & 4 & \underline{5} & \underline{8} & 6 & 7 \\
1 & 2 & 3 & \underline{4} & \underline{8} & 5 & 6 & 7 \\
1 & 2 & \underline{3} & \underline{8} & 4 & 5 & 6 & 7 \\
1 & \underline{2} & \underline{8} & 3 & 4 & 5 & 6 & 7 \\
\underline{1} & \underline{8} & 2 & 3 & 4 & 5 & 6 & 7 \\
8 & 1 & 2 & 3 & 4 & 5 & 6 & 7
\end{array}$$

The circular right shift of k places is now performed by circularly shifting right by one place k times. Let us write a program:

```
procedure Shift(n,k: integer);
  var i,j: integer;
begin
  for j:=1 to k do
    for i:=n downto 2 do Swap(i-1,i);
end; {Shift}
```

Obviously, the *Shift* algorithm requires $k\cdot(n-1)$ calls to the *Swap* procedure.

b) The second solution is based on the following observation: if portions of the table can be inverted, then the circular right shift by k places $(0 \le k \le n)$ may be accomplished by three inversions:

— invert the first $n-k$ elements;
— invert the last k elements;
— invert the entire table.

Let us demonstrate this in the case $n = 8$, $k = 3$:

the initial position	1	2	3	4	5	6	7	8
invert the first 5	5	4	3	2	1	6	7	8
invert the last 3	5	4	3	2	1	8	7	6
invert the entire table	6	7	8	1	2	3	4	5

How do we invert a portion of the table? Simply by swapping the border elements and repeating the procedure on the remainder until it is shorter than two elements. The procedure:

```
procedure Shift(n,k: integer);
{ The circular right shift of n elements by k places. }

  procedure Invert(a,b: integer);
  begin
    if b>a then begin Swap(a,b); Invert(a+1,b-1) end;
  end; {Invert}

begin {Shift}
  if n>0 then begin
    k:=k mod n; if k<0 then k:=n+k; { 0≤k<n }
    if k>0 then begin Invert(1,n-k); Invert(n-k+1,n); Invert(1,n) end;
  end; {if}
end; {Shift}
```

Although an evident misuse of the recursion, the *Invert* procedure was coded recursively, since such a solution is clearer.

Let us now determine the number of calls to the *Swap* procedure. The *Invert* procedure calls it $\lfloor (b+1-a)/2 \rfloor$ times. Therefore the *Shift* procedure calls it

$$\left\lfloor \frac{n-k}{2} \right\rfloor + \left\lfloor \frac{k}{2} \right\rfloor + \left\lfloor \frac{n}{2} \right\rfloor \le n$$

times.

314D Let us trace the program execution after reading the data intc table t. The state after each step is presented in the table:

i	j	t_1	t_2	t_3	t_4	t_5	t_6	t_7	t_8	t_9	t_{10}
	10	9	8	7	6	5	4	3	2	1	0
1	9	0	8	7	6	5	4	3	2	1	9
2	8	0	1	7	6	5	4	3	2	8	9
3	7	0	1	2	6	5	4	3	7	8	9
4	6	0	1	2	3	5	4	6	7	8	9
5	5	0	1	2	3	4	5	6	7	8	9
6	4	0	1	2	3	5	4	6	7	8	9
7	3	0	1	2	6	5	4	3	7	8	9
8	2	0	1	7	6	5	4	3	2	8	9
9	1	0	8	7	6	5	4	3	2	1	9
10	0	9	8	7	6	5	4	3	2	1	0

The program therefore outputs the sequence of the numbers in the same order as it was read.

From the explanation in the program we may conclude that the programmer intended to write a program which inverts a sequence of data. From the table we observe that the program achieved this state after the fifth step, but then proceeded to restore the initial state. This statement is true for any n. If the main loop of the program is replaced by:

```
j:=n;
for i:=1 to n div 2 do begin
  z:=t[i]; t[i]:=t[j]; t[j]:=z;
  j:=j-1;
end; {for}
```

the program inverts the sequence of the data read.

The same effect (the output of the data in inverse order) may be achieved by a shorter program:

```
begin
  readln(n);
  for i:=1 to n do read(t[i]);
  for i:=n downto 1 do write(t[i]);
end.
```

This answer was probably expected by the authors of the problem. The problem naturally allows other answers. For example: the program is correctly written and copies its data. The excess statements are included in the program because the programmer is paid by the number of code lines; the incorrect explanations make guessing what the program does harder — the programmer thus makes himself or herself indispensable.

324D When the programmer of questionable qualities brought the authors of the problems the program of problem 314D, they were not particularly kind to him. Therefore he was cautious this time, and sent the program of this problem by post. Let us examine what this program does.

The program first reads an integer table (a matrix) of data. What happens inside the double loop that follows? Consider any two values of indices $i = p$, $j = q$, $p < q$. The body of the loop first swaps the values of the elements $a[p, q]$ and $a[q, p]$ of the table a; later on, at $i = q$, $j = p$ the values of the same elements are swapped again—the elements contain their initial values. What if $p = q$? Then the body of the loop swaps the value of the element $a[p, q]$ with itself. To summarize: in the loop nothing actually happens.

The last loop outputs the table row by row. The program given thus reads and outputs an unchanged integer table of data.

Only the programmer knows what he or she had in mind when writing the program. Probably the authors of the problem had in mind the transposition of the table (the exchange of its rows and columns, that is, the reflection of the table across its diagonal). According to the above discoveries this is achieved with the following modification to the head of the middle loop:

```
for i:=1 to 9 do
  for j:=i+1 to 10 do
  ...
```

Naturally, to output a table in the transposed form there is no need to actually transpose it. This is accomplished simply by the following program:

```
begin
  for i:=1 to 10 do  for j:=1 to 10 do read(a[i,j]);
  for j:=1 to 10 do begin
    for i:=1 to 10 do write(a[i,j]);
    writeln;
  end; {for}
end.
```

Solving the problem, we intentionally skipped the request to devise suitable data and write the results. Suitable data would be the successive numbers from 1 to 100; however, this amount of data is too large to trace the program by hand. A table of size 3×3 would suffice.

514D The problem may be solved in various ways. For instance:

— produce the tables of the letter frequencies for both words; if they are equal, the words are anagrams;

— alphabetically sort the letters of both words; if the obtained "words" are equal, the words are anagrams;

— if the words are anagrams, they are either equal or the same letter may be excluded from both; the "words" obtained are again anagrams;

— if the words are anagrams, the second may be rearranged into the first.

Let us compose a function based on the last idea, which tests the given words if they are anagrams. We assume the words are at most 20 characters long. Shorter words are padded with spaces at the end.

```
const dmax = 20; dp = 21; {=dmax+1}
type word = packed array [1..dp] of char;

...

function Anagram(a,b: word): boolean;
{ Determines if the given words a and b are anagrams. }
  var
    d,da,db,i,j: integer;
    notDone,notFound: boolean;

begin
  da:=1; while (a[da] <> ' ') and (da <= dmax) do da:=da+1;
  db:=1; while (b[db] <> ' ') and (db <= dmax) do db:=db+1;
  if da<>db then Anagram:=false             { the words are of different lengths }
  else if da=1 then Anagram:=true                                   { empty word }
  else begin
    notDone:=true; i:=1; d:=da-1;
    while notDone do
      if a[i]=' ' then notDone:=false
      else begin
        j:=i; notFound:=true;
        while notFound do
          if a[i]=b[j] then notFound:=false
          else begin j:=j+1; notFound:=(j<=d) end;
        if j>d then notDone:=false
        else begin b[j]:=b[i]; i:=i+1; notDone:=(i<=d) end;
      end; {if,while}
    Anagram:=(i>d);
  end; {if}
end; {Anagram}
```

Let us consider also the solution in Logo. The method of excluding the same letters is used. The WTOL procedure translates the string w into the list of characters it consists of. The EXCLUDE procedure excludes the character c from the list w. The test is performed by the ANA and ANAGRAM procedures.

```
TO WTOL :w
  IF :w = " [OUTPUT [ ] ]
  OUTPUT SE FIRST :w WTOL BUTFIRST :w
END
TO EXCLUDE :c :w
  IF :c = FIRST :w [OUTPUT BUTFIRST :w]
  OUTPUT SE FIRST :w EXCLUDE :c BUTFIRST :w
END
TO ANA :a :b
  IF :a = :b [OUTPUT TRUE]
  IF NOT MEMBERP FIRST :a :b [OUTPUT FALSE]
  OUTPUT ANA BUTFIRST :a EXCLUDE FIRST :a :b
END
TO ANAGRAM :a :b
  IF (COUNT :a) = (COUNT :b) [OUTPUT ANA WTOL :a WTOL :b]
  OUTPUT FALSE
END
```

The solution is tested by requesting

```
    PRINT ANAGRAM "SISTER "RESIST
```

In some dialects of Logo (for instance on the IBM PC) "TRUE and "FALSE must be written instead of TRUE and FALSE.

The reader may try considering how all anagrams in a given dictionary would be found.

524D

The basic idea of the solution originates in the following property: a word is a palindrome if its first and last characters are equal, and the "word" without these two characters is still a palindrome.

```
program Test(input,output);
{ Outputs the longest palindromic start of the word. }
  var
    a: packed array [1..80] of char; { the word }
    n: integer;  { the length of the word }
    m: integer;  { the length of the longest palindrome }
    i: integer;

  function Palindrome(i,j: integer): boolean;
  { Determines if the word between the i-th and the j-th character is a palindrome. }
  begin
    if i>=j then Palindrome:=true
    else if a[i]<>a[j] then Palindrome:=false
    else Palindrome:=Palindrome(i+1,j-1);
  end; {Palindrome}
```

```
begin {Test}
{ read the string }
  n:=0;
  while input↑ <> ' ' do begin n:=n+1; read(a[n]) end;
{ determine the longest palindrome }
  m:=n;
  while not Palindrome(1,m) do m:=m-1;
{ output the longest palindrome }
  for i:=1 to m do write(a[i]);
  writeln;
end. {Test}
```

Two minor remarks:

- when *eoln=true* the statement *read* inputs a space (see solution 813A);
- the empty word is a palindrome; the condition *Palindrome*(1,0) is always true.

The *Palindrome* function is coded recursively. Some programming languages, for instance FORTRAN, do not support recursive procedures. Here we give the non-recursive version of the function:

```
function Palindrome(i,j: integer): boolean;
{ Determines if the word between the i-th and the j-th character is a palindrome }
  var p: boolean;
begin
  p:=true;
  while (i<j) and p do
    if a[i]<>a[j] then p:=false
    else begin i:=i+1; j:=j-1 end;
  Palindrome:=p;
end; {Palindrome}
```

Finally, let us code the *Palindrome* function in Logo:

```
TO PALINDROME :a
  IF (COUNT :a) < 2 [OUTPUT TRUE]
  IF (FIRST :a) = (LAST :a)
    [OUTPUT PALINDROME BUTFIRST BUTLAST :a]
  OUTPUT FALSE
END
```

It can be tested by the request

```
PRINT PALINDROME "MADAM
```

622D The basic idea of the algorithm is fairly evident:

- — a table of 1000 distinct random numbers between 1 and 1891864 is generated;
- — the records of the file with data on Slovenians whose sequence numbers are in the table are copied to the output file.

The main difficulties are caused by the requirement that the random numbers must be distinct, and the requirement from the statement of the problem that the file with the data may be searched through only once.

The second requirement is easily fulfilled by sorting the random numbers in the table ascendingly prior to copying and basing the output on the *merging* of sequences. The basis of merging is the observation that two or more sequences sorted in the same way may be arranged into a single "combined" sequence in a single pass through each sequence. Each time, the element with the smallest key value is processed. When copying our data the record sequence number is not a part of the record but is obtained by counting the records read.

The first requirement is fulfilled by inserting into the table only the numbers not in it.

The program looks as follows:

```
program Choose(census,sample);
{ Chooses a random sample of 1000 records from a given file. }
  const
    max = 1000;
    num = 1891864;
  type
    slovenian = record ··· end;
  var
    census, sample: file of slovenian;
    index: array [1..max] of integer;                { the table of random indices }
    n,i: integer;

  function Random: real; external;

  procedure Fill;
  { Fills the table of indices with num distinct random integers between 1 and max. }
    ...

  procedure Sort;
  { Sorts the table of indices in the ascending order. }
    ...
```

```
begin {Choose}
  reset(census); rewrite(sample);
  Fill; Sort;
  n:=1;
  for i:=1 to max do begin
    while n<index[i] do
      begin get(census); n:=n+1 end;
    sample↑:=census↑; put(sample);
  end; {for}
end. {Choose}
```

The introduction acquainted us with the sort algorithm, which has only to be adapted to the requirements of our program. The index table may be filled using the following algorithm:

```
  procedure Fill;
    var i,k,j: integer;
  begin
    i:=0;
    while i<max do begin
      k:=1 + trunc(num*Random);
      index[i+1]:=k; j:=1;
      while index[j] <> k do j:=j+1;
      if j = i+1 then i:=j;
    end; {while}
  end; {Fill}
```

We naturally suppose that the integers of our computer are large enough, and also that the *Random* function is good enough.

Since the current random number k is eligible only if it is distinct from all the previous, the algorithm described is of the order $O(max^2)$ (Some explanations about the complexity of an algorithm and about the symbol $O(\dots)$ may be found in the introduction to this chapter). The table may be more efficiently filled if it is represented as a hash table (see N. Wirth: *Algorithms+Data Structures=Programs*, Prentice-Hall, Englewood Cliffs 1976, pp. 264–274):

```
  ...
  const
    p = 1201;          { a prime number close to 1.2*max }
    empty = 2000000; { a value exceeding the largest allowable index }
    ...
  var
    ...
    index: array [1..p] of integer;
    ...
```

```
procedure Fill;
  var i,k,a,b: integer;
begin
  for i:=1 to p do index[i]:=empty;
  i:=0;
  while i<max do begin
    k:=1 + trunc(num*Random);
  { if the random number k is a new one, insert it into the table }
    a:=1 + k mod p; b:=1 + (k div p) mod p div 2;
    while (index[a] <> empty) and (index[a] <> k) do
      begin a:=(a+b) mod p; if a=0 then a:=p end;
    if index[a]=empty then
      begin index[a]:=k; i:=i+1 end;
  end; {while}
end; {Fill}
```

The empty places were marked with a value greater than any possible index so that after sorting these values move to the end of the table. The length of the table p must be a prime to ensure that the search passes through each element of the table. From the theory of hash tables we know that the *Fill* algorithm described above is of the order $O(max)$.

In principle, no sorting is necessary, since each sequence number n could be looked up in the index table. Due to the size of the file *census*, however, this is surely less efficient than the solution proposed above.

Perhaps the best solution would be to join filling and sorting into a single algorithm, in which the table *index* would be represented by a heap.

From computer literature the following algorithm is known, combining the effect of the *Fill* and *Sort* algorithms:

```
procedure FillSorted;
{ Fills the table index with max ascending random }
{ integers uniformly distributed over the interval 1..num. }
{ D.E. Knuth: The art of computer programming, Vol.2 – }
{ Seminumerical algorithms, Addison-Wesley, Reading 1980. }
  var i,k,n: integer;
begin
  k:=max; n:=num; i:=1;
  while k>0 do begin
    if Random<k/n then
      begin k:=k-1; index[max-k]:=i end;
    n:=n-1; i:=i+1;
  end; {while}
end; {FillSorted}
```

The algorithm described is of the order $O(num)$, and is not particularly efficient, since in our problem num is of the order max^2. But the selection itself is also of the order $O(num)$—so that (in the case of sequential files) improving the generation of the index table has no essential effect on the complexity of the overall solution. Therefore it is sensible to combine both algorithms into a single one. We obtain a new, very short solution:

```
program Choose(census,sample);
{ Chooses a random sample of 1000 records from a given file. }
  const
    max = 1000;
    num = 1891864;
  type
    slovenian = record ··· end;
  var
    census, sample: file of slovenian;
    n,k: integer;
  function Random: real; external;
begin {Choose}
  reset(census); rewrite(sample);
  k:=max; n:=num;
  while k>0 do begin
    if Random<k/n then
      begin k:=k-1; sample↑:=census↑; put(sample) end;
    get(census); n:=n-1;
  end; {while}
end. {Choose}
```

We also observe that no index table is necessary with this solution.

624D The procedure sorts the table a in ascending order using the *insertion sort* method (see introduction to this chapter and N. Wirth: *Algorithms+Data Structures=Programs*, Prentice-Hall, Englewood Cliffs 1976, pp. 68–69), based on the following idea.

The table is partitioned into a sorted and an unsorted portion. Initially, the sorted portion contains only the first element of the table $a[1]$. Then, in the i-th pass, $i=2,3,\ldots,n$ the element $a[i]$ is moved to its correct place in the sorted portion. Each time the sorted portion of the table increases by one element. So, after the algorithm terminates, the entire table is sorted.

The algorithm may be programmed in various ways. First, let us consider the FORTRAN 77 subroutine, presented in the text of the problem at the competition in addition to the Pascal version:

```
      SUBROUTINE WHAT(A,N)
      INTEGER N,A(N)
      INTEGER I,J,X
      DO 50 I = 2,N
         X = A(I)
         J = I-1
   10    CONTINUE
            IF (J.LT.1) GO TO 30
            IF (A(J).LE.X) GO TO 30
            A(J+1) = A(J)
            J = J-1
         GO TO 10
   30    CONTINUE
         A(J+1) = X
   50 CONTINUE
      RETURN
      END
```

We observe that it is simpler than the Pascal procedure. The reason the Pascal procedure is more elaborate is that the use of the **goto** statement is avoided. Even in Pascal one may write:

```
...
label 14;
...

begin
  for i:=2 to n do begin
    x:=a[i];
    j:=i-1;
    while j >= 1 do begin
      if a[j] <= x then goto 14;
      a[j+1]:=a[j]; j:=j-1;
    end; {while}
14: a[j+1]:=x;
  end; {for}
end;
```

The example shows the expressive weakness of Pascal which lacks the **exit** statement for writing loops with more exits. Other more modern languages, as well as some extensions of Pascal support this statement. The **exit** statement causes the loop in which it occurs to be exited (see Section 1.4 in the I. part). Using it, the **while** loop in the procedure would be rewritten as follows:

```
    while j >= 1 do begin
      if a[j] <= x then exit;
      a[j+1]:=a[j]; j:=j-1;
    end; {while}
```

Another possibility exists. If the value of expression a is *false*, so is the value of the expression a **and** b. Therefore, the value of expression b need not be computed. Some compilers account for that, others do not — standard Pascal allows both. Suppose that Pascal provided the logical operator **cand**:

$$a \textbf{ cand } b = \begin{cases} a & a = false \\ b & \text{otherwise} \end{cases}$$

Its sole difference from the **and** operator would be that the value of expression b would be computed only if the value of expression a would be true. In Ada the **cand** operation is called **and then**. In this case the **while** statement in the procedure might be written as follows:

```
while (j>=1) cand (a[j]>x) do
  begin a[j+1]:=a[j]; j:=j-1 end;
```

If **and** were used in this solution instead of **cand**, then during the execution the nonexistent element $a[0]$ could be used.

The algorithm may be shortened even in standard Pascal, if the table is supplemented by an additional element $a[0]$ — a sentinel (see the introduction to this chapter).

911D

a) Each program list is stored in a file whose records are composed of two fields. The first contains the program name, and the second its date. The program name may be up to 10 characters long. The date is represented by a sequence of six digits in the form yymmdd, in which the first two digits represent the last two digits of the year, the second pair of digits represents the number of the month, and the last pair the day. The date

9th January 1987 is represented by the number 870109

b) According to the problem specification, both lists are sorted by names and no name appears more than once in a single list. To avoid checking the contents of the files we assume that the same name and date represent the same program. Thus the solution may be based on merging (see N. Wirth: *Algorithms+Data Structures=Programs*, Prentice-Hall, Englewood Cliffs 1976, pp. 87–98). The details may be observed in the following program:

```
program Differences(anL,chL,output);
  type
    what = (none,andy,charlie,both);
  var
    anL, chL:
      file of record
        name: packed array [1..10] of char;
        date: packed array [1..6] of char;
      end;

  procedure Process(write,read: what);
  begin
    if      write=andy then writeln('Andy --> Charlie ',anL↑.name)
    else if write=charlie then writeln('Charlie --> Andy ',chL↑.name);
    if read in [andy,both] then get(anL);
    if read in [charlie,both] then get(chL);
  end; {Process}

begin {Differences}
  reset(anL); reset(chL);
  while not (eof(anL) and eof(chL)) do
    if             eof(anL)             then  Process(charlie,charlie)
    else if        eof(chL)             then  Process(andy,andy)
    else if anL↑.name > chL↑.name       then  Process(charlie,charlie)
    else if anL↑.name < chL↑.name       then  Process(andy,andy)
    else if anL↑.date  > chL↑.date      then  Process(andy,both)
    else if anL↑.date  < chL↑.date      then  Process(charlie,both)
    else                                      Process(none,both);
end. {Differences}
```

The condition *read* **in** [*charlie*,*both*] from the *Process* procedure could be written shorter as *read* > *andy*. However, nothing would be gained thereby, instead the program would only lose much readability and uniformity (symmetry).

The program does more than the problem requests, as it outputs the programs that Charlie should give to Andy. In this way the symmetry of the solution is preserved. The requested solution of the problem is obtained by omitting the **else** branch of the *Process* procedure.

Nevertheless the program is still not quite general—it might be useful to others as well, not just to Andy and Charlie. Therefore in the development of a more general program its variables and constants would be named differently: instead of *andy* we would probably write *firstOwner*, *secondList* instead of *chL* and so on. In a similar way the program output would be adapted.

923D Since the number of all cards is not large (30000 bits are needed), a table of bits may be used to determine the missing cards. Each bit in it records whether a particular card has been returned or not. It is reasonable to expect that some cards have not been handed out at all. The number of the last card in the series is denoted by *nCard*. Also, repeated cards will be intercepted, as well as invalid card numbers.

Let us write the program:

```
program Highway(input,output);
{ Checks the package of returned cards and outputs the missing ones. }
  const nMax = 30000;  { the maximum number of cards }
  var
    n,k: integer;
    nCard: integer;          { the number of the last card }
    missing: packed array [1..nMax] of boolean; { the table of cards }
begin
  readln(nCard);
  if nCard>nMax then writeln('Invalid last card number')
  else begin
    k:=0;
    for n:=1 to nCard do missing[n]:=true;
    while not eof do begin
      readln(n);
      if (n<1) or (n>nCard) then
        writeln('Invalid card number ',n:6)
      else if missing[n] then
        begin missing[n]:=false; k:=k+1 end
      else writeln('Duplicate card number ',n:10);
    end; {while}
    if k=nCard then writeln('No card is missing')
    else begin
      writeln(nCard-k:1,'cards are missing');
      for n:=1 to nCard do if missing[n] then writeln(n:6);
    end; {if}
  end; {if}
end. {Highway}
```

An interesting improvement to the solution would be the treatment of larger sequences of missing cards. In this case, it would be appropriate to output the results in the following way:

7–14, 21, 28–31, ...

The improvement is left to the reader.

934D The program *FindOut* is a slightly flawed program for the *bubble sort* (see N. Wirth: *Algorithms+Data Structures=Programs*, Prentice-Hall, Englewood Cliffs 1976, pp. 65–66). It differs from the usual algorithm in two details:

— it exchanges equal neighbours as well;
— it records the index of the later element of the last exchanged pair as the limit of the unsorted portion of the table.

Each of the two changes by itself would just slightly increase the number of steps in the program execution; when introduced both together they cause the loop does not terminate in some cases.

If the table contains equal items, the program exchanges them, and stores the index of the later of them as the limit of the unsorted portion of the table (the index i). Therefore it repeats the sort up to this point in the table again and again.

The data given contain a pair of equal numbers (50). Therefore the program does not terminate and so gives no output, even if it sorts the table correctly.

1024D The basic idea of the solution lies in the conclusion that the sum of all numbers on the tape plus the missing number equals the sum of all integers between 1 and 1 000 000.

It is known that

$$S_n = 1 + 2 + 3 + \cdots + (n-1) + n = \frac{n(n+1)}{2}$$

so that

$$S_{1\,000\,000} = 500\,000 \cdot 1\,000\,001 = 500\,000\,500\,000.$$

Only rare programming languages (on some computers) allow computation with such large numbers in their basic arithmetic. Our computer uses 64-bit integers, enough to represent the number $S_{1\,000\,000}$. We may also expect that such large integers may be handled by Pascal on this computer. The following program, then, solves the problem:

```
program Find(tape,output);
  var
    tape: file of integer;
    num: integer;
begin
  reset(tape); num:=500000500000;
  while not eof(tape) do begin num:=num−tape↑; get(tape) end;
  writeln('The missing number is ', num:1);
end. {Find}
```

In a more imaginative solution, the missing number — the difference between $S_{1\,000\,000}$ and the sum of the numbers on the tape — may be computed in the following "balanced" way.

```
program Find(tape,output);
  var
    tape: file of integer;
    k,n: integer;

begin
  reset(tape); k:=0; n:=0;
  while not eof(tape) do begin
    n:=n−tape↑; get(tape);
    while n<=0 do begin k:=k+1; n:=n+k end;
  end; {while}
  writeln('The number missing is ', n:1);
end. {Find}
```

It is not difficult to prove that with the assumptions of the problem statement the absolute values of variables n and k never exceed 1 000 000, and that after the loop terminates, $k = 1\,000\,000$ and n equals the missing number. This program may be executed on the majority of computers.

1031D

We observe the following property of the binary notation of numbers (the bits are counted from the least to the most significant): in the set of all 20-bit numbers the number of those with the i-th equal to 0 equals the number of those with the i-th bit equal to 1.

Let S denote a set of 20-bit numbers in which some are missing. Denote by $S_0(i)$ the set of those numbers from S with the i-th bit equal to 0, and by $S_1(i)$ the set of those with the i-th bit equal to 1. A number must be missing in the smaller of both sets. This leads us to the following concept of the algorithm (in each step of the algorithm below the symbol S_0 denotes the above set $S_0(i)$, and similarly S_1):

```
S:= { a set of 20-bit numbers (some are missing) };
x:=0; i:=0;
while S ≠ Ø do
   divide S into S0 and S1 with respect to the i-th bit;
   if |S0| ≤ |S1| then S:=S0
   else x:=x+2^i; S:=S1;
   i:=i+1
endwhile
```

When the algorithm terminates, the variable x contains one of the missing numbers.

The program in Pascal follows:

```
program Find(data,output);
{ Determines a number missing from the given set. }
  var
    tape: array [1..3] of file of integer;  { the files with the number sets }
    data: text;          { the file with the given numbers }
    source: integer;  { the number of the file with the current set S }
    x: integer;          { the missing number }
    bit: integer;        { the current bit value of the missing number }
    m,k: integer;
    n,                   { the cardinalities of the current sets S0 and S1 }
    onto: array [0..1] of integer;
                         { the numbers of the files with the sets S0 and S1 }

begin
{ copy the data to a tape }
  reset(data);
  rewrite(tape[1]);
  while not eof(data) do
    begin readln(data,tape[1]↑); put(tape[1]) end;
{ determine a missing number }
  source:=1;
  onto[0]:=2; onto[1]:=3;
  m:=1; x:=0;
  repeat
    n[0]:=0; n[1]:=0;
    reset(tape[source]);
    rewrite(tape[onto[0]]); rewrite(tape[onto[1]]);
    while not eof(tape[source]) do begin
      bit:=(tape[source]↑ div m) mod 2;
      n[bit]:=n[bit]+1;
      tape[onto[bit]]↑:=tape[source]↑; put(tape[onto[bit]]);
      get(tape[source]);
    end; {while}
    if n[0] <= n[1] then bit:=0
    else begin bit:=1; x:=x+m end;
    k:=source; source:=onto[bit]; onto[bit]:=k; m:=2*m;
  until n[bit]=0;
  writeln('The number ',x:1,' is missing on the tape.');
end. {Find}
```

1034D Let us observe what happens in the central loop of the program:

```
x:=1; s:=0;
repeat s:=s+f[x]; x:=x+1 until s>=(n div 2);
```

for some sets of data:

a)	200×1,	400×2,	400×3
b)	400×1,	200×2,	400×3
c)	400×1,	400×2,	200×3

a)

s	x
	1
0	
200	
	2
600	
	3

b)

s	x
	1
0	
400	
	2
600	
	3

c)

s	x
	1
0	
400	
	2
800	
	3

We observe that in the last case the program works incorrectly. That is, we would expect that in case (c) 2 would be chosen as the boundary value, since 400 is closer to half of all data read than 800. In this case, the boundary value determined by variable s has escaped too far.

When the **repeat** loop terminates we must therefore verify that the boundary does not escape. This is achieved by the following **if** statement

```
if ((n div 2)-s+f[x-1]) < (s-(n div 2)) then
  begin x:=x-1; s:=s-f[x] end;
```

inserted immediately after the **repeat** statement. See also solution 712G.

Let us conclude by translating the above into mathematical language. Define the function $s(x)$ for x between 1 and m as:

$$s(x) = \sum_{j=1}^{x} f_j - \sum_{j=x+1}^{m} f_j = 2 \cdot \sum_{j=1}^{x} f_j - n$$

adding that $s(0) = -n$. In $s(x)$ the first sum counts the elements not greater than the boundary value, and the second the larger elements. Since function s strictly increases, and $s(0) = -n$, $s(m) = n$, the numbers x^- and x^+ exist such that

$$x^- = \max\{x : s(x) \le 0\} \quad \text{in} \quad x^+ = \min\{x : s(x) > 0\}$$

Further, define the function $r(x)$:

$$r(x) = |s(x)|$$

measuring the difference in the sums from the definition of the function s. Function r is non-negative everywhere, we denote its minimum by x^*. It is easily seen that x^* equals either x^- or x^+. The program in the statement of the problem should compute x^*, but finds x^+; the improved program correctly decides between x^- and x^+.

Chapter E

Graphs

A **graph** $G = (V, L)$ consists of a non-empty set of **vertices** V and a set of **lines** L. Each line joins a pair of vertices from V — the **endpoints** of the line. The lines may be **directed** or **undirected**; in the former case they are called **arcs** instead of lines, and in the latter they are called **edges**. By $p(u, v)$ we denote that the arc p leads from its **initial vertex** u to its **terminal vertex** v; by $q(x{:}y)$ (or equivalently, $q(y{:}x)$) we denote that the edge q joins the vertices x and y. This may be drawn as follows:

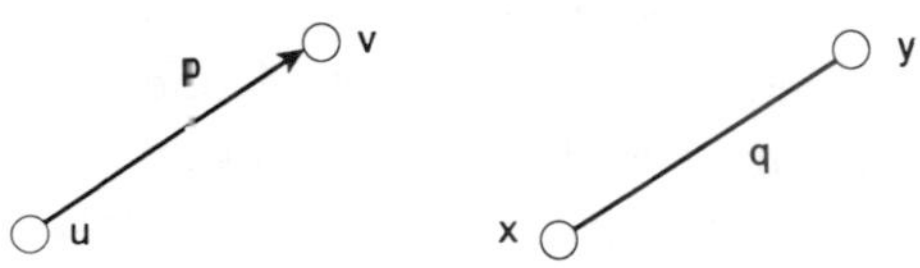

Figure E1: An arc and an edge

When both endpoints of a line are equal (the same vertex), the line is called a **loop**.

A graph is **undirected** if all its lines are undirected; and is **directed** if all its lines are directed. An undirected graph is **simple** if there are no loops in it, and there is at most one edge joining each pair of its vertices, while a directed graph is simple if each pair of its vertices is joined by at most one arc in each direction.

The type of a line determines the direction of movement along it — as in a road: along an edge we may move in both directions, while along an arc we may only move from its initial towards the terminal vertex. A sequence of successive moves along lines leading from one vertex of a graph to another is called a walk.

More precisely, a **walk** through a graph G is a finite sequence of vertices and lines of a graph

$$S(v_0, v_k) = v_0 p_1 v_1 p_2 v_2 \ldots v_{k-1} p_k v_k$$

where $p_i(v_{i-1}, v_i)$ or $p_i(v_{i-1} : v_i)$ for any $i = 1, 2, \ldots, k$. The vertex v_0 is called the **start**, the vertex v_k is the **end**, and k is the **length** of the walk. A walk leading from a vertex back to itself is called a **closed walk**. A walk is **elementary** if all its vertices excluding the start and the end are distinct. A simple walk is called a **path**, while a simple closed walk is called a **cycle**.

A vertex u is **reachable** from a vertex v if there is a walk in G starting at v and ending at u. A graph is **strongly connected** if for any pair of its vertices the first is reachable from the other; it is (**weakly**) **connected** if for any pair of its vertices the first is reachable from the second regardless of the directions of the lines.

A graph G is described by defining the set of its vertices V and the set of its lines L. For each line, its endpoints as well as its type must be given (directed/undirected). The description may be considerably compacted if all lines are of the same type, and if the labels (the names) of the vertices are of no interest. In this case, the vertices are represented by successive numbers $1, 2, 3, \ldots, n$; the lines are represented by the pairs of their endpoints. If a pair of vertices is joined by several lines, the corresponding pair of endpoints repeats an appropriate number of times. A still more compact representation is obtained by grouping together all lines starting at a given vertex. This set of lines is called the **star** of a given vertex. In the description of a star, the common vertex may be "taken out". The description of a graph using the stars of its vertices forms the basis of most representations of graphs in a computer.

In Figure E2, two notations of a given directed graph by stars are presented. The first one is simpler, but is appropriate only if the graph does not change significantly during computation; the second is much more flexible, but requires much caution in programming. In the first representation, the graph is expressed by the number of vertices v, a table of starts s, and the table of adjacent vertices a. The elements of the table a from the $s[i]$-th to the $(s[i+1]-1)$-th form the list of the vertices adjacent to the vertex i. If $s[i] = s[i+1]$, the vertex i has no adjacent vertices. The second representation also includes the number of vertices v, and the table of starts s, which contains pointers to circular lists of adjacent vertices. Each element of this list in turn consists of the number of the adjacent vertex as well as a pointer to the successive element in the list. Solution 823E describes how the input data for a graph may be prepared and read from a file.

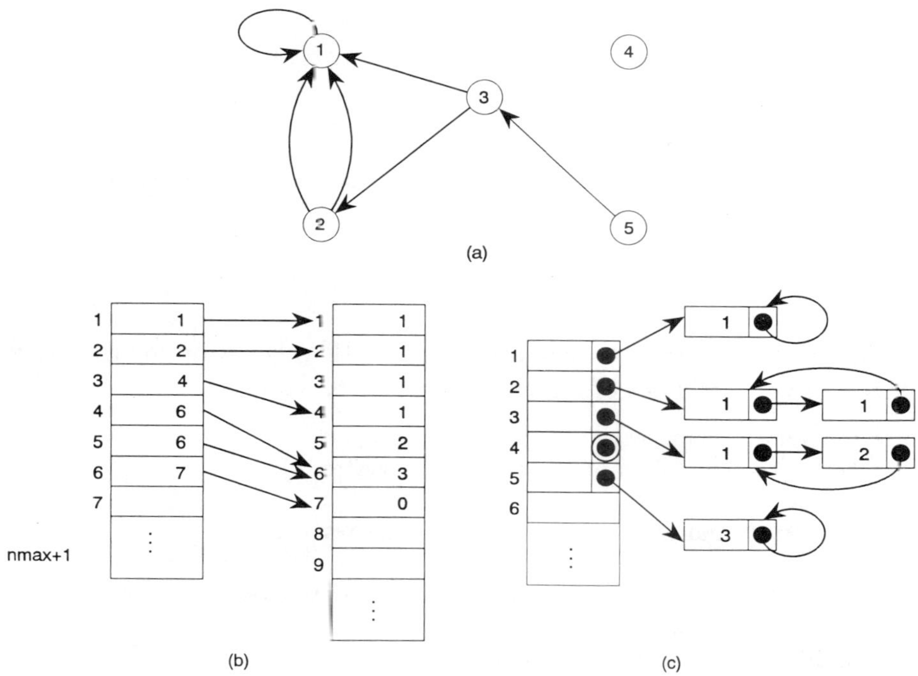

Figure E2: An example of a graph and a pair of its representations

To represent simple graphs, or if multiplicity of lines is not important, a graph may be represented by a table — the **adjacency matrix**:

```
var a: packed array [1..nmax,1..nmax] of boolean;
```

whose values are determined as follows:

$$a[i,j] = \begin{cases} \textit{true} & \text{there is a line leading from the vertex } i \text{ to } j \\ \textit{false} & \text{otherwise} \end{cases}$$

If we substitute 1 for *true* and 0 for *false*, the following matrix represents the graph from the Figure E2(a):

	1	2	3	4	5
1	1	0	0	0	0
2	1	0	0	0	0
3	1	1	0	0	0
4	0	0	0	0	0
5	0	0	1	0	0

In this representation, the fact that the arc (2,1) is a duplicate is lost.

The characteristics of particular types of graphs allow special representations. For instance, a **tree** may be described by defining the "father" of each vertex:

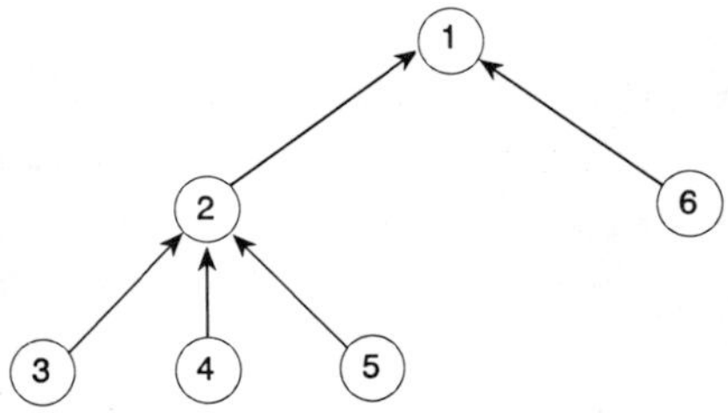

1	0
2	1
3	2
4	2
5	2
6	1

Figure E3: An example of a tree

Many algorithms in graph theory are based on the algorithm for the **traversal** or **search** of vertices/lines of a graph from a given vertex v:

```
use the vertex v; traversed:={v}; open:=Star(v);
reached:={the endpoints of the star of the vertex v};
while not all traversed do
   take (select and remove) a line p from the set open;
   use the line p;
   if an untraversed endpoint t of the line p exists then
      use the vertex t;
      add all lines not yet in the set open
        from the star of the vertex t to this set;
      reached:=reached ∪ {the endpoints of the lines added};
      traversed:=traversed ∪ {t};
   endif
endwhile
```

The details of each problem are contained in the procedures "use the vertex" and "use the line". One of them may be empty as well.

The type of the traversal is determined by the answers to the following questions:

— *What is a star composed of*? If it consists only of the lines leaving a given vertex, the algorithm traverses all vertices/lines reachable from the vertex v; if also the entering lines are added, the algorithm traverses all vertices/lines in the connected component of the graph to which the vertex v belongs.

— *When has everything been traversed*? If the traversal finishes when the set of open lines becomes empty, the algorithm traverses all (reachable) lines; if the traversal terminates when the set of the traversed vertices becomes equal to the set of all vertices, all (reachable) vertices are traversed.

In a strongly connected graph, or, if the directions of arcs are ignored, in a weakly connected graph, the following is true:

$$open = \emptyset \;\Rightarrow\; traversed = V$$

In this case, all statements referring to the set of reached vertices may be removed from the search algorithm.

Another possibility for structuring the algorithm is provided by the representation of the set of open lines and by the principle for adding and selection of the lines from it. If this set is represented by a list, and the last line to be added is always selected first, we deal with a stack. This algorithm is called the **depth-first traversal**. It is closely connected to recursive implementations of the traversal, in which the set of the open lines may be managed by the recursion mechanism. We may, however, decide to select the lines in the same order as they have been added to the list. In this case, we deal with a queue; the algorithm is called the **breadth-first traversal**. When all lines are provided with some value, and in each step the line with the largest value is selected, the **priority traversal** is obtained. The value of an line may be determined according to the nature of the problem; or else they may be determined randomly at the time of adding to the set. In this case, the algorithm is called the **random traversal**.

223E The first idea of the algorithm is probably the following:

— read and prepare the data;
— choose the direction of travel, and try touring the road with each car k, $k = 1, 2, \ldots, n$ until a solution is found;
— if the attempt was not successful, try in the opposite direction;
— output the travel.

Reconsidering, we see that the **if** in the algorithm is superfluous — the road may always be toured in the direction chosen.

Let us choose the direction of the tour. Assume the following data are available for each car i and the direction selected:

dist[i] — the distance to the subsequent car in the selected direction
reach[i] — the distance which may be traversed using the fuel in its tank

The key conclusion is: *a car exists with enough fuel to reach the next car in the selected direction.*

Suppose there is no such car. Then, for each car i, the following would be true:

$$reach[i] < dist[i]$$

and summing for all cars:

the total travel of all cars < the length of the road

This contradicts the statement of the problem that all cars together have enough fuel for a single tour.

Suppose the car k can reach its successor k'. According to the text of the problem, all the fuel may be transferred from the car k' to the car k. The problem is now equivalent to a problem without the car k', in which

$$reach[k] \leftarrow reach[k] + reach[k']$$
$$dist[k] \leftarrow dist[k] + dist[k']$$

We obtained a problem of the same kind with $n - 1$ cars. Our conclusion still holds. The procedure may thus be repeated, and a problem with $n - 2$ cars obtained, etc. This is repeated until a single car is left, which is capable of touring the entire circle.

The reasoning above leads us to an effective solution. Some more remarks are due:

In the *dist* table, the positions (its distance from a preselected point) of each car are stored at first. We assume that these data are sorted increasingly. An additional table is used:

next[*i*] ... the number of the next car

which permits a more effective implementation of the algorithm.

One final remark is due before we deal with the program. We assume that the data are integers, so that the problems with real arithmetic are avoided. As known, the following may be true in a computer:

$$\frac{1}{3} + \frac{1}{3} + \frac{1}{3} < \frac{1}{4} + \frac{1}{4} + \frac{1}{2}$$

Thus, the computer might neglect our proof (see the solution 1134B). It would be interesting to find real data, for which the program below works incorrectly.

```
program CircularTour(input,output);
{ Determines the car which can tour the entire circle, and }
{ outputs the tour. }
  const nmax = 100;
  var
    n,i,k,j,length,r,fuel: integer;
    dist,reach,tDist,tReach: array [1..nmax] of integer;
    next: array [1..nmax] of integer;
begin
{ read the data }
  n:=0;
  while not eof do
    begin n:=n+1; readln(dist[n],reach[n]) end;
{ prepare the data }
  r:=dist[1]; length:=reach[n];
  for i:=1 to n-1 do
    begin dist[i]:=dist[i+1]-dist[i]; length:=length+reach[i]; next[i]:=i+1 end;
  dist[n]:=length+r-dist[n];
  next[n]:=1;
{ determine the starting point - the car which may tour the entire circle }
  k:=1; tDist:=dist; tReach:=reach;
  for i:=1 to n-1 do begin
    while tDist[k] > tReach[k] do k:=next[k];
    j:=next[k];
```

```
  { exclude the j-th car }
    tDist[k]:=tDist[k]+tDist[j]; tReach[k]:=tReach[k]+tReach[j];
    next[k]:=next[j];
  end; {for}
{ output the tour }
  fuel:=0;
  writeln('      from    to     fuel    distance   remainder');
  for i:=1 to n do begin
    fuel:=fuel+reach[k]; j:=(k mod n)+1;
    write(k:7,j:7,fuel:10,dist[k]:10);
    fuel:=fuel-dist[k]; k:=j;
    writeln(fuel:10);
  end; {for}
end. {CircularTour}
```

423E Observe an example of such a circular route:

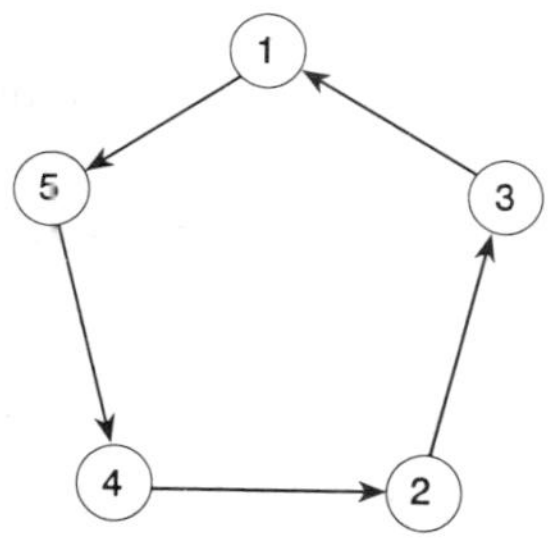

Figure E4: A circular route

It may be described by the following sequence of numbers (first, the number of stops, then the pairs (stop, next stop)):

5   5 4   1 5   4 2   3 1   2 3

The text of the problem also states that the data are correct — therefore we must output n stops. Since the route is circular, we may start the "ride" on any stop. We choose the stop 1.

The Pascal program follows:

```
program Route(input,output);
{ Output the numbers of bus stops on a circular route. }
  const nmax = 1980;
  var
    p: array [1..nmax] of integer; { the table of stop successors }
    n,i,k: integer;
```

```
begin
  read(n); for i:=1 to n do read(k,p[k]);
  k:=1;
  for i:=1 to n do begin writeln(k); k:=p[k] end;
end. {Route}
```

525E Denote by s the starting point and by f the final point. The set of points is partitioned into the set of the reached points and the set of the remaining ones. In the set of the reached points, we further distinguish the subset of open points, for which we have not yet seen what can be reached from them. The set of the points reachable from s is obtained by the following algorithm:

```
reached:={s}; open:={s};
while open ≠ ∅ do
  select a point t from the set of open points;
  determine the unreached neighbours of the point t;
  open:=open ∪ neighbours \ {t};
  reached:=reached ∪ neighbours
endwhile
```

If the point f is reachable from s, it will appear in the set of reached points. The search may be then terminated.

When coding the above algorithm in Pascal, the deficiencies of Pascal in set manipulation become evident. In the determination of the unreached neighbours, the following form of the **for** statement would be appropriate:

```
for x in S do A;
```

performing the statement A for each element x of the set S. Instead, it must be expressed with available means, at the price of lesser readability and effectiveness of the program. Suppose that *sf* is the first and *sl* is the last element of the scalar type over which the set S is defined. Then, the above statement is expressed as

```
for x:=ss to sf do if x in S then A;
```

To select a point from a set the function $min(S)$ would be appropriate, returning as its value the minimum element of the set S. Actually, any point may be chosen. If the function $min(S)$ was provided, it would probably be the best way of selection; in our case, it is probably better to select the first succeeding point.

Some compilers may impose further limitations on the set size. The Pascal program follows:

```
program Reach(input,output);
{ Determines whether a given final point may be reached }
{ from a given starting point. }
  const nmax = 100;
  var
    n,             { the number of points }
    s,f,           { the starting and the final point }
    i,t,r: integer;
    a: real;       { the maximum allowed length of a segment }
    x,y: array [1..nmax] of real; { the point coordinates }
    reached,neighbours,open: set of 1..nmax;

  function D(u,v: integer): real;
  { Computes the distance between the points u and v. }
  begin
    D:=sqrt(sqr(x[u]-x[v]) + sqr(y[u]-y[v]));
  end; {D}

begin {Reach}
  read(n);
  for i:=1 to n do read(x[i],y[i]);
  read(s,f,a); reached:=[s]; open:=[s]; t:=s-1;
  while (open<>[ ]) and not (f in reached) do begin
    repeat t:=(t mod n)+1 until t in open;
    neighbours:=[ ];
    for r:=1 to n do
      if not (r in reached) then  if D(t,r)<a then neighbours:=neighbours+[r];
    open:=open+neighbours-[t]; reached:=reached+neighbours;
  end; {while}
  write('The point ',f:3,' is '); if not f in reached then write('not');
  writeln(' reachable from the point ',s:3);
end. {Reach}
```

A tree rooted at s corresponds to any search. As we have mentioned, such a tree may be represented by a table in which the i-th element contains its "father" — the element from which the i-th element was reached. This enables us to improve the program to output the path from the starting to the final point, if it exists at all.

To do this, we use the table

```
father: array [1..nmax] of integer;
```

and precede the **while** loop by the statement

```
father[s]:=0;
```

Also, the statement **if** in the **for** loop must be extended

```
if D(t,r)<a then begin neighbours:=neighbours+[r]; father[r]:=t end;
```

and at the end, the path printed out

```
    if f in reached then begin
      t:=f; repeat writeln(t); t:=father[t] until t=0;
      writeln(s);
    end; {if}
```

722E The problem requests that all subsequences leading from a crossing to itself are removed from the given sequence of crossing numbers. In the following program this is done at the same time as the data are read:

```
program Path(input,output);
{ Shortens a given walk through a labyrinth into a simple walk. }
  const nc = 101; { = 1+max crossings }
  var
    a,n,i: integer;
    c: array [1..nc] of integer;
begin
  writeln('The walk through a labyrinth');
  n:=0;
  while not eof do begin
    readln(a); writeln(a); n:=n+1; c[n]:=a;
    i:=1; while c[i]<>a do i:=i+1;
    n:=i;
  end; {while}
  writeln('The shortened walk');
  for i:=1 to n do writeln(c[i]);
end. {Path}
```

The advantage of the solution described is that it only needs a table for a single element longer than the number of distinct crossings of the walk, regardless of the actual length of the original walk.

If the walk is already present in the first m elements of the table c, it may be "shortened" as follows:

```
  ...
  n:=0;
  for f:=1 to m do begin
    n:=n+1; c[n]:=p[f];
    i:=1; while c[i]<>p[n] do i:=i+1;
    n:=i;
  end; {for}
  ...
```

823E The problem is based on the following well known theorem of the graph theory (see G. Chartrand, *Introductory Graph Theory*, Dover, New York 1985, pp. 155-159):

In any tournament, a Hamilton path exists.

Here, a tournament is a graph of a special form, in which any pair of vertices is connected by an arc. The Hamilton path through a graph is a walk, which leads through all vertices of a graph, and passes through each exactly once. It will be briefly encountered in solution 1032B. The proof of this theorem is constructive, and may be used as the base of the algorithm to determine the requested path.

The proof proceeds with the mathematical induction. In the case of two towns, the path is determined by the arc that joins them. Assume that the path through n towns may be found. We shall prove that the path through $n + 1$ towns can also be found.

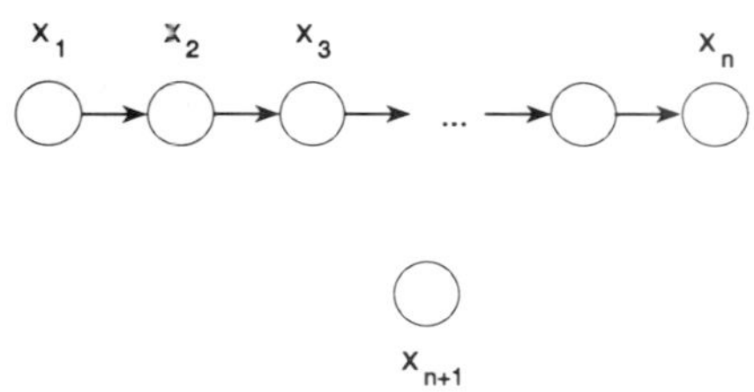

Figure E5: The path through n towns

There are three cases to consider:

a) if the arc (x_n, x_{n+1}) exists, the path may be extended at its end;
b) if the arc (x_{n+1}, x_1) exists, the path may be extended at its start;
c) neither (a) nor (b) is true — in this case (see Figure E6) the arcs (x_{n+1}, x_n) and (x_1, x_{n+1}) exist.

Let x_{r+1} denote the first vertex of the path at which the line (x_{n+1}, x_{r+1}) exists.

Such a point must certainly exist — if there is no other, x_n is appropriate. Then, the arc (x_r, x_{r+1}) is removed from the path and replaced by the arcs (x_r, x_{n+1}) and (x_{n+1}, x_{r+1}). Thus, a path through all $n + 1$ vertices has been obtained.

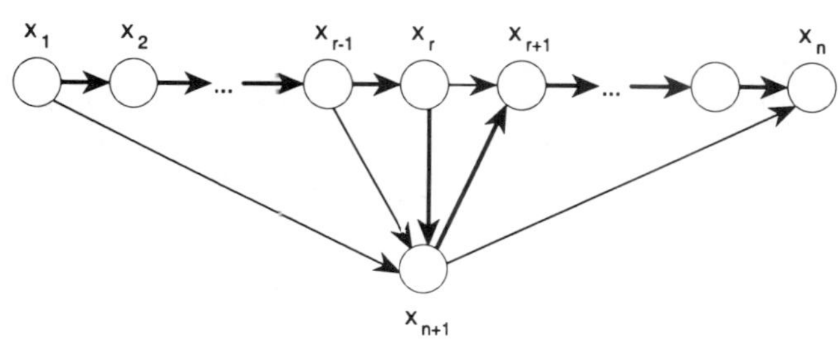

Figure E6: The path through $n + 1$ towns

On the input file, the data for the connections between towns are represented as a sequence of integers. The first integer specifies the number of all towns, while the meaning of the rest follows:

— if the number is negative, it starts the list of the numbers of towns which may be reached from the town with the numbers equal to the absolute value of the number read;

— if the number is positive it is an element of a list of towns.

The data from the text of the problem would thus be written as:

$$5 \quad -1\ 2\ 3\ 4\ 5 \quad -2\ 3\ 4 \quad -3\ 4\ 5 \quad -5\ 2\ 4$$

In the program, the connections are represented by a logical table — the adjacency matrix a

$a[i,j] \Leftrightarrow$ a road leads from the town i to the town j

and the requested path is represented by the table *path*

$path[i] \Leftrightarrow$ the number of the town to which the path leads from the town i on

and two indices sTw in eTw, denoting the numbers of towns at which the path starts and ends. The path $1,5,2,3,4$ from the text of the problem would be represented as shown in Figure E7.

sTw=1 eTw=4

path	5	3	4	0	2
	1	2	3	4	5

Figure E7: The representation of a path

The program follows:

```
program Hamilton(input,output);
{ Determines the Hamilton path. }
  const nmax = 100;  { the maximum number of towns }
  type
    adjMatr = packed array [1..nmax,1..nmax] of boolean;
    pathT = array [1..nmax] of integer;
  var
    n: integer;       { the number of towns }
    a: adjMatr;       { a[i,j] <==> there is a road leading from the town i to the town j }
    path: pathT;      { path[i] is the number of the town to which the path leads from the tov
    sTw: integer;     { the number of the first town on the path }

  function ReadData(var n: integer; var a: adjMatr): boolean;
  { Read the data (with some effort to make reading robust). }
    var
      m,j: integer;
      ok: boolean;
```

```
  procedure SkipSpaces;
  { Skips all unnecessary spaces and new-lines to make reading }
  { of numbers and testing for end of file work correctly. The }
  { reading strictly adheres to Pascal standard and is probably }
  { too complicated for the majority of compilers. }
    var done: boolean;
  begin
    done:=false;
    while not done do begin
      if eof(input) then done:=true
      else if input↑<>' ' then done:=true
      else get(input);
    end; {while}
  end; {SkipSpaces}

  function RdTest(min,max: integer; var x: integer): boolean;
  { Reads an integer x and tests whether min<=abs(x)<=max. }
  begin
    read(x); SkipSpaces;
    RdTest:=(abs(x)>=min) and (abs(x)<=max);
  end; {RdTest}

begin {ReadData}
  ok:=true;
  SkipSpaces;
  if eof(input) then
    begin writeln('Empty input file'); ok:=false end
  else if not RdTest(1,nmax,n) then
    begin writeln('Invalid number of towns ',n:1); ok:=false end
  else if n<0 then
    begin writeln('The number of towns is negative ',n:1); ok:=false end
  else begin
    for m:=1 to n do
      for j:=1 to n do a[m,j]:=false;
    m:=0;
    while not eof(input) and ok do begin
      if not RdTest(1,n,j) then
        begin writeln('Invalid town number ',j:1); ok:=false end
      else if j<0 then m:=-j
      else if m>0 then a[m,j]:=true
      else begin writeln('No road starts in town ',j:1); ok:=false end;
    end; {while}
  end; {if}
  ReadData:=ok;
end; {ReadData}

function CheckArcs(n: integer; var a: adjMatr): boolean;
{ Checks whether all roads exist and whether they are one-way. }
```

```
    var
      m,j: integer;
      ok: boolean;
  begin
    ok:=true;
    for m:=1 to n do
      for j:=m+1 to n do
        if a[m,j]=a[j,m] then
          begin writeln('Invalid pair (',m:1,',',j:1,')'); ok:=false end;
    CheckArcs:=ok;
  end; {CheckArcs}

  procedure FindPath
      (n: integer; var a: adjMatr; var sTw: integer; var path: pathT);
  { Determines the path through all towns. }
    var
      eTw: integer;                { the number of the last town of the current path }
      k,r: integer;
  begin
    if n=1 then begin sTw:=1; path[1]:=0 end
    else begin
    { determine the path between the towns 1 and 2 }
      if a[1,2] then begin sTw:=1; eTw:=2 end
                else begin sTw:=2; eTw:=1 end;
      path[sTw]:=eTw; path[eTw]:=0;
    { add other towns }
      for k:=3 to n do begin
        if a[eTw,k] then begin path[eTw]:=k; path[k]:=0; eTw:=k end
        else if a[k,sTw] then begin path[k]:=sTw; sTw:=k end
        else begin
          r:=sTw; while a[path[r],k] do r:=path[r];
          path[k]:=path[r]; path[r]:=k;
        end; {if}
      end; {for}
    end; {if}
  end; {FindPath}

  procedure WritePath(sTw: integer; var path: pathT);
  { Output the path. }
    var r: integer;
  begin
    writeln('The path leads through the towns in the following sequence:');
    r:=sTw;  while r<>0 do begin writeln(r); r:=path[r] end;
  end; {WritePath}

begin {Hamilton}
  if ReadData(n,a) then if CheckArcs(n,a) then
    begin FindPath(n,a,sTw,path); WritePath(sTw,path) end;
end. {Hamilton}
```

Chapter F

Real-Time Process Control

The area of the problems in this chapter may be roughly defined as real-time process control. At least half of these problems originate in the topics encountered in computer operating systems, although they are sometimes transposed into a more common environment for better understanding. The topics include the following concepts:

- concurrent execution of programs, concurrent operation of several computers;
- asynchronous events and related problems:
  - resource allocation,
  - a critical section,
  - a deadlock;
- an interrupt;
- the synchronization of a computer with the environment, handshaking;
- communication between processes;
- the timer queue;
- data structures:
  - a buffer;
  - a ring buffer;
  - a queue;

The other half of the exercises poses problems originating in the principles of operation of particular devices (computer peripherals or other more or less common appliances). The following devices will be encountered:

— a telephone
— an electronic organ — a synthesizer
— a bar code reader
— an analog/digital converter, a digital voltmeter
— robots and manipulators (the feedback loop, sensors)
— a drum printer
— a logic analyzer
— a position encoder
— a Geiger-Müller meter
— a statistical multiplexer
— a calculator keyboard

At first glance, the common point of all solutions (with rare exceptions) is the never-ending execution of the program. The program has to observe the environment in a loop and act appropriately in case of particular events. In all the problems, the expected time interval between changes in the environment is large relative to the execution speed of the computer instructions. Where necessary the texts of the problems stress that the execution time is negligible, but also that the program may not depend on equal execution speed (for instance, in synchronization).

In the solutions, most cases of waiting for external events are implemented using a tight loop continuously testing a particular condition. This type of implementation is applicable only on computers executing a single process at a time. Most operating systems of more resourceful computers provide other mechanisms for synchronization and waiting for external events, which make the computer available to other processes during the wait. Examples of such mechanisms are semaphores, event flags, signals, mailboxes, interrupts, and similar. For simplicity, these mechanisms were avoided in most solutions, and the "brute-force method" was used — waiting for an event in a tight loop.

Real-time programming is rarely encountered in computer literature for high schools. Nevertheless, as the experience from the competitions shows, the problems of this type present no conceptual difficulties to the students not familiar with them. Probably the main reason these problems are neglected is that their solutions are hard to implement on mainframes with classic peripherals — when computer science fought its way into high schools, no home or personal computers were available. Young enthusiasts with home computers know such problems in detail, but they must regrettably deal with them without systematic knowledge and appropriate literature.

213F Although the solution is easy, let us first look at the problem from a general viewpoint. We deal with a pair of asynchronous processes (for example, the lifts); the first process produces something (for instance, generates data, or — in our case — supplies containers), the other consumes it (for instance, uses the data, or takes away the containers). The term *asynchronous* stresses the time independence of both processes; each runs with its own speed, independent of any other process or any common synchronization signal. Some examples of such pairs of processes are: typing — printing, entrance into a bank — bank counter; processes controlling inter-computer communication, etc. The problem requests us to provide the link between the producer and the consumer. The easiest (and the worst) solution of the connection between the producer and the consumer is the following:

```
repeat
   wait for a product from the producer;
   wait until the consumer needs the product;
   transfer the product from the producer to the consumer;
forever
```

The main problem with this solution is that it exploits both processes poorly: the consumer cannot consume until the producer makes a product available; and the producer may not produce it until the consumer has used up the previous product.

To fully employ both processes, a store of appropriate size is needed where the products are accumulated when the producer produces faster than the consumer may consume, and from where the consumer may obtain products when the producer lags behind the consumption. The most important guideline is to exploit both processes and use their entire capabilities. This is one of the fundamental concepts of computer operating systems: peripheral devices must be fully utilized and the system must immediately react when a device reports it has accomplished its task. In this way the simultaneous activity of the largest number of peripheral devices is ensured.

When one of the processes is constantly slower than the other, a mechanism is needed to stop the faster process — sometimes all that is needed is to ignore the inactivity of a process (in our problem the lifts wait, until they are sent away; also, this is the case with a fast printer which remains without anything to print). Some cases, however, require special action (for instance, the keyboard must be locked if the user constantly types faster than the printer can print). Solutions 832F and 913A describe conceptually the same problem.

Let us return to our solution. The supply lift represents the producer process, which is not synchronous to the take-away lift (which may be slower or faster); nevertheless, after the delivery of each new box it waits until it is permitted to leave. We may keep it in this way if there is not enough space in the store for any new containers. The take-away lift is the consumer process, for which the same is true. Since the size of the store is limited, two boundary cases arise:

— the store is full, and the take-away lift is absent or full. In this case the supply lift must wait to be unloaded;
— the store is empty, and the supply lift is absent or empty: the take-away lift must wait.

Neither of the boundary cases requires special action, since the lifts always wait to be sent away.

The algorithm is devised to monitor continuously the state of the environment, both lifts and the store, to avoid any lift waiting idle unnecessarily. The wait is accomplished simply by repeatedly monitoring the environment.

We might make the effort to handle the case of transferring a container directly from the supply lift to the take-away one when both arrive at the same moment—but due to the low probability of such an event and marginal saving in time in this case we neglected this possibility completely.

In our solution the ordering of the store is not important. When selecting a container to be taken away, any one may be chosen. In a real warehouse it is usually important how long the products are stored in the store since storing them for too long a period lowers their quality. From such a store the containers must always be taken out in the same sequence as they arrived.

The containers thus ordered may be considered a queue. New containers are added at its tail and taken away at its head—as in the queue at a bank counter. Such data structure is called a **queue**, or sometimes FIFO (**first in**—**first out**: first come, first served). The queue will be used in solution 832F, our solution here may avoid its use:

```
repeat
   if the take-away lift is empty and the store is not empty then
     transfer a container from the store to the take-away lift;
   if the take-away lift is full then
     send the take-away lift away;
   if the supply lift is full and the store is not full then
     transfer a container from the supply lift to the store;
   if the supply lift is empty then
     send the supply lift away;
forever
```

Let us rewrite the solution in Pascal (although the problem does not request that). A cautious reader may notice that the program is derived from the above algorithm, but also that its operation slightly differs from it although this is not evident from the operation of the robot. The difference is that the algorithm above sends the take-away lift away in the same iteration of the loop, while the program below does it in the next pass (the same is true for the supply side).

In general, the sequence of the statements in the algorithm described could be arbitrarily changed. With the changes, the internal operation of the program would change, while the robot and both lifts would still function as described above. The sequence used was chosen to make the algorithm as evident as possible.

From the program it is also evident how it records to which extent the store is occupied.

```
program Robot;
{ Transfer of containers from one lift to the other. }
  const
    maxc = 10;                                    { the size of the store }
  type
    place = (SUPPLY,TAKEAWAY,STORE);  { the location names }
    stat = (EMPTY,FULL,ABSENT);               { the state names }
  var c: integer;              { the number of containers in the store}

  function State(l: place): stat;     external;
  procedure Transfer(l1,l2: place); external;
  procedure Send(l: place);          external;

begin {Robot}
  c:=0;  { initially the store is empty }
  repeat
    case State(TAKEAWAY) of
      EMPTY: if c>0 then begin Transfer(STORE,TAKEAWAY); c:=c-1 end;
      FULL: Send(TAKEAWAY);
      ABSENT: ;
    end; {case}
    case State(SUPPLY) of
      EMPTY: Send(SUPPLY);
      FULL: if c<maxc then begin Transfer(SUPPLY,STORE); c:=c+1 end;
      ABSENT: ;
    end; {case}
  until false;
end. {Robot}
```

In addition let us observe, how the program with modified **case** statements would function:

```
  case State(TAKEAWAY) of
    EMPTY:
      if c>0 then
        begin Transfer(STORE,TAKEAWAY); c:=c-1; Send(TAKEAWAY) end;
    FULL,ABSENT: ;
  end; {case}
```

```
case State(SUPPLY) of
  FULL:
    if c<maxc then
      begin Transfer(SUPPLY,STORE); c:=c+1; Send(SUPPLY) end;
  EMPTY,ABSENT: ;
end; {case}
```

In no regular case does the change influence the operation of the robot and both lifts. But what would happen if an empty supply lift arrived, or a full take-away lift? Or in the case of a lift accidentally missing the command *Send*? What would happen if a lift got stuck? Try to find out how our program reacts to these and similar irregular events.

From our example we see that sometimes, using minimum effort, programs may be devised to react correctly to or at least predictably handle unusual events and try to lessen troubles. Especially in the case of large programs it is extremely important that portions of the programs are written robustly (*fault tolerantly*) so that they survive cases of incorrect usage or erroneous (unusual) data. Additional effort to anticipate such "impossible" events at the design time is amply rewarded both at the time of program development and during its later use. So don't be surprised to see in our programs statements or tests that seem unnecessary for the normal operation of the program.

312F

Before solving the problem let us consider some elements of automata theory. The bridge, traffic lights, sensors, cars along with the rules holding for them are called a **system**. An arrangement of cars and lights on the signals is called a **state** of the system. The evolution of the system from one state to another is achieved by an **action**.

An example of a state of the system: "cars are waiting in front of the stop signals and the bridge is empty". An example of an action: "a car drives onto the bridge from the direction A" or "$Open(A)$". Our problem may be described by a set of states and transitions between states.

When an (external) system is controlled by a computer, the information about the system must be represented in the program. The state of the system is described by the data of the program, for instance by its variables or files. This representation of the external system is called a **model**.

When a system is described in a programming language, its state is defined *both* by the values of all program variables *and* the currently executed part of the program. In our case the system is so simple that no variables are necessary to describe its state; the currently executed statement suffices.

The actions by which the system progresses from one state to another may be of two types. Some actions are actuated by the program (for instance, *Open*, *Close*), other actions are external events (car travel), which may be detected using sensors. When the reading of a sensor changes, the model of the system must advance to a new state.

In the program below, some states of the system are described by a comment. The statements in these comments are called the *invariants* of the program, since they are *always* true when the program passes the point where they are written. If the truth of these formally written invariants can be verified, the correctness of the program may be proved. An example of such proof is in solution 922F.

```
program Bridge;
{ Two-way traffic over a narrow bridge. }
  type
    present = (NO,YES);
    side = (A,B,M);

  procedure Open(x: side); external;
  procedure Close(x: side); external;
  function Sensor(x: side): present; external;

  procedure OpenDirection(x,y: side);
  { Opens the bridge for traffic in the direction from x to y }
  begin
  { state: the bridge is empty, signals are at stop }
    if Sensor(x)=YES then begin
      Open(x);
{*}    repeat until Sensor(M)=YES;
     { state: one (or more) cars from the direction x have driven onto the bridge }
      repeat until Sensor(y)=YES; { until a car is waiting from the direction y }
     { state: cars are waiting from the direction y }
      Close(x);
      repeat until Sensor(M)=NO;
     { state: the bridge is empty, the signals are at stop }
    end; {if}
  end; {OpenDirection}

begin {Bridge}
  Close(A); Close(B);
  repeat until Sensor(M)=NO;
  repeat OpenDirection(A,B); OpenDirection(B,A) until false;
end. {Bridge}
```

Finally, let us emphasize some details and boundary cases which the program must handle properly:

— drivers do not have immediate reflexes, so that some time passes from the moment the light changes to go to the moment the first car drives onto the bridge; if the loop denoted by the asterisk {*} was removed from the program, the lights would start to palpitate quickly in alternation;

— the traffic coming from a single direction should not be interrupted unnecessarily;

— a function to measure time would be necessary to handle some irregular events correctly. Some examples of such events are:

  — a car parks in front of the bridge and has no intention of crossing it;

  — a car drives on the bridge at the moment the red light goes on.

322F Assuming the speed of the reader does not change, its time to move from the start to the end of a strip is directly proportional to the strip width. Therefore, the time from one change of colour to the next will be measured — the time required by the reader to move from the start of a strip to its end (or better to the start of the next strip). If this time is longer than a certain time limit, we assume that the reader has just left a wide strip, that is, a strip representing a one, otherwise we conclude that the strip is the thin one and that it represents a zero. Since it is known that the first strip of the code is thin, and since the width of the wide strip is twice the width of the thin one, the time limit is set to 1.5 times the duration of the first (thin) strip.

To adapt to changes in the true velocity of reading, this time limit should be adjusted to the actual velocity. This is done simply by recomputing it after each strip is read (this will be used in our solution). To recompute the limit, only the time of reading the last strip might be used or more complicated methods as well, for instance methods that consider the velocity may change, while the acceleration may change only slightly. Also, these methods are less susceptible to misprints, flaws in paper, and errors in reading.

```
program BarCode(output);
{ Bar-code reading. }
  type colourT = (BLACK,WHITE);
  var
    first: boolean;  { indicates whether the first (thin) strip is being read }
    b: colourT;      { the strip colour }
    t0: integer;     { the time at the strip start }
    dt: integer;     { the time to pass over a strip }
    tBoun: real;
      { the boundary time: the shorter strips are thin, the longer ones are wide }

  function Colour: colourT; external;
  function Time: integer; external;
```

```
begin {BarCode}
  repeat until Colour=BLACK;                    { ignore the initial white }
  first:=true;
  repeat
    t0:=Time; b:=Colour;
    repeat until Colour<>b;                     { wait for the color to change }
    dt:=Time-t0;
    if first then
      begin first:=false; tBoun:=1.5*dt end                     { the first strip }
    else if dt<tBoun then
      begin writeln('0'); tBoun:=1.5*dt end                               { thin }
    else
      begin writeln('1'); tBoun:=1.5*(dt/2) end;                          { wide }
  until false;
end. {BarCode}
```

A discussion about the problems of measuring time follows in solution 412F.

412F The velocity of a train is computed from the time required by a carriage to move along the measuring sensor. As we know, the length of each carriage is 10 m, so the velocity equals $v = s/t = 10\,\mathrm{m}/t$. After the measurement, the program must wait while other carriages of the train move by, as the velocity should be only output once for a train. From the text of the problem it is not obvious that a delay of more than a minute between consecutive carriages means that the train has gone by; we must assume that, since it is the only way of determining the end of a train. Also, the text specifies no detail about the engine. We assume that the trains in question are the so-called motor trains, where the motor is built-in in one of the carriages.

```
program Train(output);
{ Train velocity measurement. }
  var
    t0: real;  { the time at the start of the measurement }
    v: real;   { the train velocity in m/s }

  function Carriage: boolean; external;
  function Time: real; external;

begin {Train}
  repeat
    repeat until Carriage;                      { wait for the first carriage }
    t0:=Time;
    repeat until not Carriage;              { wait that the carriage goes by }
    v:=10/(Time-t0); t0:=Time;
    writeln('The train travels at a speed of ',v:3:1,' m/s');
```

```
    repeat                                    { wait that other carriages go by }
      if Carriage then begin
        repeat until not Carriage;
        t0:=Time;
      end; {if}
    until (Time-t0)>60;
  until false;
end. {Train}
```

To avoid inaccuracy in measurement and to obtain a better indicator of the velocity, the average velocity could be computed from the velocities measured for each carriage or the carriages could be counted and the time from the arrival of the first carriage to the departure of the last one could be used. The modification of the program is left to the reader.

The text of the problem specifies that the *Time* function returns the number of seconds elapsed from a certain moment on. The value of the function therefore continually increases. If the *Time* function is of the type integer, the accuracy of the measurement as well as the possibility of overflowing the integer range should be taken into consideration. Using 32-bit integers this would happen after 68 years, while signed 16-bit integers impose much more severe limitation: 9 hours.

Our *Time* function is of the type real (using the floating point notation), so that the range overflow is practically not possible. However, other problems may occur. Let us consider the case when the floating point notation uses 6 decimal places of precision. After twelve days (999 999 s = 11.57 days) the value of the function does not change each second anymore! A month after the start of the measurement the value of the *Time* function would change only every 10 seconds in steps of 10. (In this calculation we assumed that decimal notation was used. Since binary notation is used much more often, the actual size of the increase would differ from the above—using the approximately equivalent 20-bit notation the time would change every two seconds).

This may be a very unpleasant property, depending on the use of such a function in our program. A similar problem is discussed in solution 1134B.

A much more predictable *Time* function is for example that of the problem 422F, which returns the time elapsed since midnight in seconds. It is true that special care is necessary at midnight, when the counting is restarted from zero on, but the program always works correctly and in the same way. This is true both for the *Type* function of the type real as well as of the type integer, as long as the number of seconds in one day may be stored in an integer variable.

In programming, we are usually more interested in the duration of an event than in the time of day. If we are sure that the duration of an event is limited, we may reset the time (a stop-watch) to zero at its start, and read the time at the end of the event. This technique would suit our problem very well. Whenever the start of a carriage was sensed, the time would be reset to zero, and at the end of the carriage the time of its travel along the sensor would be read. Unfortunately, the text of the problem provides no appropriate means to reset the time to zero.

Another word is due about the type of the *Time* function. In the text of the problem, the type real was chosen only to avoid explanation, which is the time unit in the case of an integer *Time* function — it would surely not be a second, since that would make the function too inaccurate for our purpose. In practice, integer timing is always used, since this is the only way to ensure the same accuracy (absolute error) continually, also, on most computers integer computation is faster than the floating point one. On VAX computers, for instance, 64-bit integers are used to represent time, and to measure it the unit 100 ns is used, both to represent absolute (calendar) time and relative time (the duration). In this way, appropriate accuracy is achieved, while the duration is practically unlimited (10^{18} years).

Since the problem was oriented towards the competitors in the least experienced group, the problems with time measurement were deliberately neglected to simplify their work.

422F To count the carriages, their rear edges must be sensed and counted (the front edges might be counted as well), that is, the events when the value of the *Carriage* function changes from *true* to *false*. At each such event, its time must be recorded, to output the time of the event in case the last carriage went by. The end of the train is detected by sensing no new carriage at least for a minute after the last carriage goes by (see discussion in solution 412F; also see the note about the engine there). When measuring time, the time around midnight must be properly handled.

```
program Train(output);
{ Counts the carriages in the trains going by. }
  var
    n: integer;  { the number of carriages }
    t: real;     { the time at the end of the last carriage }
    dt: real;    { the time elapsed since the last carriage }

  function Carriage: boolean; external;
  function Time: real; external;

begin {Train}
  repeat
    n:=0;
    repeat until Carriage;                    { wait for the first carriage }
```

```
    repeat
      repeat until not Carriage;                    { wait for the end of a carriage }
      n:=n+1; t:=Time;
      repeat
        dt:=Time−t;
        if dt<0 then dt:=dt+24*3600;                           { jump at midnight }
      until Carriage or (dt>60);
    until dt>60;
    writeln('The train at ',trunc(t/3600):2,':',trunc(t/60) mod 60:2,
                ' had  ',n:1,' carriages.');
  until false;
end. {Train}
```

523F The first part of the problem is easy to solve, yet the solution below is not the only one possible. Our program first tests its own proposal and then votes against all computers whose proposal differs from its own. It must be assumed that the proposals are stable during tests of other computers — that they do not change. It is the voting circuitry which by considering the majority of votes ensures that a single defective computer cannot turn off correctly functioning computers.

```
  var
    me: integer;        { the number of the own computer }
    comp: integer;      { the number of the current computer }
    myProp: integer;    { own proposal }
    prop: integer;      { the proposal of the computer comp }
  ...
  WhoAmI(me); WhatSays(me,myProp);
  for comp:=1 to 5 do begin
    WhatSays(comp,prop);
    if prop <> myProp then VoteAgainst(comp);
  end; {for}
```

The operation is more reliable if the program first determines which step is proposed by the majority , and then votes against all those computers that propose a different step. This is also the solution to the second part of the problem, since in this case the identification number of the executing computer need not be known.

```
program SpaceShuttle;
{ Turning off the malfunctioning computers in the Space shuttle. }
  const
    nComp = 5;  { the number of computers }
```

```
  var
    i,comp,p: integer;
    max: integer;          { the index of the most frequent proposal in the table step }
    prop: array [1..nComp] of integer;                  { the proposals of all computers }
    n: integer;                          { the current length of the tables step and freq }
    step:                   { the table of DIFFERENT steps proposed by computers }
      array [1..nComp] of integer;
    freq:                                  { the number of proposers of the step step[i] }
      array [1..nComp] of integer;

  procedure WhatSays(i: integer; var step: integer); external;
  procedure VoteAgainst(i: integer); external;

begin {SpaceShuttle}
  n:=0;
  for comp:=1 to nComp do begin
    WhatSays(comp,p); prop[comp]:=p;
    if p<>0 then begin                             { unless the computer is turned off }
      step[n+1]:=p; freq[n+1]:=0;                                    { post a sentinel }
      i:=1; while step[i]<>p do i:=i+1;                        { find the step in the table }
      if i>n then n:=n+1;                             { if there is no such step, add one }
      freq[i]:=freq[i]+1;
    end; {if}
  end; {for}
  if n>1 then begin                                   { unless all proposals are equal }
    max:=1;
    for i:=2 to n do                                 { find the most frequent proposal }
      if freq[i]>freq[max] then max:=i;
    for comp:=1 to nComp do begin
      p:=prop[comp];
      if p<>0 then                                                  { unless turned off }
        if p<>step[max] then                           { does not agree with the majority }
          VoteAgainst(comp);
    end; {for}
  end; {if}
end. {SpaceShuttle}
```

The table *prop* is used to avoid trouble in case a computer "changes its mind" and changes its proposal during the execution of the program.

The program does not handle the case when there is no absolute majority — for instance, given the proposals 9 2 2 7 7 the program decides to vote against the computers 1, 4, and 5.

The above program is a fairly extensive one. A description of the solution sufficed at the competition.

Finally, let us take a brief overview of the actual implementation of the problem in the Space Shuttle. During the critical phases the Shuttle is controlled by four equal computers, running synchronized programs. All the most important actuators (to move the rudder and the flaps, to control the direction of the primary driving jet-engines and similar) are mechanically implemented in such a way that the opinion of the majority overrules. A computer may not turn off either any other computer or itself — this may only be done by the crew. If all four computers fail, or a serious flaw in the program emerges, or the four computers split into two equally strong groups, the crew may switch the control to the fifth — auxiliary — computer, whose programs were designed and tested separately from the programs of the first four computers. The auxiliary computer ensures a safe lift-off and landing, though it does not perform all functions of the main computer system.

All commands available to the crew (direction controls, switches, keyboards) are solely input sensors to the computers — no command directly drives an actuator. The Space Shuttle is too unstable a craft to allow steering by hand; so the reliability of its computer system is of vital importance.

Also of interest are some data about the computers aboard the Shuttle. All five computers are equal; they are based on an old and tested processor IBM System/4 Pi, model AP–101, which has been in the marketplace since the seventies. As far as technology is involved, NASA opts for already built and well tested hardware. Each computer has 106 K 32-bit words of core memory, and its speed is 0.45 MIPS — fairly slow by today's criteria. The mass storage media are composed of two magnetic tape units, on which there are 6 copies of all necessary programs. In any moment, only programs for the current phase of the flight are in memory (the lift-off, the work in the orbit, the landing — 8 phases in all); the programs of the next phase are loaded during calm and non-critical parts of the flight.

The software is a product of an IBM team as well; the first contracts for the Shuttle software were signed in 1974. In 1984, about hundred people were involved in writing the Shuttle software, another eighty were involved in testing, and another hundred took care of the software support and simulators.

You may find more on this topic in the paper by A. Spector and D. Gifford: The Space Shuttle Primary Computer System, *Communications of the ACM*, **27**(1984)9, as well as in other papers of that issue, which was entirely devoted to computers in space.

623F The algorithm described in this problem is used in the majority of modern electronic organs and synthesizers (especially smaller and portable ones). In older implementations of an electronic organ, all tones in all octaves were generated simultaneously, and the keyboard simply connected the tone generators to the amplifier.

Microcomputer control of an organ may replace a significant part of electronics, which both simplifies the final products and makes it cheaper without harming its quality.

An important assumption in simplifying the implementation is that only a small number of keys are pressed simultaneously, so that 5 to 10 tone generators suffice for any normal playing. The microcomputer assigns free tone generators to newly pressed keys (allocation), appropriately sets the tone generators, and stops the generator when the key is released.

The concept of a temporary allocation of resources (tone generators, means, objects, etc.) to consumers (keyboard keys, users, programs) is frequently encountered in computers and in everyday life. Allocation is usually necessary when there are more possible users than there are resources available, and so a resource cannot be permanently allocated to each user (imagine a computer centre with several hundred occasional users, having several hundred magnetic tape units installed just in case on some Friday 13th all users decided to use their tape).

Here are some examples of allocation of resources:

- allocation of computer tape units to a user who needs them;
- allocation of processor time to user programs;
- allocation of free memory to user programs when they need it;
- cash desks in a large department store are temporarily "allocated" by consumers;
- taking books out from a library (book allocation).

Two ways of allocation are possible. In the first case, a subject usually exists (a man, a process, the operating system) that controls the allocation of the resources to users when needed. In the other case, the user may seize the resource himself considering established rules.

Let us return to our problem. First, let us devise the data structure used to allocate generators to keys. Since there are only a few generators, and since linear search in such a small set is effective enough, a table called *alloc* suffices. Its elements indicate whether the corresponding tone generator is allocated or free. The corresponding declaration in Pascal follows, as well as the procedures to allocate and deallocate, which are needed later in the solution:

```
const maxGen = 5;  { the number of all tone generators }
var
  alloc: array [1..maxGen] of boolean;  { allocation indicators }

function Allocate: integer;
{ The function finds a free generator and allocates it; its return value equals }
{ the number of the generator or 0 in case the allocation was unsuccessful. }
```

```
  var
    gen: integer;
    found: boolean;
begin {Allocate}
  gen:=1; found:=false;
  while (gen<=maxGen) and not found do
    if not alloc[gen] then found:=true else gen:=gen+1;
  if not found then Allocate:=0
  else begin alloc[gen]:=true; Allocate:=gen end;
end; {Allocate}

procedure Deallocate(gen: integer);
{ Deallocates an allocated generator gen. }
begin
  if alloc[gen] then alloc[gen]:=false
  else writeln('A free resource cannot be deallocated!');
end; {Deallocate}
```

All necessary tools to allocate and deallocate the generators are thus ready. Next, we must solve a small problem related to pressing and releasing the keyboard keys. The *Key* function only informs us about the state of a key, while we are primarily interested in the changes on the keyboard—the key presses and releases. To detect changes, a table *pressed* will be used to record the last read state of all keys. The changes will be detected by scanning all keys using the *Key* function and comparing the value of the function to the state recorded in the table *pressed*.

When a key is released, a tone generator must be turned off and deallocated; so for each key it must be recorded which tone generator has been allocated to it. A table *generator* is used for that purpose.

The main program:

```
  const nKeys = 60;  { the number of all keys on the keyboard }
  var
    pressed:           { the state of the keys at the time of last reading }
      array [1..nKeys] of boolean;
    generator:         { the generator corresponding to a pressed key or 0 }
      array [1..nKeys] of 0..maxGen;
    j,t,gen: integer;

  function Key(t: integer): integer; external;
  procedure Freq(gen,ton: integer); external;

begin {Organ}
  for gen:=1 to maxGen do
    begin alloc[gen]:=false; Freq(gen,0) end;
  for j:=1 to nKeys do
    begin pressed[j]:=false; generator[j]:=0 end;
```

```
  repeat
    for t:=1 to nKeys do begin
      if (Key(t)=1) and not pressed[t] then
        begin { the key t has been pressed }
          pressed[t]:=true; gen:=Allocate;
          if gen>0 then begin Freq(gen,t); generator[t]:=gen end;
        end
      else if (Key(t)=0) and pressed[t] then
        begin { the key t has been released }
          pressed[t]:=false; gen:=generator[t];
          if gen>0 then
            begin Freq(gen,0); Deallocate(gen); generator[t]:=0 end;
        end; {if}
    end; {for}
  until false;
end. {Organ}
```

The described program solves part (**b**) of the problem. To solve part (**a**), the *Allocate* procedure must be modified to act when no tone generator is free; in this case it should find the generator allocated the longest time, force its release from its key, and reallocate it. The term "longest" implies some measurement of time. However, little is required from this "time": it must only run equally fast for all generators, but it is not required to run continuously or uniformly. We declare a table *time*, which records for how long each generator has been allocated. At the time of its allocation its time is set to 0, and then the time of *all* allocated generators is incremented by 1. When necessary, the longest allocated generator is found simply by finding the one with the largest value in the table *time*.

When a deallocation of a generator is forced, the table *generator*, telling which generator (if any) is allocated to a particular key, must be updated as well. If the deallocation of the generator *gen* is forced, the table *generator* must be searched to find which key will be forced to become silent. To avoid the time-consuming search, an additional table *tone* is used to specify for each generator by which key it was activated. The table *tone* thus maps a generator number to a key number, while the table *generator* maps in the opposite direction: it maps a key number to a generator number.

This introduction of the table *tone* is a good example of trade-off decisions, which must often be adopted in programming: we may either spare the space in memory and decrease execution speed, or the contrary. In our case, the time-consuming search through the table *generator* was substituted by a simple and fast operation of indexing into a table; this forced us to use additional space in the memory, required by the table *tone*.

In his work, a programmer must continually choose between various possible algorithms and data representations applicable to the problem. Probably you have met the so-called "misery preservation" rule of life in various forms several times so far, for instance: "by improving one feature of a product another suffers", or: "by cleaning one thing another one becomes dirty" (more pessimistic interpretations are possible, see A. Bloch: *Murphy's Law Complete*, Methuen, 1986). Even in the alternative—between execution speed and memory requirements—there is frequently no third choice. In the most frequently used and time critical portions of a program, faster but more space consuming algorithms are used; in rarely executed portions, which may run slower, the memory space is saved instead of execution time.

Before deciding how to improve the efficiency of a program it is worth thinking about, whether there really is no third alternative. Sometimes an algorithm or a data structure may be found which is particularly effective precisely in our case. The computer science literature is a valuable resource of ideas in this case.

Another truth about many programs is worth noting: one fifth of the program code takes four fifths of the time, while the other four fifths execute in the remaining one fifth. It is very important that the programmer is aware which part of the program code is the most time-consuming, so he may devote his attention to its most effective implementation, while in the remaining majority of the program the main guidelines are readability, clarity and robustness of the program.

The ratio mentioned (one to four) is a rough estimate, nevertheless, it is a good approximation. The more experienced the system designer and programmer, the less outstanding are the consuming parts of the program. It is not easy to detect the most time-consuming parts of a program. Even experienced programmers are sometimes surprised when they find out which parts of their programs are the most time-consuming. Of great help in program optimization are software tools, which observe a program during execution and after its termination output the time spent by the program counter in particular portions.

The improved program:

```
program Organ(output);
{ Controlling an electronic organ. }
  const
    maxGen = 5;      { the number of all tone generators }
    nKeys = 60;      { the number of keys of the keyboard }
  var
    alloc: array [1..maxGen] of boolean;            { the allocation indicators }
    time: array [1..maxGen] of integer;          { the durations of allocation }
    tone: array [1..maxGen] of integer;       { the keys activating a generator }
    generator:                      { the generator corresponding to a key or 0 }
      array [1..nKeys] of 0..maxGen;
    pressed:                   { the state of the keys at the time of last reading }
```

```
      array [1..nKeys] of boolean;

  function Key(t: integer): integer; external;
  procedure Freq(gen,tone: integer); external;

  procedure Deallocate(gen: integer);
  { Deallocates an allocated generator gen. }
  begin
    if alloc[gen] then alloc[gen]:=false
    else writeln('A free resource cannot be deallocated!');
  end; {Deallocate}

  function ForceDeallocation: integer;
  { Forces the deallocation of the longest sounding generator and }
  { returns its number. All generators must be allocated prior to this call. }
    var i,gen,max: integer;
  begin {ForceDeallocation}
    max:=time[1]; gen:=1;
    for i:=2 to maxGen do  { find the oldest }
      if time[i]>max then begin max:=time[i]; gen:=i end;
  { force deallocation }
    Deallocate(gen); generator[tone[gen]]:=0; ForceDeallocation:=gen;
  end; {ForceDeallocation}

  function Allocate: integer;
  { Finds a free generator, allocates it, and returns its number. }
    var
      i,gen: integer;
      found: boolean;
  begin {Allocate}
    gen:=1; found:=false;
    while (gen<=maxGen) and not found do
      if not alloc[gen] then found:=true else gen:=gen+1;
    if not found then gen:= ForceDeallocation;
    alloc[gen]:=true; Allocate:=gen; time[gen]:=0;
    for i:=1 to maxGen do if alloc[i] then time[i]:=time[i]+1;
  end; {Allocate}

  procedure InitialState;
  { Initializes the global variables. }
    var j,gen: integer;
  begin
    for gen:=1 to maxGen do begin
      alloc[gen]:=false; Freq(gen,0); tone[gen]:=0; time[gen]:=0;
    end; {for}
    for j:=1 to nKeys do
      begin pressed[j]:=false; generator[j]:=0 end;
  end; {InitialState}
```

```
procedure Play;
{ Scans the keyboard and (de)activates tone generators. }
  var t,gen: integer;
begin
  repeat
    for t:=1 to nKeys do begin
      if (Key(t)=1) and not pressed[t] then
        begin { the key t has been pressed }
          pressed[t]:=true; gen:=Allocate;
          if gen>0 then { in this program the allocation always succeeds }
            begin Freq(gen,t); generator[t]:=gen; tone[gen]:=t end;
        end
      else if (Key(t)=0) and pressed[t] then
        begin { the key t has been released }
          pressed[t]:=false; gen:=generator[t];
          if gen>0 then begin  { if the key was sounding }
            Freq(gen,0); Deallocate(gen); generator[t]:=0; tone[gen]:=0;
          end; {if}
        end; {if}
    end; {for}
  until false;
end; {Play}

begin {Organ}
  InitialState; Play;
end. {Organ}
```

The solution above is fairly long. We expected the competitors to provide a conceptually correct solution; it would be too much to require a polished program.

714F The text of the problem must be supplemented by requiring that the line does not turn too sharply for the truck (it is difficult to manoeuvre successfully with such simple sensors and with a steering mechanism capable of only three positions). The requirement about the width of the line from the statement of the problem as well as the above assumption about turning must also hold for the fork.

The solution may be first written as a table. A sensor gives two responses: 1, if it senses the line and 0, if it does not. Since there are two sensors available, four cases are possible:

LEFT	RIGHT	the position of the truck
0	0	no line is visible
0	1	at the left edge of the line
1	0	at the right edge of the line
1	1	on the line

First, we deal with driving along the line that does not fork (part (**a**) of the problem). In this case the objective is to keep both sensors on the line. When either sensor does not sense the line anymore, the truck must turn towards the line.

In case (**b**), where we want the truck to continue along a given branch of a fork, a different tactic must be chosen. The described algorithm for driving along the line may lead to an unpleasant situation, for instance, that the truck overlooks the fork, or that it entirely loses the line from both sensors at the same moment. To avoid this, the sensor must drive along the edge of the line for some time before the fork.

Let us devise the instructions to drive along the left edge of the line, which causes the truck to take the left branch of the fork:

— if the left sensor senses the line (regardless of what the right sensor senses) the truck is driving too much to the middle of the line, so it must turn left;
— if the left sensor does not sense the line while the right one does, the truck must continue straight on;
— if no sensor senses the line, the truck is too much to the left, it must turn right.

Driving along the right edge is handled in a similar way.

We are now able to enhance our table by adding the actions required to make the truck steer the way it should:

LEFT	RIGHT	drive along the line	left fork	right fork
0	0	we are lost	turn right	turn left
0	1	turn right	drive straight on	turn right
1	0	turn left	turn left	drive straight on
1	1	drive straight on	turn left	turn right

The decision table above specifies the algorithm precisely. The table thus solves the problem.

The only dubious action in the table is denoted by "we are lost". In normal operation this situation should not occur, but it may well happen in life, for instance, because of a partially erased line, because of the slow mechanism for turning, or when changing the objective from "take the left/right fork" to "drive along the line." If the last edge seen could be remembered, it could be supposed on which side of the line the truck was lost. An immediate turn towards the line might help in this case, if the truck has not gone too far.

The reader might consider how a truck just switched-on would find a line. The problem is similar to the problem of determining the coordinates of the point, where a light pen first touches the screen.

Let us write the program for the improved version of following a line:

```
program Truck;
{ Directing a truck along a line (algorithm A). }
  type lmr = (L,M,R);
  var
    s: integer;  { the state of both sensors }
    posit: lmr; { the position of the truck relative to the line }

  function Sensor(l: lmr): integer; external;
  procedure Turn(l: lmr); external;

begin {Truck}
  posit:=M;
  repeat
    s:=10*Sensor(L)+Sensor(R);
  { determine the position of the truck }
    case s of
      00: ; { no change }
      01: posit:=L;
      10: posit:=R;
      11: posit:=M;
    end; {case}
  { turn the wheels correctly }
    case posit of
      L: Turn(R);
      R: Turn(L);
      M: Turn(M);
    end; {case}
  until false;
end. {Truck}
```

Finally, let us remark that the algorithm to drive along an edge of the line suits the first part of the problem as well, although the driving according to the first algorithm is "smoother." For those who like to experiment and think, we provide some more questions:

— How may the truck directly switch from the algorithm, "drive along the left edge" to the algorithm "drive along the right edge?" Can this change be done in any moment of driving (regardless of the position of the truck)?

— Could a truck with a single sensor perform the same tasks as the truck with two sensors? How?

— The text of the problem states that the distance of the sensors is less than the line-width. Describe (or draw) the driving according to the first and the second algorithm for the following two trucks. The sensors of the first truck are close together, while the sensors of the second one are only slightly less than the line-width apart.

— The steering mechanism may be slow or fast, the turn of the wheels may be small or large, the speed of the truck may be slow or fast. How do these parameters influence driving (stability, reliability, etc.)?

— Write a program that simulates driving of a truck. Experiment with this model to see how different parameters influence the driving of the truck. Using a dozen components and an electrically driven toy model of a car with a motor to steer the wheels you may test the algorithms in practice.

723F The robot is incapable of opening and closing the pipes when it removes or delivers a bottle. If it is not careful, it may happen that the liquid spills over the top of a full bottle, while it is busy removing or delivering another bottle. Our program uses a simple and effective method, although it is probably not always the best: before starting to remove a full bottle, the robot closes all those pipes that could spill over during the time of reloading. Then it performs the job undisturbed and reopens the pipes.

```
program BottlingPlant;
{ Controls a robot in a bottling plant. }
  const
    FULL = 0;            { the value of WhenFull if the bottle is full }
    NOBOTTLE = −1;       { the value of WhenFull if there is no bottle }
    nPipes = 10;         { the number of filling posts – pipes }
    deliveryTime = 2;    { the time needed to deliver a new bottle }
    removalTime = 3;     { the time needed to remove a full bottle }
  var j: integer;

  procedure Open(i: integer); external;
  procedure Close(i: integer); external;
  procedure Remove(i: integer); external;
  procedure Deliver(i: integer); external;
  function WhenFull(i: integer): real; external;

  procedure TakeTime(t: integer);
  { Closes the pipes (even the already closed) which may become critical }
  { in the next t time units. }
    var i: integer;
  begin
    for i:=1 to nPipes do  if WhenFull(i)<t then Close(i);
  end; {TakeTime}

  function FindPost(state: integer; var j: integer): boolean;
  { Finds the filling post j, where WhenFull(j)=state. }
  { Here the value of the variable state may be FULL or NOBOTTLE. }
  { The function returns true, if such a post was found. }
    var found: boolean;
```

```
  begin
    j:=1; found:=false;
    while (j<=nPipes) and not found do
      if WhenFull(j)=state then found:=true else j:=j+1;
    FindPost:=found;
  end; {FindPost}

  procedure OpenPipes;
  { Opens the pipes at all unfilled bottles (even if they are already open). }
    var i: integer;
  begin
    for i:=1 to nPipes do if WhenFull(i)>0 then Open(i);
  end; {OpenPipes}

begin {BottlingPlant}
  OpenPipes;
  repeat
    while FindPost(NOBOTTLE,j) do
      begin TakeTime(deliveryTime);  Deliver(j);  OpenPipes end;
    while FindPost(FULL,j) do
      begin TakeTime(removalTime);  Remove(j);  OpenPipes end;
  until false;
end. {BottlingPlant}
```

734F a) The problem represents a typical example of *resource allocation.* It should be stressed that the variable *nDev* is used by the *Request* and *Release* procedures solely to enable *Request* to determine whether all devices have been allocated. The actual allocation (choice) of a device must be performed by *Request* in some other way (for instance using a table of free devices).

Solution 1033F deals with a similar problem, and the discussion about the critical section applies to this problem as well. Also, the critical sections will be encountered in solution 832F. The text of the problem specifies that the *Request* and *Release* procedures are implemented as critical sections.

The allocation of resources to two or more concurrent processes using one or more resources may lead to the dangerous situation of *deadlock.* The problem is most easily explained by the example of tape unit allocation, though the entire discussion is valid for any resources (for instance, for any devices, memory space, files, records in files, buffers, common variables, etc.). Suppose there are two tape units, and that two processes A and B are executing concurrently. They request the units in the following sequence:

process A requests a unit; it obtains the unit 1;
process B requests a unit; it obtains the unit 2;
process A requests another unit; it waits, since there is no free unit;
process B requests another unit; it waits, since there is no free unit;

The processes A and B therefore await each other indefinitely. This state is called *deadlock* or the *deadly embrace.* The main problem with such a state is that during the wait for a new unit it is not evident whether the unit will ever be obtained. Even when there are more than two processes, it is not necessarily evident whether their wait will ever terminate or not. An everyday example of a deadlock is the situation when at the junction of roads vehicles from each direction meet. This situation may only be resolved by indulgence, insolence or a traffic accident (is this where the phrase "deadly embrace" comes from?).

There are more solutions to the problem described. The problem cannot arise if waiting is prevented: a process either obtains the unit requested or releases all units allocated (since it aborts). This solution is not practicable in our case, but it might be used under some other circumstances in which a deadlock might occur. In our case the correct solution is to require each process to allocate all units it intends to use at the same time.

If the number of the units needed by the process varies considerably (if the process needs, say, 10 units for an instant of its execution time, and a single unit otherwise) it may happen that the units are withheld unnecessarily. In this way it may happen that a process occupies more units than it actually needs most of the time. To overcome that (in case there are many units) the above solution may be combined by the proposed algorithm: each process must, once and for all, declare in advance the maximum number of units it will ever require. When it needs the units, it allocates them in a way similar to the one proposed in the problem. Using the additional information about the maximum number of units required we may check whether the allocation may lead to deadlock. Such allocations are deferred, instead, the process must wait. The description of the algorithm is left to the reader. One of the solutions described is probably appropriate in the proposed case of the tape unit allocation.

More frequently deadlocks occur in alternate circumstances, when processes allocate different resources. A typical example is the allocation (locking) of records in a data-base (or any other files). Often, the following simple rule is used to prevent deadlock: the resources must always be allocated in the same sequence. The effect of such allocation is equivalent to the simultaneous allocation of all resources needed. In our case of tape unit allocation, this rule would be illustrated by processes allocating a particular unit (and not the next available). If all processes allocate the units so that each process allocates units in the ascending order of their sequence numbers, no deadlock is possible. Similar to this is the situation with groups of resources, where each process may allocate a single unit of each group: no deadlock can occur if all processes allocate the units in the same order of groups. In this way the allocation of records on files may frequently be implemented.

In spite of uttermost care, it may occasionally happen that deadlock cannot be prevented. In this case, it is very important to know how to decide whether a normal wait is in question, or the waiting should be (violently) interrupted, since it would otherwise never terminate. Usually, this is the duty of the operating system, which may check from time to time whether processes are in a deadlock. If it detects this unpleasant situation, a victim process must be selected, which will terminate the deadlock by releasing its units. The problems of detecting a deadlock and of selecting a victim are far from being simple, primarily due to the large computational extent required in case of a large number of allocations (which usually happens in practice). On systems where deadlock detection was (is) left to the system operators, the measuring of their reaction time was (is) a favourite entertainment of idle users.

b) The second part of the problem describes a situation almost contrary to the one stated in the problem, i. e., that both procedures execute without being interrupted. In the case of a multiprocessor computer system, any access of other processors to our data structures may be considered an interrupt. To implement a critical section in the case of a multiprocessor system, it is not enough that interrupts are disabled; entirely different methods are necessary. This is the core of the problem, occurring for example when a single unit is left for allocation. Two processors test approximately at the same moment whether there is a free unit. They both find one free, and allocate it concurrently. This is avoided by implementing the *Request* and *Release* procedures not only *uninterruptedly* but also as *critical sections* as described in the solution 1033F.

812F The program below probably needs no special explanation. It is only worth noting that anybody capable of connecting a fast relay (e. g. a reed relay) to a home computer may test the correctness of our solution. Care should be taken to prevent the microcomputer from coming into direct contact with the telephone line. It should also be noted that the pulse duration and other timing is regulated by the local telecommunication standards and may differ from the values in the program below. These values are only rough estimates.

```
program Telephone(input,output);
{ Dialling telephone numbers. }

  procedure Lift; external;
  procedure Drop; external;
  procedure Wait(t: integer); external;

  procedure Pulse;
  { Transmits a pulse. }
```

```
  begin
    Drop;  Wait(50); { 50 milliseconds = 1/20 second }
    Lift;
  end; {Pulse}

  procedure SendDigit(n: integer);
  { Waits 1/3 s and then sends the given number of pulses. }
    var i: integer;
  begin
    if n=0 then n:=10;
    Wait(334-50); { 334 milliseconds = 1/3 second }
    for i:=1 to n do
      begin Wait(50); Pulse end;
  end; {SendDigit}

begin {Telephone}
  write('Enter the number to dial: ');
  Lift;
  while not eoln(input) do begin
    if input↑ in ['0'..'9'] then SendDigit(ord(input↑)-ord('0'));
    get(input);
  end; {while}
end. {Telephone}
```

822F

The problem requests us to devise a convention specifying the meaning of the state of both signal lines: to what rules must the transmitter conform when transmitting a character, and what rules must be observed by the receiver when receiving a character. This convention (set of rules) is called a **protocol**.

Since the solution may not rely on equal program execution speed on either computer, the protocol used must depend solely on the exchange of signals over both control wires, and not on the duration of the signals. After each action, the transmitter must wait for the reaction of the receiver and vice versa. Some of the time the transmitter is "the boss" and the receiver must wait for it, then, the receiver takes over and decides about the continuation of the communication. This exchange of roles is called **handshaking**.

In our case, we define the meaning of both control signals as follows:

The signal from the transmitter to the receiver:

- — the value 1 means that a valid character is on the data line, and that the transmitter expects the receiver to read it and confirm the reception;
- — the value 0 means there is no valid character on the data line.

The signal from the receiver to the transmitter:

— the value 1 means that the receiver has read the character on the data line and that the transmitter may get ready to transmit the next character;

— the value 0 means that the receiver is ready to receive the next character;

The time diagram in Figure F1 illustrates the protocol used.

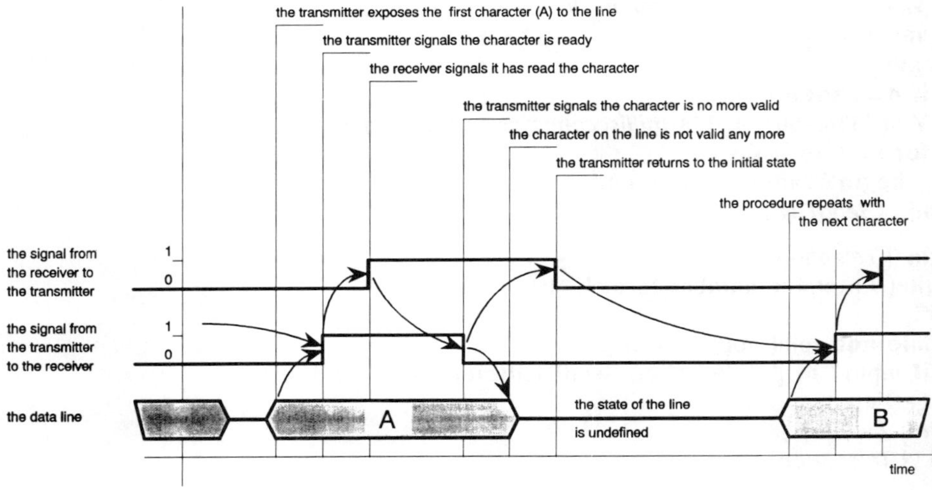

Figure F1: The time diagram of the signals

Actually, the important events in our protocol are not the states of the signal lines, but the changes of the signals. In the solution, you may observe the following loop:

```
    repeat State(s) until s=1;
```

which waits for the moment when the signal observed changes from 0 to 1. This change (or, in general, the change from the inactive to the active level) is called the **leading edge**; the change of the signal from 1 to 0 (from the active to the inactive level) is called the **trailing edge**.

The detection of a signal transition is often encountered in process control problems. There are examples of it in problems 312F, 322F, 412F, 422F, 612A, 623F, 912F, 932F, 1013F and 1132F.

As an illustration, we may observe another possible protocol. In the previous protocol, it was the level of a signal that had a specific meaning, while the changes of the level only denoted the transitions between states. In the example of Figure F2, it is the change of the signal that is significant, regardless of the direction of the transition (from 0 to 1 or vice versa).

A deficiency of the second protocol is that there may be problems at the start of the communication, if the transmitter starts to transmit before the receiver starts to examine the state of the signal line.

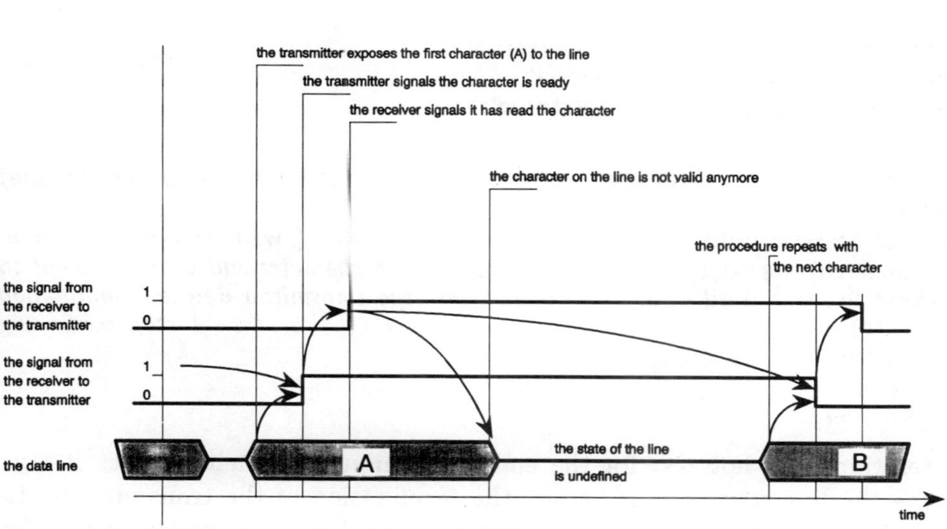

Figure F2: An example of a different protocol

The programs implementing the first protocol described follow:

```
program Transmitter(input);
{ One way communication between two computers. }
  var
    ch: char;
    s: integer;

  procedure Expose(ch: char); external;
  procedure Signal(s: integer); external;
  procedure State(var s: integer); external;

begin {Transmitter}
  Signal(0);                    { assert the initial state (just in case) }
  repeat
    read(ch);
    repeat State(s) until s=0;              { wait until the line is free }
    Expose(ch); Signal(1);                       { expose a character }
    repeat State(s) until s=1;  { wait for confirmation of the reception }
    Signal(0);                 { the character is not exposed any more }
  until false;
end. {Transmitter}

program Receiver(output);
{ One way communication between two computers. }
  var
    ch: char;
    s: integer;
```

```
  procedure Examine(var ch: char); external;
  procedure Signal(s: integer); external;
  procedure State(var s: integer); external;

begin {Receiver}
  Signal(0);                                { assert the initial state (just in case) }
  repeat
    repeat State(s) until s=1;                            { wait for a new character }
    Examine(ch); Signal(1);           { receive the character and confirm reception }
    repeat State(s) until s=0;     { wait until the transmitter detects confirmation }
    Signal(0);                                                    { stop confirming }
    write(ch);
  until false;
end. {Receiver}
```

The solution does not test for the end of the input file, neither does it try to preserve the line structure or handle the termination of the transmission. It is left to the reader to improve the programs to enable transmission of files from one computer to the other.

831F When selecting an appropriate data structure, an important piece of information is the amount of data the program must store. Since the problem specifies only that there may be "plenty" of data, we must make our own estimates. In the solution we assume that all data may be stored in computer memory, and that the time to search a linearly ordered list is acceptable for addition to the list, but not for the continual search for candidates to be awakened.

If the insertion time had to be short as well, we would probably resort to the binary search or the heap data structure. In the case of a still larger amount of data, which had to be stored in a file, we might use an indexed-sequential file and leave the majority of the problems to the file handling part of the operating system. There are many more possibilities, we have only mentioned some of the most evident.

To store the wake-up requests, the linked list data structure is used. The elements of the list are called "events", and they record the telephone number of the subscriber and the time to wake him up. The events in the list are sorted by increasing wake-up time, so that we may quickly determine whom to wake-up when the time comes. To accomplish this ordering, some more work must be done to insert an event at its correct position in the list.

Some problems may arise in time comparisons. Since only hours and minutes are stored, the times cannot be compared by their numeric values. The time 7:30 is before 20:00 if observed early in the morning. If the comparison is done in the afternoon, 20:00 is before 7:30 (of the next day), since past events are never stored in our data structure.

The limitation specified in our problem, allowing orders for at most 24 hours in advance to be inserted, solves the problem. The relation between two times (which one is earlier) depends on the current time. In time comparisons, 24 hours are added to all times, which are less than the current time. When inserting new events as well as when removing events from the list, care must be taken when observing the clock to avoid the time interval of the events in the list being extended over 24 hours.

```
program WakeUp;
{ Waking-up telephone subscribers at ordered time. }
  type
    pEvent = ↑event;
    event =
      record
        tel: integer;      { the telephone number }
        t: real;           { the wake-up time }
        next: pEvent;      { the pointer to the next event in the list }
      end;
  var
    list: pEvent;          { the pointer to the start of the list }
    time,time1: real;      { the current time interval }
    y: integer;            { indicates presence of input }
    tel: integer;          { the number to be called }
    t: real;               { the wake-up time }
  procedure Clock(var time: real); external;
  procedure Dial(number: integer); external;
  procedure Read
    (var dataReady: integer; var number: integer; var time: real); external;
  function RelTime(t: real): real;
  begin
    if t<time then RelTime:=t+24 else RelTime:=t;
  end; {RelTime}
  procedure Insert(tel: integer; t: real);
  { Inserts an event into an ordered list. }
  { tel is the telephone number, t is the wake-up time }
    var
      this,cur,prev: pEvent;
      found: boolean;
  begin {Insert}
    New(this); this↑.tel:=tel; this↑.t:=t; cur:=list; prev:=nil; found:=false;
    while (cur<>nil) and not found do
      if RelTime(t)<=RelTime(cur↑.t) then found:=true
      else begin prev:=cur; cur:=cur↑.next end;
    this↑.next:=cur;
{*} if prev=nil then list:=this else prev↑.next:=this;
  end; {Insert}
```

```
procedure Wake(t: real);
{ Wakes all subscribers on the list with time <= t. }
  var
    less: boolean;
    q: pEvent;
begin {Wake}
  less:=true;
  while (list<>nil) and less do
    if RelTime(list↑.t)>RelTime(t) then less:=false
    else begin
      Dial(list↑.tel); q:=list; list:=list↑.next; Dispose(q);
    end; {if,while}
end; {Wake}

begin {WakeUp}
  list:=nil; Clock(time);
  repeat
    Read(y,tel,t); if y=1 then Insert(tel,t);
    Clock(time1); Wake(time1); time:=time1;
  until false;
end. {WakeUp}
```

Some remarks are due about the *Insert* procedure which inserts an element into an ordered list. This simple operation of inserting an element at its correct place in a list is frequently encountered in various programs, and programmers keep "reinventing the wheel" again and again. The result is that every new solution to the same easy problem is slightly different, and that many of them are wrong. We therefore suggest that the above "recipe" is studied carefully, since it is short, clear, and efficient. Special attention should be paid to the line marked with the asterisk {*}. It solves the problem of the insertion of an element before the first element of the list, which has no predecessor.

With the procedure above the new element is inserted after the preceding one and before the current one. The procedure is safe and efficient; it only needs a pointer to the previous element; to maintain it, either additional effort is needed during the search, or a doubly linked list must be used. Now and then in computer literature (see, for example, N. Wirth: *Algorithms+Data Structures=Programs*, Prentice Hall, Englewood Cliffs 1976, p. 172), a method may be encountered which inserts an element into an ordered list without the additional pointer to the preceding element. In this method, the element is first inserted *after* the current element, and then their values are exchanged. This exchange *is very dangerous*! Not only does it waste computer time by copying in the case of large list elements, it *physically changes the contents of elements*, to which some other pointer may point. This algorithm, using the exchange of values, may therefore be used only *with uttermost caution when you know precisely what you are doing.*

832F In this problem, the concept of program interrupts is presented. Before solving the problem, let us observe what the interrupt mechanism is intended for and how it works.

The notion of an *interrupt* or a *program interrupt* denotes a temporary suspension of the normal execution flow of a program, caused by an external event (sometimes called an interrupt as well)—usually by an electrical signal on a special processor line.

Usually, the interrupts are caused by the computer peripheral equipment when they need a special service or attendance. Some cases when a peripheral needs attendance are:

— when the data requested have been transferred from the disk to the memory;
— when a new character has been typed on the keyboard;
— when the printer has terminated its work;

and similar.

The purpose of the interrupt mechanism is to enable the peripheral equipment to attract the attention of a program (the operating system or the user program direct) when they need it. In this way, the computer may devote its attention to execution of user programs without continually observing all peripherals.

Let us describe a simple interrupt mechanism on the example of accepting a character from a keyboard.

When the interface connected to a terminal observes that a new character has been received, it requests, using a special *electrical signal*, the central processing unit (CPU) to interrupt the execution of a program.

After executing each instruction, the CPU checks whether an interrupt has been requested. When it detects such a request, it *saves the state of the program counter* (and sometimes the state of some other registers as well) to the memory (usually on the stack).

Then, the *address* of the interrupt service routine responsible for servicing the interrupt, is moved *to the program counter* and execution proceeds at the new address (that is, at the start of the interrupt service routine. The address of the service routine is usually stored at a fixed location in memory, called the *interrupt vector.*

The service routine examines the state of the peripheral and does what is necessary — in our case, for instance, it reads the character received and stores it to the buffer containing the current line of text from the keyboard.

When the service routine finishes its task, it uses a special instruction to request the *return from interrupt.* This instruction *moves the saved* contents of the program counter from the memory (the stack) back to the *program counter.*

After this operation the interrupted program *continues* its work without even noticing an interrupt has happened.

The program interrupt mechanism described slightly differs with various computers; many of them even distinguish various types of interrupts. But the main characteristics remain:

— the program executing at the moment of interrupt is temporarily suspended; after the interrupt completes, its execution is resumed;

— the call to the service routine responsible for servicing the interrupt is implemented artificially. To the interrupt service routine it seems as if it is called from the interrupted program, although there is no call instruction to it at the point of interruption. This deception is implemented by special circuitry in the central processing unit.

This long introduction helps us to understand the problem and its solution. Now we know that the *Typed* and *Printed* procedures are service routines of two different interrupts. The first is called when the terminal interface receives a character from the keyboard and causes the interrupt; the second is called, after the printer interface has sent a character to the printer and is ready to receive the next character.

In our solution, the *Typed* procedure supplies the received characters to the *Printed* procedure through a buffer without the help of any other program. The programming language Pascal is not particularly appropriate to describe interrupts, asynchronousness, and multiprocessing environment of a computer. In our case, there is no real sense in writing a main program; if one must be provided, the program should first set the initial values and then loop indefinitely or perform some more useful task; it must not terminate, since that would mean that the program with all variables and both interrupt routines would be removed from memory; this would violently disrupt the interrupt mechanism itself (probably with fatal consequences for our process or even the operating system).

The *Typed* procedure supplies characters to *Printed* through a queue, implemented by a ring buffer. The *Typed* procedure adds the characters to the queue, and *Printed* takes them out and prints them.

The queue is represented by the following data structure:

— a table *queue*, in which characters are stored;

— the index *head* points to the oldest character in the queue, that is, the one to be printed next;

— the index *tail* points to the newest character in the queue, that is, the one which was last received from the keyboard and inserted at the tail of the queue;

— the number *length* which specifies the current length of the queue — the number of characters currently in the table *queue*.

Both indices (*head* and *tail*) are incremented circularly. When they reach the end of the table, they are moved to its start. The counter of the characters in the queue (*length*) is not actually required, as all tests can be performed by the indices at the expense of one character less in the queue — try writing such a solution yourself! The counter increases readability of the program and simplifies testing of boundary conditions.

Another important fact must not be overlooked: the *Printed* procedure is only called once when the printer becomes idle. If there is no character waiting to be printed, we must record that the printer has been stopped (the variable *stopped*), since the service routine *Printed* will not be called automatically again. The printer should be revived when a character to be printed becomes available. The *Typed* procedure must test whether the printer has been stopped, and revive printing if necessary. There are several ways to implement the revival:

— it may call the *Print* procedure and supply it with a character to print (after the character is printed the printer will call its interrupt routine again, so printing will continue automatically);
— it may call the *Printed* procedure itself and thus simulate an interrupt;
— some computers allow a program to cause an interrupt. If this is the case, the *Typed* procedure might itself make the interrupt otherwise caused by a character printout.

For the correct execution of the program it is vital that neither of the *Printed* or *Typed* procedures is called until all initializations at the start of the program have been performed. Also, it is important that when either program executes the other cannot start executing (this is ensured by the text of the problem), since this could lead to a partly updated and therefore invalid content in the data structure. The access to the data structure describing the queue should therefore be implemented as a **critical section**. See also solution 1033F.

For simplicity, this solution neglects the problems of asynchronous execution of procedures. To solve such problems, the mechanisms and tools provided by the operating system are ordinarily used.

```
program Interrupts;
{ Interrupt routines to print typed characters. }
  const
    maxQueue = 64;    { the maximum queue length }
  var
    queue: packed array [1..maxQueue] of char; { the buffer }
    head: integer;    { the index of the oldest character of the queue }
    tail:  integer;   { the index of the last inserted character of the queue }
```

```
    length: integer;      { the number of characters in the queue }
    stopped: boolean;     { no automatic call of Printed expected }
  procedure Print(ch: char); external;

  procedure Printed;
  { The printer interrupt service routine. }
  begin
    if length=0 then stopped:=true
    else begin
      Print(queue[head]); stopped:=false;
      if head<maxQueue then head:=head+1 else head:=1;
      length:=length-1;
    end; {if}
  end; {Printed}

  procedure Typed(ch: char);
  { The keyboard interrupt service routine. }
  begin
    if length>=maxQueue then queue[tail]:='?'
    else begin
      if tail<maxQueue then tail:=tail+1 else tail:=1;
      queue[tail]:=ch; length:=length+1;
    end; {if}
    if stopped then Printed;
  end; {Typed}

begin {Interrupts}
  length:=0; head:=2; tail:=1; stopped:=true;
{ At this point the program interrupts should be enabled. }
  repeat until false;     { the main program loops indefinitely }
end. {Interrupts}
```

The text of the problem ensures that, on average, typing is slower than printing. Still, the *Typed* procedure tests for overflow of the buffer *queue*. If an overflow occurs, the last character of the queue is replaced by a question mark, so that it is evident from the printout where some characters of the input have been lost. This is another example of safe programming, as we try to deal with an unexpected situation with the least harm.

It is interesting to compare an equivalent program written in the Ada programming language, which provides standard means for the implementation of interrupt service procedures; it also provides means of preventing the interrupt routines from being interrupted and intermixed in execution. All this is provided by the task concept of Ada. In our case a single task with two entries *Typed* and *Printed* was used, thus ensuring that during the servicing of one interrupt the servicing of the other one cannot start. The main program is missing; its sole purpose would be to enable interrupts and then, for example, wait in a loop.

```
package Interrupts is
  task Interrupt_Service is
    entry Printed;
    entry Typed(ch: character);
  -- initialize the interrupt vectors:
    for Typed use at 8#60#;
    for Printed use at 8#64#;
  end Interrupt_Service;
end Interrupts;
package body Interrupts is
  task body Interrupt_Service is
    maxQueue: constant:= 64;                           -- the maximum queue length
    subtype queue_r is integer range 1..maxQueue;      -- the queue index range
    queue: string(queue_r);                            -- the buffer
    head: queue_r:= 2;                                 -- the index of the longest queued character
    tail: queue_r:= 1;                                 -- the index of the last queued character
    length: integer range 0..maxQueue:= 0; -- the number of queued characters
    stopped: boolean:= true;                           -- no automatic call of Printed expected
    ch: character;
    procedure Print(ch: character);  pragma Interface(ADA,Print);
  begin -- Interrupt_Service
    loop
      select          -- Either Printed or Typed may be executing at the same time
        accept Printed;                         -- an interrupt from the printer is waiting
        if length=0 then stopped:= true;
        else
          Print(queue(head)); stopped:= false;
          if head<maxQueue then head:= head+1;
          else head:= 1; end if;
          length:= length-1;
        end if;
      or
        accept Typed(chr: character) do     -- an interrupt from the keyboard is waiting
          ch:= chr;                -- accepts a parameter and interrupts the rendezvous
        end Typed;
        if stopped then Print(ch); stopped:= false;
        elsif length>=maxQueue then queue(tail):='?';
        else
          if tail<maxQueue then tail:= tail+1; else tail:= 1; end if;
          queue(tail):= ch; length:= length+1;
        end if;
      or
        terminate;
      end select;
    end loop;
  end Interrupt_Service;
end Interrupts;
```

Finally, we present a Modula-2 version of the solution:

```
IMPLEMENTATION MODULE Service [7];

  FROM SYSTEM IMPORT
    ADDRESS,PROCESS,NEWPROCESS,TRANSFER,IOTRANSFER;
  FROM Storage IMPORT ALLOCATE;
  FROM Hardware IMPORT Print,Accept,EnableInterrupts;

  CONST
    keyboardVector = 60B;                    (* the keyboard interrupt vector *)
    printerVector = 64B;                     (* the interrupt printer vector *)
    spaceL = 200B;                           (* the memory size for each process *)
    maxQueue = 64;                           (* the maximum queue length *)

  VAR
    space: ADDRESS;                          (* to allocate workspace to processes *)

    queue: ARRAY [1..maxQueue] OF CHAR;      (* the buffer *)
    head: CARDINAL;          (* the index of the oldest character in the queue *)
    tail: CARDINAL;     (* the index of the last inserted character of the queue *)
    length:  CARDINAL;               (* the number of characters in the queue *)
    stopped: BOOLEAN;                (* no interrupt from the printer expected *)

    Main,                                    (* the main process *)
    Printer,                  (* the process to deliver characters to printer *)
    Keyboard: PROCESS;   (* the process to accept characters from the keyboard *)

  PROCEDURE Printed;
  (* The body of the process Printer, services printer interrupts. *)

  BEGIN
    LOOP
      IOTRANSFER(Printer,Main,printerVector);
      IF length = 0 THEN stopped:= TRUE
      ELSE
        Print(queue[head]);
        stopped:= FALSE;
        IF head < maxQueue THEN INC(head) ELSE head:= 1 END;
        DEC(length);
      END;
    END;
  END Printed;

  PROCEDURE Typed;
  (* The body of the process Keyboard, services keyboard interrupts. *)
    VAR ch: CHAR;
```

```
  BEGIN
    LOOP
      IOTRANSFER(Keyboard,Main,keyboardVector);
      Accept(ch);
      IF stopped THEN Print(ch); stopped:= FALSE
      ELSIF length >= maxQueue THEN queue[tail]:= '?'
      ELSE
        IF tail < maxQueue THEN INC(tail) ELSE tail:= 1 END;
        queue[tail]:= ch; INC(length);
      END;
    END;
  END Typed;

BEGIN
  length:= 0; head:= 2; tail:= 1; stopped:= TRUE;
  ALLOCATE(space,spaceL);
  NEWPROCESS(Typed,space,spaceL,Keyboard);
  ALLOCATE(space,spaceL);
  NEWPROCESS(Printed,space,spaceL,Printer);
  TRANSFER(Main,Keyboard); TRANSFER(Main,Printer);
  EnableInterrupts;
END Service.
```

The main program is omitted in this case as well; it should only invoke the module *Service*, and then wait or do something more useful.

912F

The main program of our solution reads consecutive lines of text from the input file. If necessary, it splits the lines longer than the printer drum into more lines. For each line it then calls the *PrintLine* procedure, which triggers the hammers at appropriate moments and advances the paper to the next line after all characters have been printed. The *PrintLine* procedure examines the rotation of the drum, and, when a new character appears under the hammers, triggers appropriate hammers. Thus the available speed of the printer is fully utilized; each line is printed in at most one revolution of the drum; sometimes it may even happen that more lines are printed in a single revolution, when no characters from one line appear in the next lines. Our program ignores space characters in the line since printing them should produce no imprint on paper. It would be a waste of space on the printer drum as well as a waste of time to activate the hammers and actually "print" the spaces like other printable characters.

```
program DrumPrinter(input);
{ Controls a drum printer. }
  const
    maxLen = 132;  { the length of the printer drum }
```

```
  var
    line: packed array [1..maxLen] of char;  { the text line }
    len: integer;        { the length of the current line }

  procedure Advance; external;
  procedure Location(var ch: char); external;
  procedure Strike(j: integer); external;

  procedure PrintLine;
  { Print a line on the drum printer. }
    var
      i: integer;
      c,c0: char;
      unprinted: integer;          { the number of characters still waiting to be printed }
  begin {PrintLine}
    unprinted:=0;
    for i:=1 to len do
      if line[i]<>' ' then unprinted:=unprinted+1;
    Location(c0);
    while unprinted>0 do begin
      repeat Location(c) until c<>c0;        { wait for a new character on the drum }
      for i:=1 to len do
        if line[i]=c then
          begin Strike(i); unprinted:=unprinted-1 end;
      c0:=c;
    end; {while}
    Advance;
  end; {PrintLine}

begin {DrumPrinter}
  while not eof do begin
    len:=0;
    while not eoln and (len<maxLen) do
      begin len:=len+1; read(line[len]) end;
    if eoln then readln;
    PrintLine;
  end; {while}
end. {DrumPrinter}
```

If the text contains a character that is not on the drum, our solution finds itself at a standstill. In this case, the program loops, waiting hopelessly for the awaited character to appear. The improvement of the program is left to the reader.

It is not difficult to write the *Advance*, *Location* and *Strike* procedures to write to the screen of a terminal as the drum printer does on paper. It is funny to observe such unusual text output on a screen.

922F (a) The unknown voltage is measured by connecting it to one input of the comparator (say INPUT2), and connecting the other input to an adjustable source of a known voltage, which is in our case provided by the output wire OUTPUT. By changing the known voltage and examining the state of the comparator (using the *Compare* procedure) we may determine the unknown voltage.

If any voltage within the allowed interval from 0 mV to 1023 mV is equally probable (case (**b**)), then the bisection requires the least number of comparisons on average. We limit the interval of the unknown voltage U by a lower and upper bound ($min \leq U < max$). On the output, we set the voltage at the middle of this interval. The comparator then tells us whether the unknown voltage is in the lower half of the interval or in its upper half. In this way, the interval may be narrowed down to that half of the current interval which bounds the unknown voltage. The procedure is repeated until the interval is narrowed down to one millivolt ($max - min = 1\,mV$), since the output voltage cannot be adjusted with finer accuracy. The relation $min \leq U < max$ still holds. In this way the unknown voltage has been determined with the accuracy of one millivolt. To be consistent, the program should output that the voltage is in the interval obtained. The solution outputs the lower bound only, and the measurer should be aware that the voltage measured may deviate from the actual value, but not by more than 1 mV.

Procedure (**c**) must be capable of measuring an arbitrary voltage in the allowed interval. For better effectiveness it may anticipate that the voltage changes slowly, meaning that the new measurement is close to the previous one. Our second algorithm proceeds as follows:

1. Set the voltage on the output to the old measured value as the starting estimate.
2. Select the direction (increasing or decreasing voltages) of the further search with regard to the outcome of the comparison.
3. Increment the voltage on the output by 1 mV in the selected direction until the outcome of the comparison changes. The voltage on the output is now within 1 mV from the unknown voltage.

There is a slight difficulty with this algorithm when the unknown voltage lies outside the allowed interval of measurement. The output voltage cannot be set outside the allowed range; the algorithm above tries that and since it is not known how the adjustable output acts in such a case, the operation of the procedure is unpredictable. In the program below, we have included the range tests to avoid overflow.

One final remark: for a pair of continuous physical quantities (for instance, voltages), we can never claim they are equal. In our solution we have tried to handle the outcome of the comparison of two "equal" voltages correctly, although this is probably irrelevant.

```
program Measurement(output);
{ The measurement of an unknown voltage. OUTPUT is connected to }
{ INPUT1, and the unknown voltage is connected to INPUT2. }
  const
    min = 0;    { the minimum output voltage }
    max = 1023; { the maximum output voltage }
  var
    u: integer;   { the measured voltage }
  procedure SetOutput(n: integer); external;
  procedure Compare(var which: integer); external;
  function Bisection: integer;
  { Measure the voltage using the bisection method. }
    var
      lower,upper: integer;              { the bounds of the measurement interval }
      u: integer;                          { the voltage compared to the unknown }
      v: integer;                  { the comparison outcome as returned by Compare }
  begin {Bisection}
    lower:=min;
    upper:=max+1;
    while upper-lower>1 do begin
      u:=(upper+lower) div 2;
      SetOutput(u);
      Compare(v);
      if v=1 then upper:=u else lower:=u;
    end; {while}
    Bisection:=lower;
  end; {Bisection}
  function Follow(estimate: integer): integer;
  { Measure the voltage by approaching in steps of 1 mV. }
    var
      u: integer;                          { the voltage compared to the unknown }
      v,vOld: integer;             { the comparison outcome as returned by Compare }
      step: integer;               { the increment in the correct direction: +1 or -1 }
      overflow: boolean;                { the voltage is outside the allowed interval }
  begin {Follow}
    u:=estimate;
    SetOutput(u);
    Compare(v); vOld:=v;
    if v=1 then step:=-1 else step:=+1;
    overflow:=false;
```

```
    repeat
      u:=u+step;
      if u<min then  begin overflow:=true; u:=min end
      else if u>max then  begin overflow:=true; u:=max end
      else begin SetOutput(u); Compare(v) end;
    until (v<>vOld) or overflow;
    if not overflow and (step=+1) then Follow:=u-1
    else Follow:=u;
  end; {Follow}
begin {Measurement}
  u:=Bisection;  writeln('The fast measurement: ',u:4,'mV');
  repeat
    u:=Follow(u);  writeln('The tracking measurement: ',u:4,'mV');
  until false;
end. {Measurement}
```

Tradition as well as experience shows that the bisection is one of the problems for which it is impossible to write a correct program at the first attempt. To ascertain that our *Bisection* procedure actually works correctly, and at the same time to demonstrate the method of formally proving program correctness, we now proceed to prove its correctness. First, we rewrite the essential part of the program to avoid the use of the *SetOutput* and *Compare* procedures; also, we denote the measured voltage by U. Also, we insert comments describing relations among variables between the statements of the program, which always hold at the point they are written. Such relations are called the *invariants*.

```
{ 1. min <= U <= max }
lower:=min; upper:=max+1;
{ 2. lower <= U < upper }
while upper-lower>1 do begin
  { 3. upper - lower > 1 }
  { 4. lower <= U < upper }
  u:=(upper+lower) div 2;
  { 5. lower < u < upper }
  if U<u then
    { 6. lower <= U < u }
    upper:=u
    { 7. lower <= U < upper }
  else
    { 8. u <= U < upper }
    lower:=u;
    { 9. lower <= U < upper }
  { 10. lower <= U < upper }
end; {while}
{ 11. upper - lower <= 1 }
{ 12. lower <= U < upper }
```

We now demonstrate each statement in turn.

Statement 1 is a consequence of the statement of the problem: the voltage is between *min* and *max* (inclusive).

Statement 2 is statement 1 rewritten with new variables.

Statement 3 holds at the start of the loop, otherwise the loop would terminate.

The start of the loop may be reached in two ways: from the program before the loop, or by the repetition of the loop. Statement 4 is true in both cases; in the first case as the rewritten statement 2, in the second, as the rewritten statement 10.

Statement 5 is most difficult to prove because of the implicit *trunc* in the **div** operation. From statement 3 it follows that $lower < upper$, so it is always

$$lower < \frac{(lower + upper)}{2} < upper.$$

if the division is performed without rounding. Two cases must be observed: when the division is even ($upper + lower$ is even) and when the division is not even ($upper + lower$ is odd). If the division is even, the quotient without rounding equals the quotient with rounding, so

$$lower < (lower + upper) \textbf{ div } 2 < upper$$

If the division is, however, not even, we have, for nonnegative *lower* and *upper*

$$(lower + upper) \textbf{ div } 2 = \frac{(lower + upper - 1)}{2}$$

Considering the statement 3 we obtain

$$lower < upper - 1$$

$$lower = \frac{(lower + lower)}{2} < \frac{(lower + upper - 1)}{2} <$$

$$< \frac{(upper - 1 + upper - 1)}{2} = upper - 1 < upper$$

In both cases we obtain statement 5 if we consider that

$$u = (lower + upper) \textbf{ div } 2$$

Statements 6 and 8 are the consequences of statements 4 and 5 and the condition in the **if** statement. Statements 7 and 9 are the consequences of statements 6 and 8 considering both assignment statements, and statement 10 is the synthesis of statements 7 and 9. Statement 11 holds since the loop terminates, and statement 12 is a rewritten statement 10 (or 2, if the loop is not executed at all).

By proving all statements in all possible courses of program execution, we have proved that all statements hold always when the program executes at the point the statement is written. Therefore, if the execution ever terminates, then *lower* $\leq U <$ *upper* which is exactly what we want.

How do we prove that the execution terminates? The only time that the execution does not terminate is when the loop does not terminate. In each iteration, the difference *upper−lower* is halved. The loop terminates when this difference is less than or equal to 1. This means that the loop terminates in a finite number of steps (the number of steps equals $\log_2(max + 1 - min)$).

A variety of literature exists on proving the correctness of programs, for instance: S. Alagić, M. A. Arbib: *The design of well-structured and correct programs*, Springer-Verlag, New York 1987.

932F The problem is fairly similar to problem 822F, so it is advisable to study that solution. First, let us think about a one-way communication (about character transmission from the transmitter to the receiver) and devise the protocol.

Since no synchronization signals are available, their role must be accomplished by changing the contents of the common location. When the transmitter writes a new value to the common location and thus changes its contents, the receiver detects the change and records the new value. The receiver must acknowledge the reception and the only means available is to change the value of the common location again.

Two-way communication is devised in a similar manner. In this case, computer 1 sometimes plays the role of the transmitter, while computer 2 is the receiver. After transmitting each character, the computers switch roles. Since the reception is acknowledged by any change of the value of the common location, the receiver may switch to transmission at the same time as the acknowledgement — the reception is acknowledged by transmitting a character in the opposite direction (from the ex-receiver to the ex-transmitter).

The problem is almost solved. A difficulty occurs when after reception of a character accidentally the same character has to be transmitted in the opposite direction. In this case, the contents of the common location *does not change*, so the other computer does not know that the reception has been acknowledged, and that a new character is ready. The problem may be solved in various ways. In our solution we assume that there are 128 characters (with codes 0..127). When transmitting, the first computer enters the exact character codes to the common location, while the second one adds 256 to each character code transmitted (sets the ninth bit). This ensures that the values entered by the first computer into the common location always differ from the values entered by the second one. After transmission the added value is removed.

Since communication may not stop even when one computer runs out of characters to transmit (and thus would not be able to confirm reception), some unused character code (say 128) is used solely to acknowledge reception; instead of printing it out, the receiver discards it.

```
program Dialog;
{ Two-way communication between two computers. }
  const
    filler = 128;        { the acknowledge-only value }
  var
    r: integer;          { the number of this computer }
    c: char;             { the character received or transmitted }
    ok: integer;         { indicates if a character is available from the keyboard }
    receive: boolean;    { the current state of the program: receive/transmit }
    d,dOld: integer;     { the new and the old value of the common location }

  procedure Assign(d: integer); external;
  procedure Inspect(var d: integer); external;
  procedure WriteCh(c: char); external;
  procedure ReadCh(var c: char; var ok: integer); external;
  procedure Computer(var r: integer); external;

begin {Dialog}
  Computer(r); d:=0;
  receive:=(r=1);            { the first computer initially receives, the second transmits }
  repeat
    if receive then
      begin
        dOld:=d;
        repeat Inspect(d) until d<>dOld;                { wait until the value changes }
        if d>=256 then d:=d-256;                        { remove the ninth bit }
        if d<>filler then WriteCh(chr(d));
      end
    else { transmit }
      begin
        ReadCh(c,ok);
        if ok=0 then d:=filler else d:=ord(c);
        if r=2 then d:=d+256;
        Assign(d);
      end; {if}
    receive:=not receive;                          { switch receive/transmit or vice-versa }
  until false;
end. {Dialog}
```

1011F The problem described is probably known to any programmer wondering how his program could go astray. At such times he has probably wished he could have observed what was happening inside the program *before* getting into trouble.

The airplane flight-recorder is intended for the same purpose: during the flight it continually records the instrument readings and the conversation of the pilots, and retains the last few minutes of the recording in case of an accident.

Electronic engineers know the problem as well, as they frequently observe the changing of a voltage *prior* to a key event on the screen of an oscilloscope. On an ordinary oscilloscope this is only possible in the case of a repeated signal. The problem is more easily solved with digital oscilloscopes or logic analyzers. The job is performed by fast memory circuitry and some other electronics using a procedure similar to the one presented later on. Such circuitry is capable of sampling the input circuitry with the frequency of several dozen million samples per second.

An important requirement of the problem is that the successive readings follow as fast as possible. To fulfil this requirement, an appropriate data structure must be selected together with a suitable algorithm. The successive readings are stored in a table *t*. Until the table is full, the readings may be stored in successive elements of the table. When the table is full, a new reading may be stored in the table only by overwriting the oldest one. For such a long table it is not practical to shift the whole table by an element towards its start, since that takes too much time. Instead, we imagine that the table is circular, that its first element follows the last one. When the table is full, we simply shift the boundary between the oldest and the most recent reading. The variable *last* always points to the last (the most recent) reading in the table, while the variable *length* stores the number of readings currently stored in the table. At the end of the reading, the index *first* is computed to ease output, pointing to the oldest reading in the table.

The output of readings is not difficult either: starting at the reading pointed to by *first*, *length* readings must be output from consecutive elements of the circular table.

A similar data structure is described in solutions 832F and 1023F.

```
program BlackBox(output);
{ Records and outputs events before interrupting the measurement. }
  const maxt = 1000;     { the maximum number of readings }
  type stateT = (MEASURE,PRINTOUT);
  var
    t: array [1..maxt] of integer;  { the stored readings }
    length: integer;          { the number of readings stored }
    first: integer;           { the index of the oldest reading stored }
    last: integer;            { the index of the newest reading stored }
```

```
procedure Measurement(var voltage: integer); external;
procedure State(var s: stateT); external;

procedure Recording;
{ Records the events while state is MEASURE. }
  var s: stateT;
begin
  length:=0; last:=0;
  repeat State(s) until s=MEASURE;              { wait for the start of measuring }
  while s=MEASURE do begin
    if last<maxt then last:=last+1 else last:=1;
    Measurement(t[last]);
    if length<maxt then length:=length+1;
    State(s);
  end; {while}
  first:=((last+maxt-length) mod maxt) + 1;
end; {Recording}

procedure Printing;
{ Prints the recorded readings. }
  var i,j: integer;
begin
  j:=first;
  for i:=1 to length do begin
    writeln(t[j]);
    if j<maxt then j:=j+1 else j:=1;
  end; {for}
end; {Printing}

begin {BlackBox}
  repeat Recording; Printing until false;
end. {BlackBox}
```

The speed of sampling depends on the type of the computer used and the quality of the program. A program on a home computer, written in an assembly language, is capable of performing several dozen thousand readings in a second (as an orientation: the processor 8088 in a PC/XT performs approximately 50 000 readings in a second).

Another remark is due. Instead of the statement

```
if last<maxt then last:=last+1 else last:=1;
```

we could write the shorter one:

```
last:=last mod maxt + 1;
```

This was not done since the computation of the modulo is usually much slower than the **if** statement above.

1013F When the measuring scale moves, the signals from the sensors change. Since the sensors are half the strip width apart, in any given moment the state of at most one sensor may change; both sensors never change simultaneously. For the measurement, the only interesting event is when the state of any sensor changes—then the weight changes for a half of the unit. How does the program detect the change of state? In the variables $a0$ and $b0$ the state of the sensors at the previous reading is stored. If the new reading differs from the previous one, the state of a sensor has changed. The skeleton of our solution thus follows:

```
var
  a,b: integer;     { the current reading of the sensors A and B }
  a0,b0: integer;  { the previous reading of the sensors A and B }

a0:=SensorA; b0:=SensorB;
repeat
  repeat { wait until the state of either sensor changes }
    a:=SensorA; b:=SensorB;
  until (a<>a0) or (b<>b0);
  Act;
  a0:=a; b0:=b; { save the last reading of the sensors }
until false;
```

Observe the point in the program where we have written *Act*. At this point we may be sure (from the termination condition of the **repeat** loop) that either sensor A or B changed its value. From the description of the balance we know that the value of *both* sensors could not change. Therefore four possible changes of the sensor states remain. Let us illustrate them in the following table:

if the sensors change	always	only when the force increases	only when the force decreases
sensor A from 1 to 0	$a0=1,\ a=0$	$b0=1,\ b=1$	$b0=0,\ b=0$
sensor A from 0 to 1	$a0=0,\ a=1$	$b0=0,\ b=0$	$b0=1,\ b=1$
sensor B from 1 to 0	$b0=1,\ b=0$	$a0=0,\ a=0$	$a0=1,\ a=1$
sensor B from 0 to 1	$b0=0,\ b=1$	$a0=1,\ a=1$	$a0=0,\ a=0$

From the table we deduce the following four conditions:

1. when the force increases: $b=a0,\ a\neq b0$
2. when the force decreases: $b\neq a0,\ a=b0$

Since the conditions for increasing force exclude the conditions for decreasing force, it does not matter which of the four are used in the solution. The final solution is as follows:

```
program Balance(output);
{ A spring balance with optical reading of the measuring scale. }
  var
    weight: real;      { the current weight }
    a,b: integer;      { the current reading of the sensors A and B }
    a0,b0: integer;    { the previous reading of the sensors A and B }

  function SensorA: integer; external;
  function SensorB: integer; external;

begin {Balance}
  weight:=0;
  a0:=SensorA; b0:=SensorB;
  repeat
    repeat a:=SensorA; b:=SensorB until (a<>a0) or (b<>b0);
    if (a<>a0) and (b<>b0) then writeln('Error')
    else if a0=b then weight:=weight+0.5 else weight:=weight-0.5;
    writeln('F = ',weight:5:1,' N');
    a0:=a; b0:=b;
  until false;
end. {Balance}
```

1023F The problem was especially up-to-date when it was posed: about a month after the nuclear power plant catastrophe at Chernobyl, USSR. In the solution, the ring buffer data structure is encountered again (see problems 832F and 1011F).

The text of the problem does not directly state the type of the *Time* function, whether it is of type *real* or *integer*. It is only known that a minute is used as the unit. To obtain an accurate average of the number of particles in the last hour, the *Time* function should return continuous time. For each particle, the time when it traverses the Geiger-Müller meter should be recorded, all the data from the last hour saved, and the average computed from these data.

In our solution we assume that the *Time* function returns discrete time, that is, an integer. The majority of competitors also assumed that the *Time* function was of type *integer*. This only enables us to compute the average every minute, which actually does not limit the use of the program, and reduces its memory usage.

The *Count* procedure examines the meter for one minute and counts the pulses. For the last sixty minutes, the table *basket* stores the number of particles in each minute. The variable *last* is the index to the newest reading in the table. When the table is filled to the end, the oldest entries are overwritten, as the data older than one hour are not needed any more. To avoid summing the elements of the table *basket* each time the average is output, the number of particles in the last hour is updated instead. Care is necessary with the time measurement around midnight, and also in computing the average during the first hour of measurement, when there are less data than for the entire hour available.

```
program Geiger(output);
{ Measures radioactivity using the Geiger–Müller meter. }
  var
    t: integer;                          { the current time in minutes since midnight }
    last: integer;                 { the index to the newest reading in the circular list }
    nMinutes: integer;   { the number of minutes for which the readings are available }
    nPtMin: integer;                       { the number of particles in the last minute }
    nPart: integer;       { the number of particles in the last hour or from the start }
    basket: array [1..60] of integer;  { the circular list }

  function Time: integer; external;
  function Pulse: integer; external;

  function Count(var t: integer; duration: integer): integer;
  { Counts pulses from the current time t to t+duration. }
  { Time is given in minutes. }
    var n,t0,dt: integer;
  begin {Count}
    n:=0; t0:=t;
    repeat
      n:=n+Pulse; t:=Time; dt:=t−t0;
      if dt<0 then dt:=dt+24*60;
    until dt>=duration;
    Count:=n;
  end; {Count}

begin {Geiger}
  writeln('The average number of particles in the last hour');
  last:=0; nMinutes:=0; nPart:=0; t:=Time;
  repeat
    if last<60 then last:=last+1 else last:=1;
    nPtMin:=Count(t,1); nPart:=nPart+nPtMin;
    if nMinutes<60 then nMinutes:=nMinutes+1
    else nPart:=nPart−basket[last];
    basket[last]:=nPtMin;
    writeln(t div 60:2,':',t mod 60:2,'   ',
            nPart/nMinutes:8:2,' particles/minute');
  until false;
end. {Geiger}
```

1033F The problem of resource allocation was already discussed in solutions 623F and 734F, while the critical section was encountered in solution 832F. The *Allocate* and *Deallocate* procedures are usually parts of the operating system, and so the ordinary computer user does not have to bother with inventing the algorithm to implement exclusive access of users (programs, processes) to common resources.

In general, there may be more resources, as well as several users who wish to use them. Our problem limits itself to a single resource (the disk) and a number of users (processes). The basic idea of the solution is as follows: a common memory location records which process currently uses the disk (the process number, a positive number). If the disk is currently unused, the value of the common location is zero. When a process wishes to access the disk, it first waits until the value of the common location becomes zero, and then assigns its number to it, thus denoting that the disk unit is in its sole use until released. When it needs the disk no more it sets the common location to zero.

The first approximation of the solution thus follows:

```
var common: integer;                          { the common location, initially 0 }

procedure Wait(Time: integer); external;
function WhoAmI: integer; external;

procedure Allocate;
{ Allocates a resource. }
begin
  while common<>0 do Wait(1);
  common:=WhoAmI;
end; {Allocate}

procedure Deallocate;
{ Deallocates an allocated resource. }
begin
  if common=WhoAmI then common:=0
  else writeln('invalid operation');
end; {Deallocate}
```

The *Allocate* procedure usually works correctly, only sometimes it is unlucky, and does not perform its duty. Suppose two processes simultaneously decide they need the disk, and that each calls its own *Allocate*. It may happen that *Allocate* in both processes finds a zero in the common location. Believing that the disk is free, they both assign their process number to *common*. The variable *common* thus first receives the value of the faster process, but is immediately overwritten with the number of the slower process, although the latter should not have done that as the common location was not zero at the time. The consequence of this is that each process believes that the disk is in its possession, so they may "step on each other's fingers".

Obviously the operation of testing the value of *common* and the assignment to it should be performed in a single step, to prevent anyone from interfering with the allocation procedure. The portion of the program from testing the value of the variable *common* up to the assignment to it is called a **critical section**. When any process executes a critical section of a program, no other process may enter a critical section of the same type (it may not examine the value of the variable *common* to change it, it may, however, perform the allocation of another resource).

Let us consider several ways of implementing a critical section. If all processes execute on the same processor, a program entering a critical section may request that the processor is assigned solely to it until it exits the critical section — for instance by inhibiting program interrupts, for which most processors provide a simple and fast machine instruction. Let us improve our solution.

```
procedure EnterCritSec; { the start of a critical section }
begin InhibitInterrupts end; {EnterCritSec}

procedure ExitCritSec; { the end of a critical section }
begin EnableInterrupts end; {ExitCritSec}

procedure Allocate;
{ Allocates a resource. }
  var
    process: integer;
    allocated: boolean;
begin
  process:=WhoAmI;
  repeat
    EnterCritSec;
    begin { the critical section }
      if common=0 then common:=process;
      allocated:=(common=process);
    end;
    ExitCritSec;
    if not allocated then Wait(1);
  until allocated;
end; {Allocate}
```

The portion of the *Allocate* procedure — from the call to *EnterCritSec* up to the call to *ExitCritSec* — is a critical section. When writing critical sections, we must strive to ensure that the program leaves the critical section as soon as possible, to avoid other programs waiting for entry to their critical sections unnecessarily. For instance, in the *Allocate* procedure it is important that the call to the *Wait* procedure is outside the critical section, forcing us to slightly complicate the program.

Some computers provide a special uninterruptible machine instruction which stores the value of its operand and then assigns a new value to it. The same thing may be achieved by an uninterruptible machine instruction that interchanges the values of two variables. Such instructions exist primarily to allow fast and effective implementation of critical sections.

As an exercise, the reader may try writing the *EnterCritSec* and *ExitCritSec* procedures using an additional memory location and a *Swap* procedure:

```
procedure Swap(var a,b: integer); external;
```

which interchanges the values of its arguments a and b with a single instruction.

All solutions so far have used additional mechanisms not described in the text of the problem (the text, however, does not prohibit them, although the authors of the problem had that in mind). Let us now show a solution which solves the problem without any additional mechanisms for two processes. The algorithm was first described by E. W. Dijkstra and written by Dekker.

```
var
{ the following variables are in the common memory: }
  onTurn: 1..2;  { should be initially 1 }
  uses: array [1..2] of boolean;  { both elements initially false }

procedure Allocate;  { resource allocation – the solution for two processes }
{ Allocates a resource. }
  var
    me,him: integer;
begin
{ assume that one process has the number 1 and the other 2 }
  me:=WhoAmI;
  him:=3–me;  { maps 2 → 1  and  1 → 2 }
  uses[me]:=true;
  while uses[him] do
    if onTurn<>me then begin
      uses[me]:=false;
      repeat until onTurn=me;
      uses[me]:=true;
    end; {if}
end; {Allocate}

procedure Deallocate;  { resource deallocation – the solution for two processes }
{ Deallocates an allocated resource. }
  var me,him: integer;
begin
  me:=WhoAmI; him:=3–me;
  uses[me]:=false; onTurn:=him;
end; {Deallocate}
```

The solution may be extended to the case of more processes; we omit it due to its length.

Finally, we note that the solutions proposed are appropriate only for multiprocessor computers, where each process executes on a separate processor. In an ordinary computer, where the processor time of a single processor is divided among several processes, the above solutions are too time consuming. The correct solution for such computers is to tightly couple the mechanisms to enter and exit a critical section with the scheduler, which is a part of the operating system.

More on this and similar problems can be found in the following books:

1. P. Brinch Hansen: *Operating System Principles*, Prentice-Hall, Englewood Cliffs 1979,
2. R. C. Holt, G. S. Graham, E. D. Lazowska, M. A. Scott: *Structured Concurrent Programming*, Addison-Wesley, Reading 1978,
3. N. Wirth: *Programming in Modula-2*, Springer Verlag, Berlin 1983.

1112F The main difficulty of the problem lies in the synchronization of the measurement with the period of the voltage measured. The program must detect the start of each period (and with it the end of the previous period). If the changing of the voltage within the period is arbitrary, it is very difficult to determine when a period starts. The text of the problem states that the voltage is approximately sinusoidal in shape, which simplifies this determination. For a period we choose the time between two consecutive transitions of the voltage from a negative voltage through zero to a positive voltage (it would be equally appropriate to choose the time between two consecutive maximal values of the voltage or something similar). Since the voltage measured is a real number, it is fairly improbable even with a slowly changing voltage that, at the start of the period, a voltage of exactly 0 V would be measured — therefore we may only rely on the change of its sign. A similar problem occurs in numerical analysis in determination of the zeros of a function.

Within each period, the squares of the voltage measured are summed and the measurements counted in a loop, and at the end of the period the square root of the average of the squares is computed and output; then the measurement of the new period is initialized.

The details are evident from the program below:

```
program MeasureVoltage(output);
{ Measurement of the effective voltage. }
  var
    u0,u: real;  { the previous and the current value of the voltage }
    sum: real;  { the sum of squares of voltages measured in the current period }
    n: integer;  { the number of measurements in the current period }

  procedure Measure(var u: real); external;
  procedure Delay; external;
```

```
begin {MeasureVoltage}
{ wait for the first change of sign from  – to + }
  repeat Measure(u0) until u0<0;
  repeat Measure(u0) until u0>0;
  sum:=0; n:=0;
  repeat
    Measure(u);
    if (u>0) and (u0<=0) then begin             { the sign changed from – to + }
    { a new period has started }
      if n>0 then               { output the effective voltage of the previous period }
        writeln('The effective period equals ',sqrt(sum/n):7:4,' volts');
      sum:=0; n:=0;                                      { start with the new period }
    end; {if}
    u0:=u; sum:=sum+sqr(u); n:=n+1;
    Delay;                          { the waiting ensures uniformity of measurement }
  until false;
end. {MeasureVoltage}
```

When adding a large number of real values numerical errors may occur. This problem is presented in more depth in solution 1134B, in our case it was overlooked on purpose.

1122F The problem describes a very common approach used to connect remote terminals to a host computer. Such division of a physical connection to several virtual connections is used in other areas of telecommunications as well (for instance, for telephone transmissions).

Simultaneous transmission of two or more messages in one or both directions over a single line is called multiplexing (in Latin "multus" means multiple, numerous; "plexus" means interweaved). There are two classic ways to divide a physical transmission line:

— frequency division multiplexing (FDM), and
— time division multiplexing (TDM).

When using frequency division multiplexing, the entire frequency band which the line is capable of transmitting (for instance, 64 kHz) is divided into several narrower frequency bands. In the case of telephone connections, a bandwidth of 3 kHz is required for each connection (link). Using electronic equipment similar to that found in radio transmitters and receivers, several connections may be broadcast over the same cable.

When using time division multiplexing, the entire transmission capacity of the line is first for a moment allocated to the first connection, then to the second and so forth, until the last line, after which the allocation restarts with the first one. Since the switching speed is considerably greater than the highest frequency to be transmitted, the switching is imperceptible.

When transmitting digital data (for instance, characters, as is the case in our problem) both methods may be used. The device at any end of the line is called a multiplexer. Using the classic time division multiplexing, the multiplexer on the terminal side would transmit sequentially and cyclically a single character from each of the terminals, (sending a predefined character to be ignored by the receiving multiplexer if the terminal is inactive). Exactly 1/8 of the transmission capacity of the line would thus be dedicated to each of the eight terminals from our exercise. The advantage of this solution is its simplicity, since no auxiliary data load the transmission line (except periodically for synchronization), and each terminal is able to transmit one character in each cycle. The disadvantage of this method is its poor utilization of transmission speed when some of the terminals are less active. The problem requires us to write a program for the so called statistical multiplexer. Contrary to the time division multiplexer, the statistical multiplexer allocates the transmission capability only to the terminals currently active. On average (statistically) both the total throughput and the utilization of the transmission line are superior to time division multiplexing.

Prior to writing the program, we must specify the protocol for sending the data over the modem line connecting the two statistical multiplexers. We have already encountered the notion of a protocol in problems 822F and 932F. The protocol is a standard, a list of rules, governing some task — in our case the communication. We must specify how the characters from each terminal will be supplied with the information necessary to identify the origin of the characters (for instance the number of the terminal from which the characters originate).

A simple but wasteful protocol might be to precede each character transmitted with a character denoting the terminal number. The disadvantage of this method is that the additional control information, accompanying the characters transmitted from the terminals, requires a considerable part of the transmission line capacity.

Thus, it is better to collect characters from each of the terminals into groups. These groups are in turn supplied with additional data about their origin — the terminal number. The additional control characters are thus reduced, as they are distributed among more characters from the terminals.

There are more alternatives to distinguish control data from the transmitted data, only some of which will be mentioned:

1. The character set for transmission over the modem line may be divided into two parts. The characters from one part (for instance, part of ASCII control characters) are used to encode control information, while characters from the other part encode the data transmitted.
2. A single character from the character set available may be reserved to introduce control data that follow.

3. Among the control data, the number of transmitted characters that follow the control data may be included. Thus no special character is required to introduce the control data—each group of data is immediately followed by the next control data.

In our solution we decided to use the third alternative. Prior to transmitting a group of characters from a terminal, its number (the first control character), and the number of characters that follow (the second control character) are sent. They are followed by the specified number of characters.

If the length of the groups (often termed the packets) is limited to 32 characters, the terminal number (three bits) and packet length (five bits) may be packed in a single eight-bit character. In this way, one character in each packet is spared. The details of this implementation are left to the reader.

The longer the data groups (packets) are, the less frequent is the control information and the better is the transmission line throughput. On the other side, longer packets cause longer waiting time from the reception of a character from the terminal to the transmission of this character. The program is devised to increase the allowable packet length in the case of larger load, increasing the transmission line throughput, while decreasing the maximum packet length when the line load decreases, thus also decreasing the average waiting time from the moment of reception of a character till its transmission.

Our protocol is almost the same as the protocol that is in fact used in statistical multiplexers. It could be improved with a capability to detect and correct errors which frequently occur in transmission lines. For that purpose, additional code (redundancy code), computed from packet contents, is frequently appended to each block. The redundancy code is computed again when the block is received and compared to the received code. If the codes differ, an error has occurred during block transmission, and the receiver may request the bad block to be retransmitted.

Various ways exist to compute the redundancy code. Longitudinal parity may be used for this purpose, as is described in solution 1113B. Another common method is to sum the data modulo 256 (when using the 8-bit redundancy code). This sum is usually called the checksum. There are other more complicated and reliable methods, among which the best known is the CRC method—Cyclic Redundancy Check.

```
program Multiplexer;
{ A part of the program to control a statistical multiplexer. }
  const
    nTerm = 8;              { the number of terminals connected to the multiplexer }
```

```
  var
    maxBl: integer;        { the maximum number of characters sent in a single block }
    notSent: integer;           { the total number of characters not sent in one cycle }
    term,n,i: integer;
    ch: char;

  procedure ReadChar(term: integer; var ch: char); external;
  procedure Waiting(term: integer; var n: integer); external;
  procedure SendChar(ch: char); external;

begin {Multiplexer}
  maxBl:=5; { the starting estimate }
  repeat
    notSent:=0;
    for term:=1 to nTerm do begin                              { examine all terminals }
      Waiting(term,n);
      if n>0 then begin
        if n>maxBl then                                    { send at most maxBl chars }
          begin notSent:=notSent + (n-maxBl); n:=maxBl end;
        SendChar(chr(term));                                { send the terminal number }
        SendChar(chr(n));                          { send the number of chars that follow }
        for i:=1 to n do                  { send n data characters from the terminal term }
          begin ReadChar(term,ch); SendChar(ch) end;
      end; {if}
    end; {for}
  { adjust the maximum packet length to the line load }
    maxBl:=notSent div nTerm + 2;
    if maxBl<4 then maxBl:=4 else if maxBl>12 then maxBl:=12;
  until false;
end. {Multiplexer}
```

It should be noted that the program assumes the *ReadChar* procedure is the only means to decrease the number of waiting characters. If that were not the case (for instance, if the waiting characters could be discarded by depressing a special key on the terminal) the program could get into trouble.

1132F If the voltages on all horizontal wires are set to 1 V, except one, which is set to 0 V, we may determine which keys in the selected horizontal line are pressed by scanning the voltages of the vertical wires. To determine the state of all keys, this procedure is repeated for each horizontal wire. The main problem has thus been solved. Since the output is required only when the key is depressed, that is, when the state of one of the keys changes from "not pressed" to "pressed", the state of the keys at the previous scan must be stored in memory. A depression of a key is reported only in the case where the key was not pressed at the previous scan. After each scan the saved state must be updated to reflect the new state.

It is worth noting that many calculator and computer keyboards use the connections and algorithms described in this problem. Often the algorithm is implemented in circuitry and not in software.

```
program Keyboard(output);
{ Scans the keyboard and outputs the coordinates when a key is }
{ depressed. Simultaneous depressions of several keys are allowed. }
  const xMax = 4; yMax = 5;
  type stateT = 0..1;
  var
    x,y: integer;     { the coordinates of the scanned key }
    state: stateT;    { the scanned state of the vertical wire x }
    p: boolean;       { indicates the key (x,y) is depressed }
    pressed:          { the last scanned state of all keys of the keyboard }
      array [1..xMax,1..yMax] of boolean;

   procedure SetState(y: integer; state: stateT); external;
   procedure ReadState(x: integer; var state: stateT); external;

begin {Keyboard}
  for x:=1 to xMax do                              { set the initial state of the keys }
    for y:=1 to yMax do pressed[x,y]:=false;
  for y:=1 to yMax do SetState(y,1);                 { set all horizontal lines to 1 V }
  repeat
  { check for each horizontal line if it is connected to a vertical one }
    for y:=1 to yMax do begin
      SetState(y,0);                             { set the voltage of the wire y to 0 V }
      for x:=1 to xMax do begin
      { check for any change on the vertical wires }
        ReadState(x,state);  p:=(state=0);
        if p>pressed[x,y] then
          writeln(x,y);                 { if the key is now pressed but was not previously }
        pressed[x,y]:=p;                       { update the state to reflect the actual }
      end; {for}
      SetState(y,1);                         { return the voltage of the wire y back to 1 V }
    end; {for}
  until false;
end. {Keyboard}
```

Chapter G

Computer Graphics

In recent years, computer graphics has become a regular guest at the competitions, not so much due to its attractiveness as to the breadth of the problems it poses to a computer scientist. The problems mainly dealt with the algorithms to process pictures, while little attention was given to the basic algorithms for drawing, for transforming the pictorial elements (lines, curves, coloured areas, etc.) into groups of coloured points. This was not a coincidence: the drawing algorithms are either simple and well known to anybody, or too difficult for a high-school student. Interesting graphical problems are encountered elsewhere: operations with geometrical figures (polygons, solids, and similar), operations on raster (filtering, raster economization, and so on), and many other applications of computer graphics.

The common denominator of most problems in this chapter is the **raster picture**, which is used to display pictures on some graphics terminals. In it, the picture is represented by a rectangular array of colour points — the **raster**, so such devices are called raster devices. In addition to these, vector (calligraphic) devices exist, which display the picture by a set of lines. Some examples: displays of home computers, matrix and laser printers, computerized type-setting machines, and film cameras are raster devices, while pen plotters are vector devices.

In a computer, the **colour** is represented by its number, so we may imagine that the raster picture is represented by the corresponding *matrix of colour numbers* in the computer and on the raster devices. The position of a particular point is specified by the distances from a chosen corner of the matrix, which are usually called the **coordinates** of the point. Plotting is accomplished by changing colour numbers of suitable points in the matrix, thus changing the colours of the points in the picture. The colour numbers may represent various *shades of grey* or different *chromatic colours.* We will keep to the convention that the background colour is black and represented by the value 0 (denoted by the constant *BLACK*), and that the white colour is represented by the largest colour number (denoted by the constant *WHITE*). Also, we will not distinguish between the shades of grey and chromatic colours, but we will just call them colours.

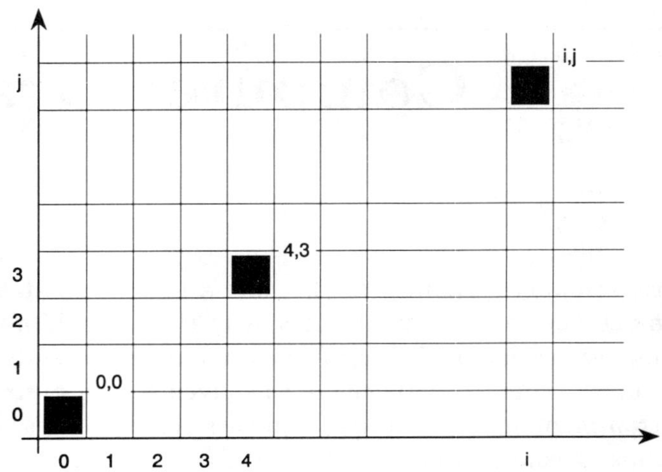

Figure G1: The raster picture

Various raster algorithms use the notion of **neighbour** points. Two kinds of neighbours are distinguished: the **strong** neighbours, of which each point may have at most four — the left, the upper, the right, and the lower one; and the **weak**, of which there are eight — the four diagonally displaced points in addition to the four strong neighbours. (By the way: can you tell which points have less than eight weak neighbours? Which points of the raster picture have the least?) For instance, point 4,8 is a weak (but not a strong) neighbour to point 5,7, while point 6,7 is its strong neighbour (and the weak as well). In solution 732G, we will encounter the strong neighbours, although the reasoning and the algorithms could easily be adapted to the case of the weak neighbours.

Related to neighbours is the notion of the **distance** between raster points. We are best acquainted with the usual — *Euclidean* — distance, which is computed using the Pythagorean theorem. In raster pictures, this distance is rather impractical, as the distance of two raster points is rarely integer, although their coordinates are always integer. Therefore, other distance measures are often used. When working with strong neighbours, the distance is defined as follows:

$d_1(A, B) = |x_A - x_B| + |y_A - y_B|$

The strong neighbours of a point A are then exactly those points W, for which $d_1(A, W) = 1$. This distance is called the Manhattan distance. It is pretty obvious why, since in Manhattan in New York, the buildings are set in a rectangular raster of streets, so that the distance above tells us how far it is from a chosen point to another, if the shortest walk through the streets is taken. For the weak neighbours, the distance is defined in a different way:

$d_\infty(A, B) = max(|x_A - x_B|, |y_A - y_B|)$

(The *max* function returns as its value the larger of its arguments.) Again, the weak neighbours are the points for which $d_\infty(A, W) = 1$. The subscripts qualifying both distances (1 and ∞) originate in mathematics. The Euclidean distance is denoted by d_2 in mathematics.

A variety of textbooks exist at different levels to introduce you to the field of computer graphics. You will find a fairly elementary introduction in the book by M. P. Hearn and D. Baker: *Computer Graphics*, Prentice-Hall, Englewood Cliffs, 1986. A more extensive treatment of the subject may be found in the text by J. D. Foley and A. Van Damm: *Fundamentals of Interactive Computer Graphics*, Addison-Wesley, 1982.

513G Imagine that the line is drawn on the screen by some kind of pen. Let the x and y variables denote its position. After the position of the pen is properly initialized, the lines are drawn simply by following the movements of the mouse, and setting the colour of the points regarding the position of the pen as well as the state of the key on the mouse. The execution speed assures that the line is connected (as the text of the problem states). The pen may escape outside the screen area, and in this case no line is drawn. The algorithm is simple:

```
repeat
   read the movement of the mouse and the state of its key;
   update the position of the pen;
   if the mouse key is pressed and
      the pen is inside the screen area then
      draw a white point;
forever
```

It is easily transcribed into the following program:

```
program Doodle(output);
{ Draw lines using a mouse. }
  const
    WID = 500;    { the screen width }
    HEI = 500;    { the screen height }
```

```
  var
    x,y: integer;      { the pen position }
    dx,dy: integer;    { the mouse movement }
    key: integer;      { the state of the mouse key }

  procedure SetColour(x,y, colour: integer); external;
  procedure Mouse(var dx,dy, key: integer); external;

begin {Doodle}
  x:=WID div 2; y:=HEI div 2;  { the initial pen position }
  repeat
    Mouse(dx,dy,key);
    x:=x+dx; y:=y+dy;
    if (key=1) and
       (0<=x) and (x<=WID) and (0<=y) and (y<=HEI) then
      SetColour(x,y, 1);
  until false;
end. {Doodle}
```

The program above is far from perfect. We immediately see some of its major deficiencies. Perhaps the least annoying is that the loop of the program never terminates, so that the drawing may only be finished violently. Can you avoid this yourself?

A much more irritating flaw of the program is that during the drawing the position of the pen is not shown, so that it is not evident where a new white line will start. To avoid this, all serious programs for drawing mark the position of the pen by a tracking symbol—the *cursor*: an arrow, a cross, an icon of a pencil or similar. Usually, the cursor also shows whether the mouse key is depressed or not: if not, the position may be shown by an arrow, otherwise by a pencil. (Can you improve the program by drawing the cursor? It is not too difficult: each time the pen moves, the cursor must be erased and redrawn at the new position. If this is done awkwardly, some of the picture may be inadvertently erased, so be careful! Which predefined function is additionally needed?)

Much more work would be necessary to enhance the program above to become a serious drawing program. Let us examine some of the most important steps.

First, the program would be improved by introducing new drawing primitives: various kinds of lines and curves, coloured areas, text, and similar. The algorithms of *raster graphics* may be used to implement this; they are described in the books mentioned in the introduction to this chapter. This part of enhancement thus poses no difficult problem.

Much more effort must be devoted to designing the *user interface*, that is, the portion of the program directly in front of the user. Since the most probable users of the program will be skilled "hand" designers, we attempt to design this part to make the *user model* of the program as close as possible to the ordinary drawing desk. The majority of the screen must certainly be assigned to the drawing area. Somewhere at its side, the most frequently used drawing tools are presented, those which the designer must have always at his disposal: pencils of various thickness, various line patterns (full, dashed, dot-dashed), and similar. Since this display plays the same role as the bill of fare in a restaurant, it is commonly called the *menu*. Less frequent tools are put away into "drawers", into pull-down menus, which open at a touch of the mouse driven cursor and enable the designer to chose from them. A line of the screen is intended for written communication and for the echo area of typed data or commands as well. The screen is thus partitioned into a number of dialogue areas (see Figure G2). It is important to enable the user to position these areas to his taste. For instance, to many, the most handy position for the tools menu is at the right of the screen, nevertheless, some (e. g. the left-handed) prefer them at the left.

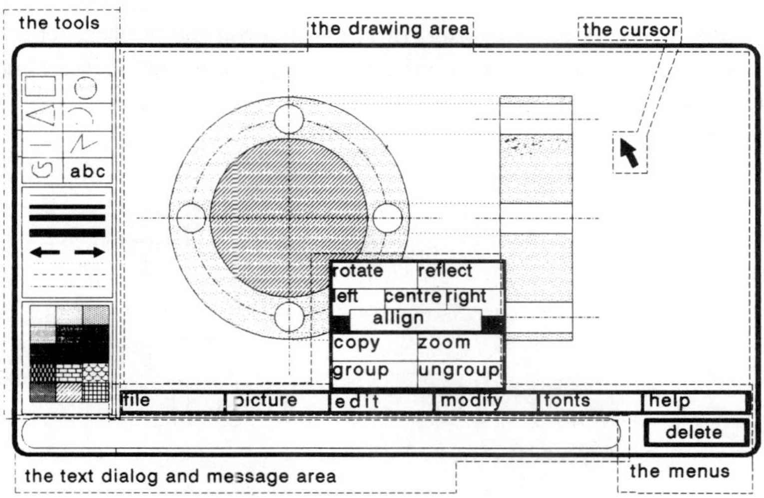

Figure G2: The dialogue areas on the screen

Other proved means are used to enhance the dialogue. Important messages are highlighted by displaying them in a different colour. The cursor has a specific shape in each dialogue area or for each particular operation: when drawing free-handed, it is displayed as a pencil, when painting, it is a paintbrush, when choosing from a menu, it only highlights the current choice. Complicated? Regardless of the programming difficulties, the program must be simple to use for those for whom it is intended and not for those who program it, otherwise it has missed its point. Most people prefer using comprehensible simple tools to powerful but unintelligible ones.

521G A rectangle with sides parallel to the coordinate axes is a very frequent aid in programming graphic problems. It is used so frequently that it deserves a name: it is called a **box**. The name originates from its use in three dimensions, where the analogous construct is indeed a box. A box is never used alone, usually some graphical object is enclosed in it (for instance, a line, a figure, a solid) and thus the box specifies its approximate bounds. When the box contains another object, it clings tightly to its outer bounds.

The projection of the box onto the horizontal axis (x axis) is an interval on this axis, extending from the abscissa of the lower left corner of the box up to the abscissa of the upper right corner. The projection onto the vertical axis (y axis) is defined analogously. Both its projections precisely define the box, since all its four corners can be determined from them. When the box encloses a connected figure (a triangle, a ring, an ellipse, an epicycloid), the projections specify the extents of the figure in the specific direction; at the same time, they are the *projections of the figure* onto the respective axis. When the figure inside a box is not connected, when it is composed of several separate islands, the box roughly describes the location of the archipelago. Finally, a question for clever heads: if a box encloses a rectangle, can the box be different from it?

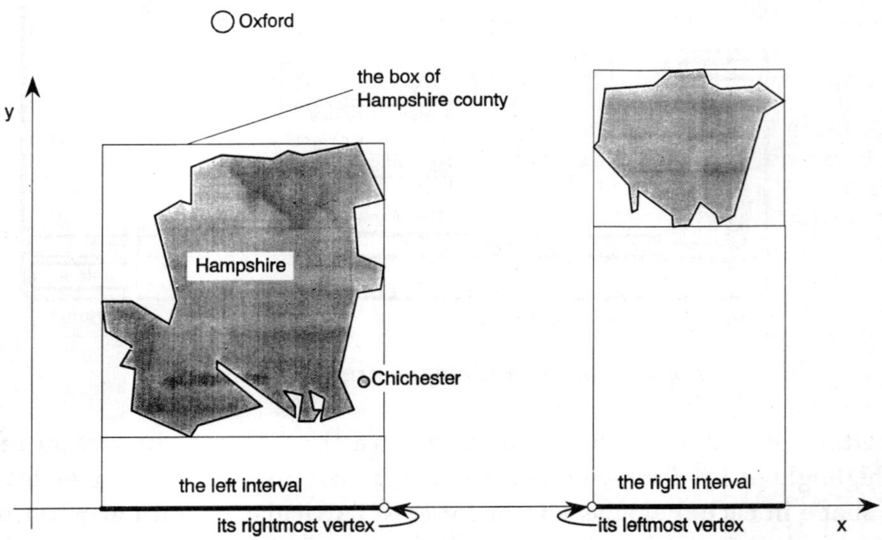

Figure G3: The box of a figure

a) To determine the enclosing box of a pair of boxes, let us observe its projections on both coordinate axes. Its projection on the x axis must contain the projection of both smaller boxes, so it must extend from the leftmost of both left endpoints to the rightmost of both right endpoints. A similar conclusion holds for the y direction. Both endpoints are computed using the *Min* and *Max* functions, which, given a pair of real numbers, determine (respectively) the smaller or the greater of the two.

b) The rectangles have a common point when their projections onto either axis intersect. As we said before, the projections are intervals. Two intervals intersect unless one is entirely to the left of the other. In the latter case (see Figure G3), the *right* endpoint of the *left* interval (or, in other words, the leftmost of both right endpoints) is to the left of the *left* endpoint of the *right* interval. So, the larger abscissa of their *lower left* corners must be smaller than the smaller abscissa of their *upper right* corners; a similar conclusion must hold for the ordinates of the corners, if the two rectangles are to have a point in common. Let us translate these conclusions into Pascal:

```
type box = record xLeft,yLower, xRight,yUpper: real end;

function Min(a,b: real): real;
  begin
    if a<b then Min:=a else Min:=b
  end;

function Max(a,b: real): real;
  begin
    if a<b then Max:=b else Max:=a
  end;

procedure EnclosingBox(a,b: box; var c: box);
{ Determines the smallest enclosing box of two boxes. }
begin
  c.xLeft:=   Min(a.xLeft,   b.xLeft);
  c.yLower:=  Min(a.yLower,  b.yLower);
  c.xRight:=  Max(a.xRight,  b.xRight);
  c.yUpper:=  Max(a.yUpper,  b.yUpper);
end; {EnclosingBox}

function HaveCommonPoint(a,b: box): boolean;
{ Determines, whether the boxes given have a common point. }
begin
  HaveCommonPoint:=
    (Max(a.xLeft,b.xLeft) <= Min(a.xRight,b.xRight)) and
    (Max(a.yLower,b.yLower) <= Min(a.yUpper,b.yUpper));
end; {HaveCommonPoint}
```

In practice, boxes are used for fast but less accurate determination of the *relative location* of geometrical figures. If, for example, the box of a polygon has no point in common with the box of a line, the line cannot intersect the polygon boundary. Similarly, a point cannot lie inside a polygon if it lies outside its box.

Tests using boxes are simple and fast operations, and they cheaply reveal evidently distinct polygons, lines and points. For example: using a not particularly accurate digitalization, the boundary of Hampshire county in England would be represented by 300 points (see figure G3). Together with the digitalization, the box of the contour would be determined once and for all, with a slight increase in memory and time requirements. Without the box of the boundary, a computer would have to compare the coordinates of Oxford to the coordinates of all 300 boundary points to determine that it lies outside the county, while that would be evident after only four comparisons if box test was used. To determine the same for Chichester, the test with boxes would have to be complemented by the comparison to the boundary, since Chichester lies too close to the Hampshire boundary. Here, comparisons to boundary points are approximately equivalent to box comparisons, only rarely must an additional calculation be performed — the algorithm is similar to that of solution 811G. For Oxford, approximately 296 comparisons are spared, while for Chichester four additional are required — an impressive improvement on average.

It is much more difficult to determine the intersection of two lines using their boxes. In comparison to the usual computational procedure it has the advantage that it uses only addition and division by 2 and may thus be implemented on a fairly simple processor incapable of integer division. Can you devise the algorithm? Since this exercise is not quite trivial, a hint will probably be welcome: from the box of a line, it is easy to determine the boxes of both halves. If one of them has no common point with the boxes of the other line, the intersection lies outside it, so the box may be omitted from further partitioning.

712G

To solve the problem, the number of occurrences of each colour in the points of the picture must first be counted, that is, we must determine the **colour distribution**. Since the number of all points in the picture is known, the boundary colour is first determined as the one at which the total number of points with the colour less than or equal to the boundary colour exceeds half the number of picture points. This boundary is too far if the preceding colour is closer to half; in this case the boundary colour is decreased. The modification of the picture is then performed in another pass through all points of the picture.

```
program TransformPicture(input,output);
{ Modifies a half-tone picture to a two-colour one. }
  const
    BLACK= 0;        { the black colour number }
    WHITE= 127;      { the white colour number }
    WID  = 512;      { the picture width }
    HEI  = 512;      { the picture height }
    HALF = 131072;  { half of the number of points in the picture, =WID*HEI/2 }
```

```
  type
    colour = BLACK..WHITE;
    picture = array [1..WID,1..HEI] of colour;
  var pic: picture;
  procedure ReadPicture(var pic: picture); external;
  procedure SavePicture(var pic: picture); external;
  function BoundaryColour(var pic: picture): colour;
  { Determines the boundary colour approximately halving the colours. }
    var
      i,j,k,boundary: integer;
      distr: array [colour] of integer;
  begin
  { Determine the colour distribution first. }
    for k:=BLACK to WHITE do distr[k]:=0;
    for i:=1 to WID do
      for j:=1 to HEI do
        distr[pic[i,j]]:=distr[pic[i,j]]+1;
  { Find the boundary colour from the distribution. }
    boundary:=BLACK; k:=distr[BLACK];
    while k<HALF do begin boundary:=boundary+1; k:=k+distr[boundary] end;
    if (boundary>BLACK) and ((k-HALF)>(HALF-k+distr[boundary])) then
      boundary:=boundary-1;
    BoundaryColour:=boundary;
  end; {BoundaryColour}
  procedure ModifyPicture(boundary: colour; var pic: picture);
  { Modifies the halftones in a picture to two colours. }
    var i,j: integer;
  begin
    for i:=1 to WID do
      for j:=1 to HEI do
        if pic[i,j]<=boundary then pic[i,j]:=BLACK else pic[i,j]:=WHITE;
  end; {ModifyPicture}
begin {TransformPicture}
  ReadPicture(pic);
  ModifyPicture(BoundaryColour(pic),pic);
  SavePicture(pic);
end. {TransformPicture}
```

The program would work correctly in most cases even without the conditional which decreases the boundary when it escapes too far (such was the "official" solution at the competition). However, it would fail for instance in the case of a two-colour picture with more than half of the points of the larger-valued colour. In this case, the program would set the boundary after the second colour and colour the entire picture with colour 0. From this error in the official solution problem 1034D originated, where you may find additional remarks.

732G First, let us define some terms. In the program, we call the colour 1 from the statement of the problem (in Figure N7 in the text of the problem it is depicted by circles) *WHITE*, and the colour 0 (squares from Figure N7) *BLACK* — the lines are thus drawn in white on a black background. Further, let the term **dot** denote a point coloured white. To solve the problem, we will follow the *recursive* definition of **connectedness**:

Any dot is connected to the starting dot, if it is either

— its neighbour, or if it is

— a neighbour of a point connected to the starting one.

The connected dots will therefore be deleted one after another: first the starting point, then its neighbours, then the neighbours of its neighbours, and so on. This is most easily done recursively by first removing the starting point and then repeating the process for the neighbour dots, using them as the new starting points. The corresponding *DeleteNeighbours* procedure follows:

```
procedure DeleteNeighbours(x,y: integer);
{ Deletes all dots connected to the given one. }

begin
  if pic[x,y]=WHITE then begin
    pic[x,y]:=BLACK;
    DeleteNeighbours(x-1,y); DeleteNeighbours(x+1,y);
    DeleteNeighbours(x,y-1); DeleteNeighbours(x,y+1);
  end; {if}
end; {DeleteNeighbours}
```

Short and clear, but slightly ineffective: only after the call to the procedure is it determined whether the neighbour is white at all. According to the problem, most neighbours are black, so many calls to the procedure will be in vain and waste precious computer time. The colour of the neighbour should therefore be checked prior to calling the procedure:

```
procedure DeleteNeighbours(x,y: integer);
{ Deletes all dots connected to the given one. }

begin
  pic[x,y]:=BLACK;
  if pic[x-1,y]=WHITE then DeleteNeighbours(x-1,y);
  if pic[x+1,y]=WHITE then DeleteNeighbours(x+1,y);
  if pic[x,y-1]=WHITE then DeleteNeighbours(x,y-1);
  if pic[x,y+1]=WHITE then DeleteNeighbours(x,y+1);
end; {DeleteNeighbours}
```

If necessary, the colour of the starting point must be determined prior to the initial call to the procedure. Our problem does not require that.

The simplicity of the proposed algorithm has its weakness. An unfortunate property of the recursion used in it (and elsewhere) is that it sometimes needlessly wastes computer time and memory. As we know, each call to a procedure uses some time and a portion of computer memory where the values of the arguments are stored together with the local variables (declared in the procedure) and the return address. Recursive calls are therefore often avoided, especially when analysis shows that the solution without recursion is faster but no less clear.

As the problem claims, the picture is composed mainly of lines, and so the algorithm above mainly encounters dots with a single neighbour dot (the successor, as the preceding dot has already been deleted). In this case, the entire line may be processed in a loop. The algorithm may now be respecified in slightly different words: instead of dots, it processes **lines**, which are sequences of dots with two neighbours (the predecessor and the successor). A line terminates either at an **endpoint**, a dot with a single neighbour (without a successor) or at a **crossing**, a dot with more than two neighbours (with more than one successor). At endpoints, deletion terminates, while at crossings it is continued recursively along all emanating lines. In this way, recursion is avoided along the lines, but still used at crossings.

To avoid continual testing as to whether the edge of the picture has been reached, the picture is surrounded by a frame of black points, which are definitely not connected to the starting one. This technique is frequently used in programming. The elements which play analogous roles to the frame above are called the **sentinels**, as they ensure that an algorithm does not *slip across a boundary*. The price paid — some additional memory — is negligible when compared to the increased clarity and simplicity as well as execution speed. In our case, two columns (0 and $n+1$) and two rows must be added, $4n+4$ points in total.

```
const
  WID    = 11;  { the width of the picture + 1 }
  HEI    = 11;  { the height of the picture + 1 }
  BLACK = 0;    { the background colour }
  WHITE = 1;    { the drawing colour }
type
  colour = BLACK..WHITE;
  picture = array [0..WID,0..HEI] of colour;
var
  pic: picture;
  nNeigh: integer;  { the number of the dot neighbours in DeleteNeighbours (!!!) }
```

```
procedure DeleteNeighbours(x,y: integer);
{ Deletes all dots connected to the given one. }
{ global }
{   nNeigh: integer; } { the number of the neighbours of a dot }
begin
  if pic[x,y]=WHITE then begin
  { Delete a line. }
    repeat
      pic[x,y]:=BLACK;
{*}   nNeigh:=pic[x-1,y]+pic[x+1,y]+pic[x,y-1]+pic[x,y+1];
      if nNeigh=1 then begin
        if      pic[x+1,y]=WHITE then x:=x+1
        else if pic[x-1,y]=WHITE then x:=x-1
        else if pic[x,y+1]=WHITE then y:=y+1
        else y:=y-1;
      end; {if}
    until nNeigh<>1;
  { Delete the lines emanating from this point. }
    if nNeigh>1 then begin
      if pic[x-1,y]=WHITE then DeleteNeighbours(x-1,y);
      if pic[x+1,y]=WHITE then DeleteNeighbours(x+1,y);
      if pic[x,y-1]=WHITE then DeleteNeighbours(x,y-1);
      if pic[x,y+1]=WHITE then DeleteNeighbours(x,y+1);
    end; {if}
  end; {if}
end; {DeleteNeighbours}
```

The trick in the line marked by the asterisk works only when the colour of the background equals 0 and the drawing colour equals 1. Otherwise, conditional statements must be used.

The *nNeigh* variable actually belongs among the local variables of the procedure above. By declaring it globally, we avoided useless copies of a variable not needed for a long time. Such economizing may be dangerous, as the value of a variable, used for another purpose in the enclosing program or still required at a higher level of the recursion, may be inadvertently changed. It is usually very difficult to discover such an error. It depends on the problem, whether the saving in space justifies the danger introduced by the loss of clarity. Here, it probably does not, and we only used the trick to demonstrate it; if *nNeigh* were a table of, say, a few dozen elements, the trick would be well worth doing. A good programmer uses these and other tricks, but always with caution—and with three exclamation marks in the comment to the trick. To stress the trick in the above program, the variable varnNeigh was "declared" global in the starting comment of the procedure.

Even at a crossing, the algorithm might continue iteratively along one of the branches, and process the others recursively. You might try adapting the program yourself. The algorithm might even be devised without recursion, using a *stack*. (You will find more about the stack in solution 115H). It proceeds as follows:

```
push the initial dot on the stack;
repeat
   pop the starting point of a line from the stack;
   delete the line;
   if the line endpoint is a crossing then
      push all its successors on the stack;
until the stack is empty.
```

Similar to the first version of the program above is one of the algorithms for raster colouring. After an area of the picture is surrounded by a connected line, an uncoloured starting point is chosen inside. Then, colouring proceeds by first colouring the chosen point and proceeding recursively with its uncoloured neighbours. In this way, all points inside the contour and connected to the starting point are coloured. This method of colouring is called the **flood fill**, since it really looks as if ink was spilled over a portion of the picture. The flood fill is the simplest algorithm for filling, but is also the slowest and the most memory consuming—unless it is improved as above.

811G Again, we stick to the conventions from the introduction. In the program, we call the colour with the value 1 *WHITE*, and the colour 0 *BLACK*. The figure is thus again drawn in white on a black background. As in solution 732G, we again surround the picture by a sentinel frame of black points, ensuring the edge of the figure is entirely inside the picture. In Figure N8 in the text of the problem, the white points are depicted by circles, and the black ones by empty spaces.

The edge points are clearly defined, since they are white. To determine the position of other points, we must recall what the notion of interior means: if we want to get outside, that is, far enough from a point inside the figure, we must cross its edge at least once. If we cross it for a second time we again enter it, so we must cross it once more. Therefore: travelling from an interior point towards the boundary of the picture, the edge of the figure is crossed an odd number of times. When travelling from an outside point, the edge is either not crossed at all, or it is crossed an even number of times. This conclusion leads us to the following algorithm:

```
set the current position to the starting point;
set the number of crossings to 0;
while not at the boundary of the picture do
   move by a step to the right;
   if the edge has been crossed then
      increment the number of crossings for 1;
endwhile
if the number of crossings is even
   then the starting point is outside the figure
   else it is inside the figure.
```

The only difficult point of the algorithm is the determination of whether the edge of the figure has been crossed. Two cases must be distinguished: the edge may either be actually crossed or only touched. Consider, for example, the point marked by a cross in Figure N8. If we travel from it to its left, there is no problem: the edge is obviously crossed, when the colour of the encountered points changes for the second time, since we first step on the edge, and then off it outside the figure. If we take the path to the right, however, the edge paralyzes our reasoning: when we step off it for the first time, we do not step outside, but inside again! What is the difference between the two sequences of the edge points travelled through? Observe Figure N8 carefully again. In the left sequence, the edge enters the starting point of the crossing from below, and exits the last above; in the right sequence, the edge enters as well as exits above. This is the key conclusion: if the directions of the edge before and after the crossing sequence are the same, the edge has been only touched, otherwise it has been actually crossed. The algorithm is ready to be coded in Pascal!

```
program Interior(input,output);
{ Determines whether the point lies inside the figure. }
  const
    WID   = 11;  { the picture width + 1 }
    HEI   = 11;  { the picture height + 1 }
    BLACK = 0;   { the black colour number }
    WHITE = 1;   { the white colour number }
  type
    position = (ONEDGE,INSIDE,OUTSIDE);
    colour = BLACK..WHITE;
    picture = array [0..WID,0..HEI] of colour;
```

```
  var
    pic: picture;
    i,j: integer;

  procedure ReadPicture(var pic: picture); external;

  procedure SetFrame(var pic: picture);
  { Encloses the picture inside a frame of black points. }
    var i: integer;
  begin
    for i:=0 to WID do
      begin pic[i,0]:=BLACK; pic[i,HEI]:=BLACK end;
    for i:=1 to HEI-1 do
      begin pic[0,i]:=BLACK; pic[WID,i]:=BLACK end;
  end; {SetFrame}

  function PointPosition(i,j: integer): position;
  { Determines the position of a point. }
    var
      start,endp: integer;
      ins: boolean;
  begin
    if pic[i,j]=WHITE then PointPosition:=ONEDGE
    else begin
      ins:=false; start:=0;          { from the left picture boundary (from outside) }
      while start<i do begin
        start:=start+1;                                       { towards the point }
        if pic[start,j]=WHITE then begin
          endp:=start;
          while pic[endp,j]=WHITE do endp:=endp+1;
          if pic[start,j+1]=pic[endp-1,j-1] then ins:=not ins;
          start:=endp;
        end; {if}
      end; {while}
      if ins then PointPosition:=INSIDE else PointPosition:=OUTSIDE;
    end; {if}
  end; {PointPosition}

begin {Interior}
  ReadPicture(pic); SetFrame(pic);
  write('The point coordinates : '); readln(i,j);
  case PointPosition(i,j) of
    ONEDGE:   writeln('The point is ON THE EDGE of the figure.');
    INSIDE:   writeln('The point is INSIDE the figure.');
    OUTSIDE:  writeln('The point is OUTSIDE the figure.');
  end; {case}
end. {Interior}
```

Finally, a question: what happens if the edge of the figure leaks, if it is not closed?

921G At first glance, the solution is evident: a position on the screen must be randomly chosen and the corresponding character written there. From here on things become complicated. To find the character corresponding to a position on the screen quickly, the entire commercial must be stored in memory. To start with, we may try to choose a random position on the screen by randomly choosing a position on the screen until a free one is found. But this is not a good method: the more characters there are on the screen, the longer it takes to find a free point. (How long does it take to find any particular point — for instance, the last free point — by searching randomly for it?) To make the display unchanging in speed, the display of each point must be guaranteed to take approximately the same number of operations. We must try a different way.

Why don't we try to shuffle the points randomly and then display them in the order obtained? In this way, the display of each point takes the same time, we only have to wait a little before the display starts. This solution will satisfy the expectations of the visitors entirely. So, in addition to the text of the commercial, the shuffled coordinates must be stored in the memory as well. The text is thus represented in the memory by a table of points, while each point is represented by the coordinates of its position and the character of the commercial to appear at this position.

The shuffling works by exchanging a particular point — say, the last one — by a point randomly chosen among all points. The last point is thus randomly chosen, and may be displayed. The shuffling proceeds in the same way in the remaining portion of the table. In a similar way, anything else may be shuffled, for instance, consecutive numbers, a deck of playing cards, or the like.

```
program Nowherton(input,output);
{ Outputs a commercial. }
  const
    WID = 80;    { the screen width }
    HEI  = 24;   { the screen height }
    ALL = 1920;  { the number of all characters of the screen, =WID*HEI }
  type
    point = record x,y: integer; z: char end;
    tScreen = array [1..ALL] of point;
  var
    screen: tScreen;
  procedure WriteAt(x,y: integer; ch: char); external;
  procedure Random(var r: real); external;
```

```
function ChooseRandomly(first,last: integer): integer;
{ Returns a random number between first and last. }
  var r: real;
begin
  Random(r);
  ChooseRandomly:=first+trunc(r*(last-first+1));
end; {ChooseRandomly}

procedure ReadCommercial(var screen: tScreen);
{ Reads the text of the commercial. }
  var i,j,k: integer;
begin
  k:=0;
  for j:=1 to HEI do begin
    for i:=1 to WID do begin
      k:=k+1;
      with screen[k] do begin
        x:=i; y:=j;
        if eoln then z:=' ' else read(z);
      end;
    end; {for i}
    readln;
  end; {for j}
end; {ReadCommercial}

procedure WriteCommercial(var screen: tScreen);
{ Randomly outputs the commercial on the screen. }
  var
    k,n: integer;
    t: point;
begin
  for n:=ALL downto 1 do begin
    k:=ChooseRandomly(1,n);
    t:=screen[k]; screen[k]:=screen[n]; screen[n]:=t;
    with t do WriteAt(x,y, z);
  end; {for}
end; {WriteCommercial}

begin {Nowherton}
  ReadCommercial(screen);
  WriteCommercial(screen);
end. {Nowherton}
```

The *WriteCommercial* procedure may be easily complemented by the *EraseCommercial* procedure, which erases the commercial on the screen in a similar way.

933G The proposed way to represent a raster picture is quite common in computer picture processing; it is called the **quadtree**. This way of storing a picture usually requires much less storage than storing the raster (the matrix), especially when large areas of the same colour occur in the picture. In addition, some operations on the picture run faster (for instance, the determination of the boundary colour, see solution 712G). On the other hand, the operations requiring access to particular colour points are slower, since they depend on the size of the picture. (Can you find out what kind of dependence this is? A hint: the operations are slower because more steps are needed to reach a particular point. Determine how many more steps are needed to reach a point of the picture with a side twice the size of the original one in the case of a raster picture and in the case of a quadtree).

a) The *data structure* immediately imposes itself: a four-branch tree must be represented. Its elements are either the **leaves**, in which only the colour of the single-colour square is stored; or the **branch nodes**, which store pointers to the four subtrees representing the four subsquares. The tree node is therefore a record with five fields: a colour and four pointers. When the node is a branch node, the colour is undefined and the pointers point to the roots of the subtrees. When the node is a leaf, the pointers are nil, and the colour determines the colour of the square. Since it is usually difficult to represent an undefined colour in addition to the full set of valid ones, the program below determines whether the node is a leaf by testing whether any of the pointers to the subtrees points nowhere, when it equals **nil**.

b) It is easiest to devise the algorithm to *build the quadtree from the raster* recursively. A square is split into four subsquares, which are recursively tested to see whether all are of the same colour. If not, a new branch node is produced and the pointer to it returned. In the opposite case the entire square is of the same colour, and so only its colour is returned. The description of a leaf node may only be constructed when we return to the branch node that points to it. Try guessing why—find out what would happen otherwise. Observe carefully how the *BuildQuadTree* program below functions.

c) The *colour of a point* is determined recursively as well. If a single-colour square has been reached, that is, a leaf node, the colour of the point equals its colour; otherwise we determine in which of the four subsquares the point lies and repeat the procedure.

```
program QuadTree(input,output);
{ Builds a quadtree from a raster and traverses it. }
  const
    SIZE    = 7;                  { the side of the raster square-1 }
    BLACK   = 0;                  { the black colour number }
    WHITE   = 255;                { the white colour number }
  type
    coor    = 0..SIZE;
    colour  = BLACK..WHITE;
    raster  = array [coor,coor] of colour;
    pQTree  = ↑ndQTree;
    ndQTree = record
                c: colour;
                t1,t2,t3,t4: pQTree;
              end;
  var
    x,y: integer;
    pic: raster;                  { the raster picture }
    t: pQTree;                    { the root of the quadtree }
    c: colour;                    { the colour of the quadtree }

  procedure ReadPicture(var pic: raster); external;

  procedure BuildQuadTree
     (x,y: coor;                  { the lower left corner }
      side: integer;              { the square side }
      var c: colour;              { the square colour }
      var t: pQTree);             { the subtree root }
  { Builds a quadtree from the raster picture. }
    var
      c1,c2,c3,c4: colour;        { the subsquare colours }
      t1,t2,t3,t4: pQTree;        { the subtree roots }
      halfSide: integer;          { half of the square side }
  begin
    c:=pic[x,y];
    if side=1 then                { a raster point }
      t:=nil
    else begin                    { examine each subsquare }
      halfSide:=side div 2;
    { the algorithm works correctly only for pictures with sides 2↑n points long }
      BuildQuadTree(x,          y,          halfSide, c1, t1);
      BuildQuadTree(x+halfSide, y,          halfSide, c2, t2);
      BuildQuadTree(x,          y+halfSide, halfSide, c3, t3);
      BuildQuadTree(x+halfSide, y+halfSide, halfSide, c4, t4);
      if      (t1=nil) and (t2=nil) and (t3=nil) and (t4=nil) and
              (c1=c2) and (c2=c3) and (c3=c4) then
        begin c:=c1; t:=nil end                { All squares are of the same colour. }
      else begin                                    { Squares of different colours. }
```

```
    { Make leaf nodes if necessary. }
      if t1=nil then begin new(t1); t1↑.c:=c1; t1↑.t1:=nil end;
      if t2=nil then begin new(t2); t2↑.c:=c2; t2↑.t1:=nil end;
      if t3=nil then begin new(t3); t3↑.c:=c3; t3↑.t1:=nil end;
      if t4=nil then begin new(t4); t4↑.c:=c4; t4↑.t1:=nil end;
    { Make the branch node for the entire square. }
      new(t); t↑.t1:=t1; t↑.t2:=t2; t↑.t3:=t3; t↑.t4:=t4;
    end; {if}
  end; {if}
end; {BuildQuadTree}

function PointColour
   (x,y: integer;            { the point coordinates }
    side: integer;           { the square side }
    t: pQTree                { the root of the tree }
   ): integer;
{ Determines the colour of a given point. }
  var halfSide: integer;     { half of the square side }
begin
  if t↑.t1=nil then          { leaf node }
    PointColour:=t↑.c
  else begin                 { The colour is determined by the quarter }
    halfSide:=side div 2;    {  in which the point lies }
    if x<halfSide then
      if y<halfSide then
        PointColour:=PointColour(x,            y,            halfSide, t↑.t1)
      else
        PointColour:=PointColour(x,            y-halfSide,   halfSide, t↑.t3)
    else
      if y<halfSide then
        PointColour:=PointColour(x-halfSide,   y,            halfSide, t↑.t2)
      else
        PointColour:=PointColour(x-halfSide,   y-halfSide,   halfSide, t↑.t4);
  end; {if}
end; {PointColour}

begin {QuadTree}
  ReadPicture(pic);
  BuildQuadTree(0,0, SIZE+1, c,t);
  if t=nil then
    begin new(t); t↑.c:=c; t↑.t1:=nil end;                 { single-coloured raster }
  while not eof do begin
    readln(x,y);
    writeln(x,y, PointColour(x,y, SIZE+1, t));
  end; {while}
end. {QuadTree}
```

As already mentioned, the recursive calls are best avoided if they are not necessary. They are replaced by a suitable loop; this replacement also requires that all necessary data are saved on stack explicitly. This might be done in both cases above. Especially the determination of the point colour (or any downward *search* of the quadtree without backtracking) is easily written nonrecursively:

```
consider the entire tree as the current square;
while the current square is not single-coloured do
   determine the quarter in which the point lies;
   compute the relative coordinates of the point within this quarter;
   consider this quarter as the current square;
endwhile
the colour of the point is the colour of the current square.
```

The building of the quadtree (or any up-and-down *traversal* of the tree) is slightly more complicated, since a stack must be used. Try writing it yourself. As a hint, see solution 115H first.

1022G The subpicture will be copied row-by-row, and each of them from one end towards the other.The only problem occurs when the original and the copy overlap. In this case, the original must be copied before the copy overwrites it. If the copy is to the right of the original, and so $nx > x$, the rows must be copied right-to-left, and vice-versa otherwise. Similarly, the subpicture must be copied bottom-up, if the copy lies below the original, and so $ny > y$.

```
const
  N = 16;           { the picture size }
  BLACK = 0;        { the minimum colour number }
  WHITE = 31;       { the maximum colour number }
type
  colour = BLACK..WHITE;
  picture = array [1..N,1..N] of colour;

procedure CopySubpicture
   (w,h: integer;     { the width and height }
    x,y: integer;     { the position of the original }
    nx,ny: integer;   { the position of the copy }
    var a: picture);  { the raster picture }
{ Copies a rectangular subpicture. }
```

```
var
  ox,oy: integer;  { the position of the original point }
  cx,cy: integer;  { the position of the copied point }
  dx,dy: integer;  { the directions of copying }
  i,j: integer;    { counters }
begin {CopySubpicture}
 if (x<>nx) and (y<>ny) and (w>0) and (h>0) then begin
 { determine the directions of copying }
  if x>nx then dx:=1
  else begin x:=x+w-1; nx:=nx+w-1; dx:=-1 end;
  if y>ny then dy:=1
  else begin y:=y+h-1; ny:=ny+h-1; dy:=-1 end;
 { copy }
  oy:=y; cy:=ny;
  for j:=1 to h do begin
    ox:=x;
    cx:=nx;
    for i:=1 to w do begin
      a[cx,cy]:=a[ox,oy];
      ox:=ox+dx; cx:=cx+dx;
    end;
    oy:=oy+dy;
    cy:=cy+dy;
  end; {for}
 end; {if}
end; {CopySubpicture}
```

1131G At first sight, the solution seems difficult, but only until we learn the gymnastics with indices. Let us denote the picture side, that is, the order of the matrix, by $N + 1$, and let the coordinates run from 0 to N to ease computation. Imagine that the two diagonals partition the picture and observe the four triangles obtained (see Figure G4). They are congruent, and the altitude of each equals N **div** 2.

When the picture is rotated, any point of a triangle moves to the same point in the next triangle. As soon as we can determine the coordinates of the points at the same position in all four triangles, we know how to rotate the entire picture. Therefore, observe the i-th row of the top triangle. The coordinates of its leftmost point are i, i; the coordinates of point k places right are $i, i + k$. The rotation moves this line to the i-th column. Its leftmost point moves to the cross diagonal, to the position with the coordinates $N - i, i$. The point displaced by k places is rotated k rows above, so that its coordinates become $N - i - k, i$. With some additional effort we see that the coordinates of the points with the same positions in each of the four triangles are the following (replacing the sum $i + k$ by j):

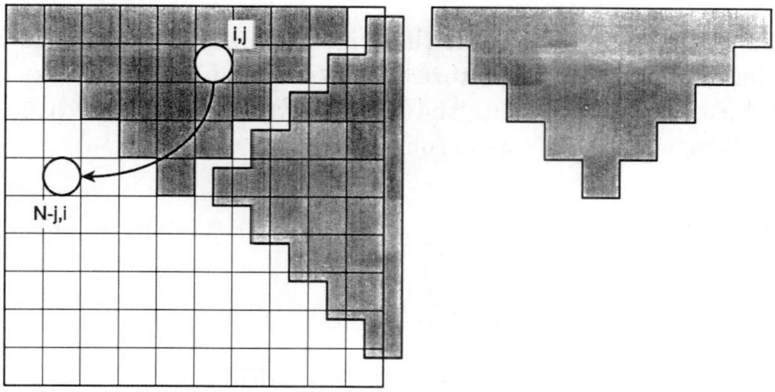

Figure G4: Rotating the picture

1. triangle $i, \quad j$
2. triangle $N-j, \quad i$
3. triangle $N-i, \quad N-j$
4. triangle $j, \quad N-i$

To rotate by the right angle, these four points must be circularly exchanged. The circular change is most easily performed by swapping in the direction contrary to the rotation: we temporarily save the last point, overwrite it by the next-to-last, and so around until we return to the first one, which is overwritten by the saved copy of the last. (You can find more about circular shift in solution 224D.)

```
const N = 999;
type picture = array [0..N,0..N] of integer;

procedure Rotate(var pic: picture);
{ Rotates the raster picture by the right angle counter-clockwise. }
  var
    i,j: integer;
    sav: integer;
begin
  for i:=0 to N div 2 do
    for j:=i to N-i-1 do begin
      sav          := pic [i,   j  ];
      pic [i,   j  ]:= pic [j,   N-i];
      pic [j,   N-i]:= pic [N-i,N-j];
      pic [N-i,N-j]:= pic [N-j,i   ];
      pic [N-j ,i  ]:= sav;
    end; {for}
end; {Rotate}
```

Suppose the picture is so large that there is not enough space in the memory to store it. Therefore, the entire picture is stored on a file and accessed by square chunks similar to the above using the *GetChunk*(i,j,*pic*) and *PutChunk*(i,j,*pic*) procedures. How would you rotate such a picture?

Chapter H

The Remaining Problems

Finally, the problems outside any other group remain to be solved. As in the group of the straightforward problems, these problems have nothing particular in common; they are just slightly more difficult.

113H This problem takes us back to the old days of computers, when a computer was a mysterious black box to most users. It ate punched cards at one end, and produced paper at the other; also, interactive use was a luxury dream of the most daring. The problem is unfortunate in composition and any honest author of competition problems would be ashamed of it nowadays. But all this may be excused by its purpose at the time of its creation. Namely, experience with the "programmers" of that time showed that most knew nothing about the principles of operation of a computer, so that they had no idea about what happened to their programs after they handed their deck of punched cards to the operator. Frequently, they were hopelessly frustrated by errors of the most commonplace nature. We have no intention of saying that the problem is extinguished today. Quite the contrary, as the use of computers increases, so does the crowd of "programmers", who, using learned recipes, produce interesting effects using the black box while they do not have even the slightest idea what happens inside the computer. So, it is worth testing such knowledge even today, but this is usually done in conversation, as it is difficult to define the correctness of a written solution.

Nonetheless the problem is rather outdated, since computers with card readers are rarely found today. This would probably be the main reason for not obtaining any results from the card deck. Nevertheless, let us forget the time gap and summarize some solutions (reasons for not obtaining expected results), which were listed by the competitors and given consideration at the time:

— an error in the control cards,
— a syntax error in the program,
— an algorithmic error in the program,
— incorrect data,
— an error in reading the deck,
— an error in data transmission,
— an error in the system software,
— a hardware failure,
— the results are correct, but unexpected.

The last reason listed above is no joke. A variety of programs exist for which the results cannot be anticipated (e. g. a simulation of a physical experiment in a computer), but may only be predicted or not even that. In this case, careful checking is necessary to confirm the correctness of the results or to detect an error.

Finally, it is worth mentioning that the type of computer heavily influences the probability distribution of the errors. On professional mainframe systems a hardware failure or an error in the system software is extremely improbable; quite the contrary is the case with the software for home and personal computers, about which long stories might be told by their passionate users.

115H

The notation from the problem is called the **prefix Polish notation**; Polish, since it was first studied in detail by the Polish mathematician Łukasiewicz; prefix, since the operator *precedes* both operands. Similar to it is the **postfix** or **reverse** Polish notation, used in some types of hand calculators. Both notations are interesting since neither the conventions about the priority of operators (the multiplication has priority over the addition in the usual notation) nor the parentheses to avoid them are necessary; we must only know how many operands an operator has, its "arity"(is it unary, binary, ternary, etc.).

a) Let us compute the value of the expression from the problem. The operands used in the current step of the computation are printed in boldface.

$$
\begin{aligned}
& * \; 2 \; * \; + \; 2 \; 2 \; + \; 2 \; * \; \mathbf{2} \; \mathbf{2} \\
= & * \; 2 \; * \; + \; 2 \; 2 \; \mathbf{+} \; \mathbf{2} \; \mathbf{4} \\
= & * \; 2 \; * \; \mathbf{+} \; \mathbf{2} \; \mathbf{2} \; 6 \\
= & * \; 2 \; * \; \mathbf{4} \; \mathbf{6} \\
= & * \; \mathbf{2} \; \mathbf{24} \\
= & \; 48
\end{aligned}
$$

In the usual **infix** notation, where the operator is written between its operands, the expression looks as follows:

$$* \ 2 * + \ 2 \ 2 + 2 * 2 \ 2 = 2 * (2 + 2) * (2 + 2 * 2)$$

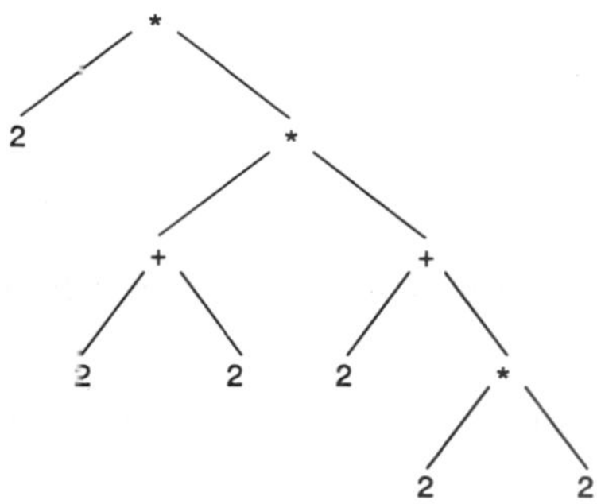

Figure H1: The tree of an arithmetic expression

An arithmetic expression may be represented by a binary tree (Figure H1). The prefix Polish notation is obtained by the *preorder* printout of the tree (first the label of the father, then the left and finally the right subtree, respectively). In the output of the tree in *inorder* (the left subtree, the label of the father, and the right subtree), parentheses must be used. Special care must be taken to avoid unnecessary parentheses — can you devise such output?

b) The algorithm is most easily devised recursively. When an operator is read, it is used on a pair of expressions that follow in the notation and are computed by a recursive call to the same subprogram. The value computed is returned as the value of the expression in which the operator occurs. If a number is read, its value is returned.

```
function Expr: integer;
{ Computes the value of an expression written in the prefix Polish notation. }
  var
    n: integer;
    ch: char;
begin
  while (input↑=' ') and not eoln(input) do
    get(input);
  if eoln(input) then
    begin Expr:=0; writeln('Error in the expression.') end
  else if input↑ in ['0'..'9'] then
    begin read(input,n); Expr:=n end
  else if input↑ in ['+','−','*','/'] then
```

```
      begin
        read(input,ch);
        n:=Expr;
        case ch of
          '+': Expr:=n+Expr;
          '−': Expr:=n−Expr;
          '*': Expr:=n*Expr;
          '/': Expr:=n div Expr;
        end; {case}
      end
    else
      begin Expr:=0; writeln('Illegal character in the expression.') end;
  end; {Expr}
```

There is an interesting point to note. When we first wrote it, the case statement appeared as follows:

```
read(input,ch);
case ch of
  '+': Expr:=Expr+Expr;
  '−': Expr:=Expr−Expr;
  '*': Expr:=Expr*Expr;
  '/': Expr:=Expr div Expr;
end; {case}
```

When it was tested on one computer, it worked correctly. Later, the test was repeated on another computer, where it gave incorrect results for subtraction and addition. In the current version it works correctly on both computers. Can you explain why? What about the sequence of expression evaluation?

The non-recursive solution is less evident, but as it is an excellent (and frequent) example of stack usage, it is worth presenting here. The **stack** is a real pile of data: new data may only be added at the top of it, and the stacked data may only be removed from the top. In a computer, it is most easily represented by a table and the index of the top element. In our case, all operators read are put on the stack; a number is put on the stack unless it is the second in a pair of consecutive numbers, and thus allows at least one of the operations to be performed. In the latter case, the stack is undone by performing all possible operations. The result is again put on the stack after the last operator not yet executed.

```
function Expr: integer;
{ Computes the value of an expression written in the prefix Polish notation. }
  type
    oper = record op: char; va: integer end;
```

```
  var
    val: integer;                                   { the value of the expression }
    top: integer;
    stack: array [0..100] of oper;                                  { the stack }
begin {Expr}
  top:=0; stack[0].op:=' ';                                       { a sentinel }
  repeat
    while (input↑=' ') and not eoln(input) do
      get(input);
    if eoln(input) then
      begin top:=0; val:=0; writeln('Error in the expression.') end
    else if input↑ in ['+','-','*','/'] then
      begin top:=top+1; read(stack[top].op) end
    else if input↑ in ['0'..'9'] then
      begin
        read(input,val);
        while stack[top].op='0' do begin
          case stack[top-1].op of
            '+': val:=stack[top].va+val;
            '-': val:=stack[top].va-val;
            '*': val:=stack[top].va*val;
            '/': val:=stack[top].va div val;
          end; {case}
          top:=top-2;
        end; {while}
        if top>0 then                   { push the partial result on the stack }
          begin top:=top+1; stack[top].op:='0'; stack[top].va:=val end;
      end
    else begin
      top:=0; val:=0;
      writeln('Illegal character in the expression.');
    end;
  until top=0;
  Expr:=val;
end; {Expr}
```

An alternate name for the stack is the acronym LIFO (last in — first out), since the last element to enter it is the first to leave. The acronym FIFO (first in — first out) denotes another frequent data structure, the queue. You may find an example of its use in solutions 213F and 832F.

The evaluation of the expressions in the postfix Polish notation is left as an exercise. The situation here is inverse to the above: the iterative solution is easy and straightforward, while the recursive one is obscure. Also, you may try finding out how an expression in the usual notation would be translated to the postfix notation. An example:

3 + (7 * 2 − 1) * 8 = 3 7 2 * 1 − 8 * +

This notation is used in a variety of hand calculators for numerous reasons. Both execution and keying of expressions are easy, the parentheses are unnecessary, the partial results may always be examined, and so on.

221H Let us denote the order of the matrix by m and illustrate the problem geometrically:

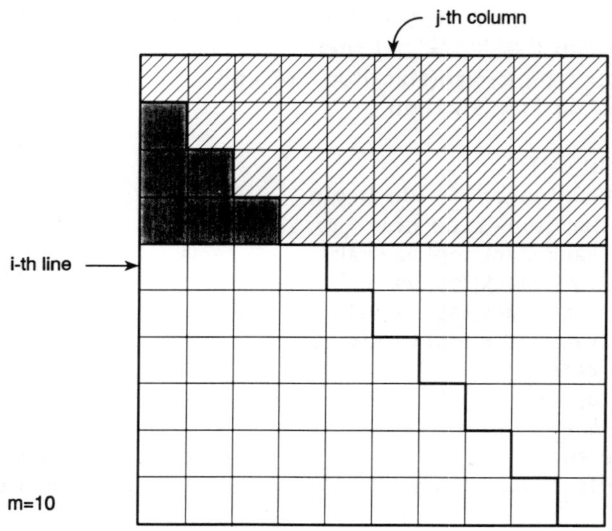

Figure H2: The computation of indices in an upper triangular matrix

To determine the sequence number of the i,j-th element, the number of the elements in the hatched portion must first be determined, and the sequence number of the i,j-th element in the i-th row. In the hatched portion there are

$$(i-1)\cdot m - \frac{(i-2)\cdot(i-1)}{2}$$

elements, since there are $(i-1)\cdot m$ of them in the entire upper rectangle, while there are $(i-2)\cdot(i-1)/2$ in the dark triangle.

The i,j-th element is at the $j-(i-1)$-th place in the i-th row, since $(i-1)$ elements are missing at the start of the i-th row. The sequence number of the i,j-th element is therefore

$$k = j + \frac{(i-1)\cdot(2m-i)}{2}$$

It is much more difficult to compute i,j from the sequence number k of the element. We may clarify the solution by the algorithm that computes i and j when given k:

```
j:=k; u:=m; i:=1;  { u is the length of the i-th row }
while j>u do
  begin i:=i+1; j:=j−u; u:=u−1 end;
j:=j+i−1;  { add the length of the empty part of the line }
{ i and j are the indices k-th element of the schema }
```

It is rather difficult to derive the expressions to compute the indices i and j from k, so we will only sketch it here. The three indices are combined into two inequalities, which restrict the values of k in the i-th row of the matrix. To solve them, we take into account that i is a nonnegative integer, as well as other known relations about i, j, k, and m. In this way the row index i is computed, and the column index j is then computed from the above equality. The formulas obtained follow:

$$i = m - \left\lfloor \frac{1}{2}\left(\left\lfloor \sqrt{1 + 8\left(\frac{m\cdot(m+1)}{2} - k\right)}\right\rfloor - 1\right)\right\rfloor$$

$$j = k - \frac{(i-1)\cdot(2m-i)}{2}$$

The brackets $\lfloor$ and $\rfloor$ in the expressions denote the integer part of the enclosed expression.

Storing the triangular schema in such a way seems clumsy and impractical in relation to the matrix.

Nevertheless, it is sometimes well worth storing the schema in a compact way although the access to the data is somewhat slower. This exercise is only one among many aspects of a common problem, as to how a special form of a matrix schema may be most compactly stored. A characteristic and frequent example is the diagonal and tridiagonal matrices, which are stored in a single vector or in three vectors (tables), respectively. In other problems, large but almost empty matrices (which have little non-zero elements) occur. Such schemas are stored in the so-called *sparse matrices* (see E. S. Page, L. B. Wilson: *Information Representation and Manipulation in a Computer*, Cambridge University Press, Cambridge 1973, p.58) or *hash tables* (N. Wirth: *Algorithms+Data Structures=Programs*, Prentice-Hall, Englewood Cliffs 1976, pp. 264-274), mentioned in solution 622D. Using such structures, the main organizational problem is fast and effective addressing of their elements.

511H This is an easy problem in information theory. If 256 light intensities are distinguished in each point, 8 bits are needed for the data about the light intensity in each point ($2^8 = 256$). For the entire image

$$3 \cdot 256 \cdot 256 \cdot 8 = 1\,572\,864$$

bits are needed. If this number of bits is transferred in 5 220 seconds, the transmission speed equals

$$\frac{1\,572\,864}{5\,220} = 301.3$$

bits per second.

The problem was stated soon after Voyager I passed the planet Saturn (on November 12, 1980). The data about the transmission speed were reproduced from a popular magazine, from which the time could be understood either as the duration of the transmission or as the time required to reach Earth from Saturn. Later, it was discovered that the latter was the case.

The correct data about the Voyager are the following: its camera records the image with 800×800 points, the image is black and white, and the resolution is 8 bits in each point. The transmission speed is adjustable and is adapted to the capabilities of the receivers on Earth (the data must be separated from noise). The transmission speed used from Saturn was unknown to us. From Uranus, which Voyager II encountered on 24th January 1986, the transmission speed of 14 400 bits per second with 90% reliability could be achieved using a single antenna, and 29 900 bits per second by combining signals from three antennas. In fact, the speed of 21 600 bits per second was used. The images from Uranus were transferred in a compacted form, considering that the neighbour points differ little in light intensities; in this way the transmission time was reduced to half. The transmission errors, which are much more fatal when packing is involved, were recovered using a special redundancy code (Reed-Solomon), which allows recovery of a limited number of transmission errors (an example of a simple such code is presented in solution 1113B).

It is interesting to note that the initial flight plan did not include the encounter with Uranus, which was incorporated only after the encounter with Saturn. The encounter was planned by a large group of scientists in the little more than four years of flight from Saturn to Uranus. During this time, most software for the computers aboard Voyager II was changed. The problems encountered were quite unusual for ordinary situations. One of the more annoying problems was the vibration of the space probe caused by the magnetic tape unit of the computer being switched on and off. Only six days before the encounter with Uranus it was discovered that a single bit malfunctioned in the memory of one of the two computers (core memory is used). The usage of the damaged bit was avoided at the last minute by reprogramming. You can imagine how pleasant such programming is, considering that the radio signal travels approximately an hour and a half to Uranus...

814H As usual, the interchange is performed in three steps: first, the value of the X variable is transferred to an auxiliary variable A, then the value of Y is transferred to X, and finally, the value of A is transferred to Y. Since the computer provides no move instruction, the transfer must be implemented by the increment and decrement instructions. We must only ensure that the value of any variable transferred equals zero prior to the transfer. Then this variable is incremented at the same time the other one is decremented, until the latter becomes zero.

The program therefore consists of four loops: the first one ensures that A is zero at start and the other three transfer values from X to A, from Y to X and from A to Y, respectively.

```
START:
L1:     BRZE   A, L2    ; A := 0
        DECR   A
        BR     L1
L2:     BRZE   X, L3    ; A := X,  X := 0
        INCR   A
        DECR   X
        BR     L2
L3:     BRZE   Y, L4    ; X := Y,  Y := 0
        INCR   X
        DECR   Y
        BR     L3
L4:     BRZE   A, STOP ; Y := A
        INCR   Y
        DECR   A
        BR     L4
STOP:
```

In the program above, the semicolon denotes that the remainder of the line is a comment and not a part of the program.

It is sometimes worth trying to reduce the number of operations; therefore we note the basic idea of another solution: both numbers are decremented and A incremented until the smaller becomes zero. Then, the remainder of the larger is transferred to the other. Finally, both numbers are incremented along with decrementing A, until it becomes zero. You might try writing the corresponding program. Can you estimate how many operations (increments, decrements, or comparisons, all of the same duration) were spared? Is the procedure described always more effective?

924H The string is copied character by character left to right, in the same sequence as it is input. Imagine it is split into three portions. The first portion represents the part of the string in which no substitution may occur any more. Thus, we are through with it, so it may be output. In the second portion, substitutions may still occur, so it must be stored somewhere at hand. The third portion has not been dealt with yet. Denote the three portions by p, q and r respectively. Then, our string is the **concatenation** of the three strings $p+q+r$, the string p has been output, the string q must be stored because of possible substitutions in it, while the string r is waiting on input to be processed.

The string is processed by comparing the last character of the string q to the first character of the string r. If nothing special is detected, the character is only moved from the string r to the string q. A substitution must be made, if the last character of q equals the first character of r, and both equal either A or B. In this case, both characters are removed, and the substitution character is added at the start of r. Since it may happen that another substitution may be needed after this one, the substitution character may not be added to the end of q. As soon as the starting character is neither A nor B, it cannot cause any substitution, so it can be moved to q, and the obtained q output, that is, moved to p and forgotten. Since, theoretically, the length of q is not limited in any way, as new and new characters without peculiarities may be added to it, it seems that the problem cannot be solved.

But... The string q may be emptied in two ways: by successive substitutions or by output. It may be filled in a single manner: by alternately adding the character A and B to it. As we have seen, any other character empties q, while consecutive equal characters A or B cause substitution and thus cannot occur in q. Therefore, it suffices to know the first character of q (denote it by s) and the length of the string q (denote it by n). Also, denote by t the input character (the starting character of r). Then, the following action table entirely describes the copying procedure. In it, let X denote any character not equal to A or B, and let A,B or B,A denote one of the two characters.

t	n	odd(n)	s	Action
X				*Empty*(s,n); n:=0; *write*(t);
A,B	=0			s:=t; n:=1;
A,B	>0	false	$=t$	n:=n+1;
A,B	>0	true	$\neq t$	n:=n+1;
A,B	>0	false	$\neq t$	n:=1; s:=t;
A,B	>0	true	$=t$	n:=1; s:=B,A; { the other character }

The program to perform the copy follows:

```
program CopyString(input,output);
{ Copies a string substituting characters. }
  var
    s: char;       { the starting character of the alternating string }
    n: integer;    { the length of the alternating string }
    t: char;       { the input character }

  procedure Empty(s: char; n: integer);
  { Outputs the alternating sequence. }
    var i: integer;
  begin
    for i:=1 to n do begin
      write(s);
      if s='A' then s:='B' else s:='A';
    end; {for}
  end; {Empty}

begin {CopyString}
  n:=0;
  while not eof do begin
    read(t);
    if (t<>'A') and (t<>'B') then
      begin Empty(s,n); n:=0; write(t) end
    else if n=0 then begin n:=1; s:=t end
    else if odd(n)<>(s=t) then n:=n+1
    else begin
      n:=1;
      if s<>t then s:=t
      else if s='A' then s:='B'
      else s:='A';
    end; {if}
  end; {while}
  Empty(s,n);
end. {CopyString}
```

At second glance, the problem seems nicely solved. The only problem which is still not under control is the length n of the string q, since it may become arbitrarily large. The capacity of any computer memory is limited, so it cannot hold a number of arbitrary size. Theoretically, we may still compose a string of alternating characters A and B long enough to exceed the capacity of the available computer memory.

Just for fun, let us estimate how long that string would be, and how much time would a fast computer take to read it. Suppose our computer uses 100-bit numbers in computations. Such arithmetic may be easily programmed (see solution 613B). The largest number which may be represented on such a computer is $2^{100} - 1$, which approximately equals 10^{30} (since 2^{10} approximately equals 10^3). If 3 mm wide characters of a string of this length were to be written side by side, it would take 10^{19} seconds or $3 \cdot 10^{11}$ years for the light to travel from its start to its end. A super-fast computer, receiving 10^7 characters per second (the existing computers access the data in their memory this fast) would need 10^{23} seconds (approximately $3 \cdot 10^{15}$ years) to read the entire string. (For comparison, let us list some cosmic numbers: our Earth is a modest $3 \cdot 10^8$ years old according to some estimates; the universe is three times older.)

The hundred-bit numbers above were selected by sheer coincidence, and obviously we reached much too far. It would therefore be interesting to invert the computation and determine the number of bits needed to represent the length of the string whose transmission time would exceed our lifetime (say 100 years), using the above estimate about the transmission speed. Try doing that yourself.

1021H "The clock runs with triple speed and the time to announce the winners of the computer science competition inexorably approaches. The competition committee, sweating with effort, finally realizes that the solutions cannot all be corrected on time. What can be done to determine at least the winners before the announcement?"

This thrilling situation, encountered each year at the competitions, is the actual background to the problem about the passionate dicers. The solution to such a dilemma is obvious: the solutions of those competitors who cannot win in any way (for instance, who have no points from three exercises corrected out of four in total) are put away for a moment, and are perhaps corrected later, while all effort is directed towards the possible prize winners.

Let us return to the passionate dicers. Problems asking for the *best* among possible solutions (according to a selected criterion), are usually called *optimization* problems. In general, it is difficult to ascertain that a given solution is actually the best. In our case, the number of rounds (being optimized) depends on throwing dice, so we may only find the least number of throws on average. Two algorithms to play would therefore be compared by observing a large number of games and declaring the one with the least number of rounds on average to be better. The somewhat loose formulation of the least number of throws from the statement of the problem must be understood in this way. The average number of rounds may be discussed only if the probabilities of particular numbers are known. For dice, it may be safely assumed that the outcomes of particular throws are independent (that the die is honest), and that the probabilities of particular outcomes are equal, while this is certainly not true for the results of the competition problems. Since detailed formal discussion of the optimality of the solution exceeds the scope of this book, we are satisfied with a solution which at least looks good.

From the statement of the problem it is not perfectly clear how precisely the rules of the game are formulated. There are two possibilities. The first is that all players play the first (k-th round), and then, based on the results obtained, the players for the next round are selected. The other possibility is that the first player may throw all 30 rounds, then the second, third, etc. throw; each one until he finishes the game or he is eliminated. In fact, the exercise prescribes no order for throwing, and we will see that for a serious optimization total freedom is required to set the throwing order. First, we present a program for the second variant of the algorithm (in which each player is treated separately). This is a more practicable procedure (especially if you imagine several hundred passionate dicers striving for the die) and the program is easily devised as well. Let us also observe how we determine when a dicer may be eliminated from the further game. Since not even the slightest mistake may be made in the determination of the winner, a particular player may not be eliminated until he is incapable of overtaking the best, even if he wins the full score in the remaining rounds.

```
program Game(input,output);
{ The players play in turn. }
{ Each one is allowed to throw until he may overtake the current leader. }
  const
    maxRound = 60;          { the maximum score of a round }
    allRounds = 30;         { the number of rounds }
  var
    n: integer;             { the number of all players }
    i: integer;             { the current player number }
    j: integer;             { the number of the remaining rounds }
    sum: integer;           { the sum of points of a single player }
    round: integer;         { the result of a round }
    leader,max: integer;    { the leader and his result }
  begin
    write('The number of players: '); readln(n);
    max:=0; leader:=0;
    for i:=1 to n do begin
      sum:=0; j:=allRounds;
      while (sum+j*maxRound>=max) and (j>0) do begin
        write('Player ',i:1,', round ',allRounds-j+1:1,': '); readln(round);
        sum:=sum+round; j:=j-1;
      end; {while}
      if sum>max then begin max:=sum; leader:=i end;
    end; {for}
    writeln('The winner is ',leader:1,' scoring ',max:1,' points');
  end. {Game}
```

In this program, as well as in the problem, it was intentionally "forgotten" that there might be several winners. This inconsistency may be easily corrected by adding a table of logical values indicating the winners, while a single winning score suffices. Naturally, all winners are output at the end.

Such a program was an acceptable solution at the competition. If we wished to devise an algorithm which would be a real help in similar problems (for instance, in correcting the solutions at the competition), it is worth improving it a little. The most upsetting feature of the program above is that its effectiveness heavily depends on the moment when the prime cheat of the club takes his turn. Since he is the one to win, the other players are eliminated effectively only after his turn. Obviously, it would be best to guess the winner in advance, so that he would be the first to throw. This is of course impossible; we may try approximating this by giving preference to those players who currently score the best. In this way, we soon obtain high scores necessary for fast elimination of inferior players. Three values are necessary to rate the players:

— the *total minimum score*, which equals the current score plus the minimum possible score of the remaining rounds of a player;
— the *total maximum score*, which equals the current score plus the maximum possible score of the remaining rounds of a player;
— the *total expected score*, which equals the current score plus the average score of the remaining rounds of a player;

The last prediction and with it the criterion are naturally inappropriate if there are swindlers in the club; also, both work poorly in the case of correcting the exercises. The optimality criteria are different for gambling (uniform random distribution of the outcomes, if the die is honest) and for competition or sport, where the results (hopefully) are not accidental. Sometimes it is more realistic to expect that, on average, the player has the same success in all rounds. Such expectation incorporates more information about the nature of the problem than the case of the uniform probability of all cases. In this case, we may actually improve the algorithm to be more effective. In any case, the choice of the next player depends on some *expectation*, so we may only speak about higher or lower *probability* that, on average, the new algorithm gives superior results to the previous one. In such optimization problems, the specific nature of the problem must be considered, or the program allowed to adapt the expectations to the course of the game.

We present the basic idea of the algorithm without further discussing its optimality:

— the candidates for the next round are all those players who have neither finished nor been eliminated (who may still overtake the leader);

— among these, the candidate with the highest (current) score is chosen to play.

A player is eliminated when his total maximum score falls below the largest total minimum score of all other players.

The data about the players are stored in a table, from which the most promising player is chosen in each round. The players that have finished or have been eliminated are moved to the end of the table and ignored. All the time, the total minimum score of one of the leaders is observed. Since all data about the players are stored in the table, no extra effort is needed to look after all winners. After the game terminates, they are simply looked up in the table and output.

```
program FasterGame(input,output);
{ Determines the sequence of the die throws }
{ considering the expected results. }
  const
    nMax = 100;     { the maximum number of players }
    allRounds = 10; { the number of rounds }
    maxRound = 60;{ the maximum number of points in a round }
    minRound = 10; { the minimum number of points in a round }
    avRound = 35;  { the expected number of points in a round }
                   { (minRound+maxRound) div 2 }
  type
    playerT = record
                number: integer;  { the player sequence number }
                max,min: integer; { the maximum, minimum, and }
                aver: real;       { average total score }
                rounds: integer;  { the number of remaining rounds }
              end;
    table = array [1..nMax] of playerT;

  var
    player: table;                { the player table }
    n: integer;                   { the number of players }
    winScore: integer;            { the player score }
    i: integer;

  procedure InitialState(var player: table; n: integer);
  { Initializes the player table. }
    var i: integer;
  begin {InitialState}
    for i:=1 to n do with player[i] do begin
      max:=allRounds*maxRound;
      min:=allRounds*minRound;
      aver:=allRounds*avRound;
      rounds:=allRounds;
      number:=i;
    end; {for}
  end; {InitialState}
```

```
procedure Game;
{ Controls the competitions by choosing the players. }
  var
    leaderMin: integer;
      { the total minimum score of one of the current leaders }
    remaining: integer;   { the number of players still in the game }
    cand: integer;        { the next candidate to play in the current round }
    score: integer;       { the score of the round }

  function Select: integer;
  { Selects the most promising of the remaining players. }
    var
      promising: integer;  { the index of the most promising player }
      p: real;
      i: integer;
  begin {Select}
    p:=player[1].aver;
    promising:=1;
    for i:=2 to remaining do
      if player[i].aver>p then
        begin p:=player[i].aver; promising:=i end;
    Select:=promising;
  end; {Select}

  procedure Eliminate(i: integer);
  { Eliminates the i-th player and shortens the active portion of the table. }
    var
      auxilry: playerT;
      last: integer;        { the index of the last active player in the table }
  begin {Eliminate}
    last:=remaining;
    auxilry:=player[i];
    player[i]:=player[last];
    player[last]:=auxilry;
    remaining:=remaining-1;
  end; {Eliminate}

begin {Game}
  leaderMin:=allRounds*minRound;
  remaining:=n;
  while remaining>0 do begin
    cand:=Select;
    with player[cand] do begin
      if (rounds<=0) or (max<leaderMin) then
        Eliminate(cand)
      else begin
        write('Player ',number:1,', round ',allRounds-rounds+1:1,': ');
        readln(score);
        min:=min+score-minRound;
```

```
        max:=max+score-maxRound;
        aver:=aver+score-avRound;
        rounds:=rounds-1;
        if min>leaderMin then
          leaderMin:=min;
      end; {if}
    end; {with}
  end; {while}
  winScore:=leaderMin;
end; {Game}

begin {FasterGame}
  write('The number of players: '); readln(n);
  InitialState(player,n);
  Game;
  for i:=1 to n do
    with player[i] do
      if min=winScore then
        writeln(' The winning score ',winScore:1,
                ' was achieved by the player number ',number:1);
end. {FasterGame}
```

To make the program more understandable, we intentionally avoided the use of more elaborate data structures. A more elegant and, for a larger number of players, much faster algorithm would be obtained, if the *heap* structure was used to select the best candidate. The heap is a binary tree in which the value of the father is always larger than or equal to the values of the successors (see for instance N. Wirth: *Algorithms+Data Structures=Programs*, Prentice-Hall, Englewood Cliffs 1976). Usually we assume that the tree is complete, so that it may be represented in a one-dimensional table without wasting any space (the node with the index i is the father to the successor nodes with indices $2i$ and $2i+1$).

The improved program is fairly similar to the previous one. The initial table is already a heap, so no rearrangement is necessary. The *Select* procedure becomes unnecessary, since the "largest" element is always the first in the table due to the properties of the heap. After any change to this element (that is, at the end of the **while** loop), the table must be updated to become a heap again. This is done by "sinking" the changed element down to its correct place in the heap according to its key value, *aver*. This is performed by the following procedure, described in the literature listed:

```
procedure UpdateHeap(var player: table; var length: integer);
{ Updates the active portion (length) to become a heap by sinking
  the top element, which may not suit the heap requirement
  (is no more the largest), to its correct position in the tree. }
```

```
  var
    father,son: integer;
    x: playerT;

begin {UpdateHeap}
  father:=1; son:=2;
  x:=player[1];
  while son<=length do begin
    if son<length then
      if player[son].aver<player[son+1].aver then
        son:=son+1;
      { the variable son is now the index of the largest son }
    if x.aver>player[son].aver then
      son:=length+1 {exit}
    else
      begin player[father]:=player[son]; father:=son; son:=2*father end;
  end; {while}
  player[father]:=x;
end; {UpdateHeap}
```

The statement *son*:=*length*+1 substitutes the **exit** statement not provided by standard Pascal. Usually, it would be replaced by a **goto** statement; nevertheless, we refuse to use this harmful and dreadful statement in our solution. In such cases, the decision is left to individual taste. At the same time one should be aware that the replacement of the **exit** statement is the sole legal use of the **goto** statement that may be afforded without violating the rules of good programming.

1124H

The procedure to provide a working compiler proceeds as follows:

a) The written compiler is first transferred to Professor Branes' computer.
b) The source is then compiled using Professor Branes' working compiler. A working compiler is thus obtained, running on Professor Branes' computer, but generating code for Professor Hasting's computer.
c) The source is compiled again, this time using the compiler just obtained. The resulting code provides a compiler, which may be executed on Professor Hasting's computer.
d) The executable code is finally transferred to Professor Hasting's computer.

The procedure described is called **bootstrap**. At the competition and before, this simple procedure proved to be far from obvious for those who had not encountered it before. Different variations of this procedure are almost always used for compiler writing in practice. The most popular way to write a compiler for some programming language is as follows:

a) First, a compiler is written to translate the programming language to an intermediate code. The intermediate code must be relatively simple, but it is not necessary that it is executable on any real computer. We may imagine that we operate a computer with the instruction set adapted to the programming language. It is not necessary that this compiler is a complete one, since the only program to be compiled with it is the compiler itself (up to step (e)).
b) The compiler described is compiled on any other computer. In this way, we obtain a compiler which runs on the other computer and translates programs to the intermediate code.
c) The source is translated again, using the compiler just obtained, providing the translation of the compiler to the intermediate code.
d) An interpreter for the intermediate code is written on the target computer. This interpreter actually simulates (i.e. emulates) the fictitious computer adapted to our programming language. Since the intermediate code is simple, an interpreter for it is easily written using any language.
e) The compiler in intermediate code is transferred to the target computer and linked to the interpreter. A compiler is obtained, translating to the intermediate code and executing on the target computer. Since the compiler is partly interpreted (the intermediate code is interpreted), it is slow, and so are other translations. The primary advantage of the procedure so far is that all further work may be done on the target computer.
f) The compiler into intermediate code is altered to translate to the actual instruction set of the target computer instead of translating to the intermediate code. By translating this compiler twice, a new compiler for the target computer is obtained, the one we wished to produce in the first place.

In practice, all steps are repeated many times. There is another variation of step (f), in which an additional compiler is written, translating the intermediate code to the target one, instead of altering the initial compiler. The intermediate code thus remains an intermediate phase of the compilation. The phase (f) usually represents the majority of the work on the compiler, especially the optimization of the target code (which requires most of the work necessary for a good compiler).

The amount of work required to produce a working compiler varies a lot. Small compilers may be produced in several weeks (a fine example is the compiler for the PL0 programming language from the book by N. Wirth: *Algorithms+Data Structures=Programs*, Prentice-Hall, Englewood Cliffs 1976, pp. 280-347), a working compiler for Pascal may be written by one programmer in approximately one year (one man year of work is needed), for some other compilers an incredible amount of work was needed (2000 man years of work for the PL/1–G compiler). The popularity of the Pascal programming language is mostly due to the existence of Pascal–P compiler, translating from Pascal to the so called P-code, for which it is easy to develop an interpreter. Many compilers for the C programming language are based on a common compiler to an intermediate code, while a separate compiler from the intermediate to the target code had to be provided for each particular target computer.

Literature

A. V. Aho, J. E. Hopcroft, J. D. Ullman: *The Design and Analysis of Computer Algorithms*, Addison-Wesley, Reading 1974

W. Ahrens: *Matematische Unterhaltungen und Spiele*, Leipzig 1918

S. Alagić, M. A. Arbib: *The design of well-structured and correct programs*, Springer-Verlag, New York 1987

E. Ashcroft, Z. Manna: *The Translation of Goto Programs to While Programs*, IFIP71, Ljubljana 1971

D. Baker and M. P. Hearn: *Computer Graphics*, Prentice-Hall, Englewood Cliffs, 1986

E. T. Bell: *Men of Mathematics*, Simon and Schuster, New York 1965

A. Bloch: *Murphy's Law Complete*, Methuen, 1986

I. Bratko: *Prolog Programming for Artificial Intelligence*, (2nd edition) Addison-Wesley, Reading 1990

P. Brinch Hansen: *Operating System Principles*, Prentice-Hall, Englewood Cliffs 1979

G. Chartrand: *Introductory Graph Theory*, Dover, New York 1985

D. I. A. Cohen: *Basic Techniques of Combinatorial Theory*, John Wiley, New York 1987

W. J. Dahl, E. W. Dijkstra, C. A. R. Hoare: *Structured Programming*, Academic Press, New York 1972

E. W. Dijkstra: Go to Statement Considered Harmful, *Communications of the ACM*, **11**(1968)3

J. D. Foley, A. Van Damm: *Fundamentals of Interactive Computer Graphics*, Addison-Wesley, 1982

D. Harel: *The Science of Computing*, Addison-Wesley, Reading 1987

R. C. Holt: G. S. Graham, E. D. Lazowska, M. A. Scott: *Structured Concurrent Programming*, Addison-Wesley, Reading 1978

J. E. Hopcroft, J. D. Ullman: *Introduction to Automata Theory, Languages and Computation*, Addison-Wesley, Reading 1979

B. W. Kernighan, P. J. Plauger: *Software Tools in Pascal*, Addison-Wesley, Reading 1981

D. E. Knuth: *The Art of Computer Programming, Vol. 1: Fundamental Algorithms*, Addison-Wesley, Reading 1968

D. E. Knuth: *The Art of Computer Programming, Vol. 2: Seminumerical Algorithms*, Addison-Wesley, Reading 1981

E. S. Page, L. B. Wilson: *Information Representation and Manipulation in a Computer*, Cambridge University Press, Cambridge 1973

W. W. Rouse Ball, H. S. M. Coxeter: *Mathematical Recreations and Essays*, University of Toronto Press, Toronto 1974

I. Sommerville: *Software Engineering*, 2nd ed., Addison-Wesley, Reading 1985

A. Spector and D. Gifford: The Space Shuttle Primary Computer System, *Communications of the ACM*, **27**(1984)9

R. R. Stoll: *Set Theory and Logic*, Freeman, San Francisco 1961

N. Wirth: *Algorithms + Data Structures = Programs*, Prentice-Hall, Englewood Cliffs 1976

N. Wirth: *Programming in Modula-2*, Springer Verlag, Berlin 1983

Index

The index collects the most important notions and characteristic keywords appearing in the introductory part, in the problems, or in the solutions. The number in parentheses denotes the Chapter number from part I, while a letter in parentheses denotes an item mentioned in the introduction to the chapter specified. Numbers without parentheses refer to the exercises (and not to pages).

Problems & Solutions Index

170130

06 69